CHIMERAS
and other writings

This is the first in a series of **IPTAR Books**, written by members of *The Institute for Psychoanalytic Training and Research* and selected by a committee chaired by Dr. Steven Ellman.

CHIMERAS
and other writings

SELECTED PAPERS OF
SHELDON BACH

IPBOOKS.net
International Psychoanalytic Books

IPTAR
Institute for Psychoanalytic Training and Research

International Psychoanalytic Books (IPBooks),
25–79 31st Street Astoria, NY 11102
Online at: www.IPBooks.net

Bach, S., & Schwartz, L. (1972). A dream of the Marquis de Sade: Psychoanalytic reflections on narcissistic trauma, decompensation, and the reconstitution of a delusional self. Journal of the American Psychoanalytic Association 20, 451-475, reprinted by permission of Sage publications.

Bach, S. (1977). On the narcissistic state of consciousness. International Journal of Psychoanalysis 58:209-233, reprinted by permission of Wiley-Blackwell.

Bach, S. (1998). Two ways of being. Psychoanalytic Dialogues 8:657-673, reprinted by permission of the International Association for Relational Psychoanalysis and Psychotherapy, www.iarrp.net.

Bach, S. (1998). On treating the difficult patient In *The Modern Freudians: Contemporary Psychoanalytic Technique*, eds. C. S. Ellman, S. Grand, M. Silvan, & S. Ellman. Northvale, NJ: Jason Aronson, pp. 185-195.

Bach, S. (2001). On being forgotten and forgetting one's self. Psychoanalytic Quarterly 70:739-756, reprinted by permission of Wiley-Blackwell.

Bach, S. (2006). The Language of Perversion and the language of love, chapters reprinted by permission of Rowman & Littlefield Publishers.

Bach, S. (2006). Getting from Here to There: Analytic Love, Analytic Process, chapters reprinted by permission of Taylor & Francis.

Bach, S. (2008). On digital consciousness and psychic death. Psychoanalytic Dialogues 18:784-794, reprinted by permission of the International Association for Relational Psychoanalysis and Psychotherapy, www.iarrp.net.

Bach, S. (2011). Chimeras: Immunity, Interpenetration, and the true self. Psychoanalytic Review 98(1):39-56, reprinted by permission of Guilford Press.

Strand, M. (2014). Collected Poems. New York: Knopf. Poem reprinted by permission of Random House.

Interior book design by Maureen Cutajar
www.gopublished.com

ISBN: 978-0-9969996-4-9

For P who illuminates my life.

Contents

ON NARCISSISM AND ALTERED STATES
OF CONSCIOUSNESS

ON SADOMASOCHISM

HOLISTIC CLINICAL MANAGEMENT

Acknowledgments

My thanks are due primarily to the many patients who have consistently been my best and most patient teachers. They have lived in my mind and heart throughout the last sixty years and I am extremely grateful to them for both spiritual and financial sustenance. I am equally grateful to the many students and supervisees from whom I have learned more than I have taught.

Amongst friends and colleagues I especially want to thank Delia Battin and Eugene Mahon, Carol Bandini and Robert Mammerella, Carolyn and Steven Ellman, Madelon and Jerry Grobman, Susannah and Michael Lewis, Arlene and Arnold Richards, Lynne Rubin, Katherine and Kenneth Snelson, Susan Schulson, Annie and Warren Weisberg and many others too numerous to mention but who know of my gratitude.

I am lucky enough to have had a peer group that has been ongoing for more than fifty years and that included Steven Ellman, the late Norbert Freedman, Mark Grunes, Martin Nass and the late Irving Steingart. Newer colleagues and more recent writing and supervision groups have helped me to understand the changing world and to renew my links to and faith in the younger generations of psychoanalysts. So thanks to Carolyn Ellman, Allan Frosch, Carina Grossmark and Robert Grossmark, Douglas Van Der Heide, Elizabeth Kandall, Rachael Karliner, Michael Moskowitz, Aaron Thaler, Neal Vorus and Lissa

Weinstein. And a special thanks to Steve Ellman who wrote the kind of introduction that helped me to get a better perspective on my work.

My wife Phyllis Beren has nourished my body and mind for decades now and without her, life and work would be unimaginable. I am also profoundly grateful to Rebecca, Matthew and Julia who, each in his and her own way, have shared with me so much life and love.

I want to thank Alexandra Petrou who did such a great job editing the manuscript and also Tamara and Larry Schwartz who have been so consistently helpful with the details of publication.

I have decided that it is better to reprint most of these papers without change, although I am aware, for example, that there is more recent research on de Sade's father, that Snell's position on early Greek mentation has been questioned, etc. The analytic atmosphere has changed so dramatically over the past fifty years that I hope my readers will consider the epoch in which each of these papers was written.

Acknowledgements are due to the many periodicals and publishers that have given permission for reprinting.

I hope that this book provides both pleasure in reading and raises worthwhile questions about psychoanalysis, the vocation to which I have dedicated my life and that I love so much.

Foreword

The reader who has not read the papers in this volume is in for a rare treat: the discovery of new worlds revealed within what were thought to be familiar spaces. I believe that those who have already read some of the chapters in this volume will have the experience of rediscovering precious clinical and theoretical gems that have influenced many therapists and analysts. In fact, Bach's influence has quietly spread throughout the field often without various authors fully acknowledging or perhaps realizing his impact on their concepts. I feel certain that readers will share my excitement in reading the chapters in this current volume.

I, of course, have read Bach's papers for many years and have always been impressed by the originality of his concepts. Thus the chimera, the digital self and his ideas about two ways of being are but a fraction of some of his pioneering thoughts describing the human condition. For some, it might be important to connect his concepts to the ideas of other major analysts, such as Freud, Kohut or Winnicott as well as to a variety of contemporary contributors from various theoretical orientations.

Normally, this type of discussion, that is, of theoretical positions touching and mutually influencing each other, would interest me (Ellman, 2010). However, in the present context, I was searching for a different perspective to help me clarify both my emotional and intellectual reaction to Bach's work. I was fortunate to stumble upon Oliver

Sacks' recent book, *On the Move* (2015), which reminded me of his previous work, *Awakenings* (1973), where patients who were encephalitic came alive psychologically with doses of L-dopa. In a manner parallel to *Awakenings*, it struck me that each time I hear or read about Bach's patients a new aspect of human experience comes alive for me. His vivid descriptions of a patient's experience always leave me with new ways of thinking about various topics and experiences. For me, much of psychoanalytic thought and clinical work is vivified through his clinical concepts and descriptions. He narrates awakenings of different aspects of the self or ego and shows how psychoanalysis can allow unconscious derivatives to be experienced in ways that enliven rather than fragment a person's sense of self. He also implicitly, and at times explicitly, shows how theories touch and can be integrated in new and valuable ways. I will first present some clinical examples of the type of awakenings that Bach characteristically describes, and then briefly discuss some of his concepts about early development and psychoanalytic technique.

Let us begin with Jeffrey (Chapter 2) who would constantly ask whether or not he had previously mentioned a name or incident in his analysis. He consistently expected that Bach would not remember what "he had said yesterday or the day before" (p. 24). In fact, as the narrative unfolds, Jeffrey is not certain how he is present in many parts of his reasonably complicated life. His multiple phobias (flying, elevators, claustrophobia etc.), all seemed related to being or not being remembered, "as if the act of being remembered by someone was very literally what was keeping him alive" (p. 26). One can watch Jeffrey come alive in his analysis when his discrete images are transformed into a series of images with "continuous connected movement" (p. 32). Bach gives us a picture of a patient coming alive through the process of reciprocal perception. The perceptual reciprocity allows a cognitive (ego) function to be liberated so that Jeffrey is both able to remember and to be remembered, but the process is not only a cognitive one. As Bach importantly demonstrates, the feeling of being present in someone else's mind is crucial for a child's psychological survival. This survival affects not only the child's sense of security but large parts of the way the world is experienced.

Conversely, Bach states, "It seems to me that one way of summarizing what I learned is to say that a parent may actually destroy a child, both psychically and even physically, by not constructing or holding that child's memory or representation in a particular way" (p. 34). In other terms,

> What Jeffrey had experienced throughout his childhood, and what he conveyed to me via transference enactments, was that his mother had given him no real concept of process. In practice, this meant to Jeffrey that if you let anything get even a little bit out of control, it could turn into its opposite—i.e., if you sneezed, that meant you were sick and going to die, or if you asked a question, that meant you were stupid and did not belong in the present company. (p. 28)

Bach is describing a regulating factor that is crucial when the child experiences being present in the other's (usually parent's) mind. However, when Jeffrey could feel himself in his mother's mind, it was too terrible to tolerate. Somehow Bach could bring to Jeffrey a way for the analytic couple to tolerate each other's presence. Tolerate is probably a transitional word since clearly Jeffrey came to utilize the other in a new way and this functioned as a gateway towards new transformations, as Jeffrey gradually became alive in the presence of the other .

I wonder whether most therapists when reading Bach's papers are containing their excitement, as they rush to the section where he relates how it happens clinically. One might ask: "What does one do to bring about these new states?" Interestingly, Bach is implicitly asking and then answering this question throughout his descriptions, but before we move towards this pivotal point, let us look at some of the experiences that he has described and then implicitly explained. Bach teases us with a paper (Chapter 4) that seems to start as a theoretical discussion of psychological states: what is a state, how does one define a state, etc? These are questions that he asks from a number of theoretical perspectives and then answers in an interesting manner. However, true to form, he shows us the deeper meaning of the concept of states in a clinical discussion that blends Mahler, Winnicott, and Bach. He provides a clinical illustration that brings alive the idea of self and other or alternatively the Apollonian and the Dionysian mode or, if you wish, subjectivity and objectivity. However, both before and after the clinical illustrations that Bach provides, he discusses the difficulties of being simultaneously in touch with both objective and subjective aspects of the self. Here he ranges far and wide in showing the difficulties in maintaining a dual perspective. In addition to his clinical illustrations, Bach provides a sociological illustration. Towards the end of Chapter 4 he uses the French as a "people who appreciate method and logic" (p. 71). Despite this characteristic proclivity he points out that (when he wrote this paper) that "more French men and women believe in the devil than a decade ago" (p. 71). Using the French (and others) as illustrations, Bach concludes that the movement towards integrating subjective and objective modes does not necessarily lead to higher levels of synthesis but often an integration takes place but "at something of a price." The price is at times the inability to fully utilize both perspectives.

This chapter covers a good deal of intellectual ground, yet it is anchored by Bach's clinical illustrations. He first reminds us that in Winnicott's original description of the transitional object such as a piece of blanket, it is literally permeated and suffused with the handling and odor of both caretaker and child. Thus, it conterminously provides both a safe haven of attachment to the object and a means of separation from that very object. However, when this developmental sequence does not take place optimally (or well or "good enough"), then one finds frozen dichotomies of subject and object where the person is unable to tolerate both polarities at the same time. Bach gives an interesting example of a woman (originally diagnosed with multiple personality) who begins to tolerate the coexistence of subjective and objective vantage points but she experiences on a mournful note. He writes that after several hectic years she calls and says:

> Dr. Bach, I just wanted to keep you informed that, in addition
> to the many other things that psychoanalysis has deprived me

of, I now seem to have lost the ability to commit suicide. I can never be positive that I had it, but I certainly scared myself a great number of times and was convinced that I was about to suicide. But yesterday, I had probably the most painful day of my life, but I never seriously considered suicide—that is, I never even for a moment flipped out or, as you call it, split off...I never seemed able to forget that I was the mother of little children and other things as well, and this was something that formerly didn't seem relevant to me and would never even have come into my mind. (p. 67–8)

One can only wonder about the original pain that this woman experienced when subject and object collided early in her development, as subject and object only rarely seemed able to be seen in the same space again. The birth of a new integrative capacity was a painful one for her, but a necessary one for her if she were to truly love the lives that surrounded her. Despite her pain, one can only surmised that this woman is grateful for this birth (or rebirth) of her integrative capacity. Bach gives other examples of two halves struggling to come together and in each of the examples it is as if a new aspect of life has begun.

Bach's central concerns are linked to what he has called narcissistic states. Perhaps his most startling paper was an early publication with his friend and colleague, Dr. Lester Schwartz (Chapter 6). It is only with his profound understanding of narcissistic states that he is able to find in Marquis de Sade a person whom one can understand and, indeed, even empathize with despite his sadism. As Bach and Schwartz write,

What is most interesting about de Sade is not his psychiatric diagnosis, nor yet the repeated provocative behavior which led to a life of incarceration, but rather those qualities which allowed him to survive the long years of imprisonment, to maintain his unique sense of identity, and to produce his eccentric and extraordinary work. Chief among these qualities are certain grandiose and megalomaniacal trends, with such a remarkable emphasis on issues of power and self-assertion that we were inevitably led to further consideration of narcissistic phenomena.

In our reading of de Sade we were impressed by what seemed to be a persistent and vastly hypertrophied grandiose self-image crucial to his view of himself, and clearly defensive and compensatory in nature. (p. 145)

This complex formulation is further amplified in Bach's paper but more completely in a paper by Bach on Narcissistic states of consciousness (Chapter 5).

In chapter 5 Bach begins by repeating an oft-cited complaint of the analytic community about treating narcissistic patients. One might say that this complaint or comment begins with Freud who, as Kohut pointed out, in the case of narcissistic patients logically confounded the possibility of a transference relationship with the concept of object love (see Ellman, 2010). Bach points out that analysts frequently report that they have difficulty in "getting through" to patients who are considered to be narcissistic. These patients often display the types of reactions that Bach has detailed in terms of a lack of continuity of experience, seeing the world in one way or the other, or in either feeling grandiose or totally devastated. Bach begins to think of these characteristics as part of what he terms a "narcissistic thought disorder."

To arrive at the concept of a narcissistic state, Bach explores the idea of states of mind from a number of perspectives. To reproduce his erudite synthesis is beyond the scope of my introductory remarks; I will only mention that he cites authors from Freud to Piaget, to Winnicott, to Lacan, to Laplanche and Pontalis, Ferenczi, Dixon, Escalona, Mahler, Spitz, Simon, Gedo and Goldberg, and perhaps most importantly Rapaport, who provided the theoretical tools for the structure of the concept of state of mind. By providing a model for the normal (optimal in my view) development of reflective capacity and eventually the capacity for the love of another, Bach is paving the way to show where in development narcissistic conflicts reside. One might easily have made a volume from this chapter alone. Bach's chapter is a true psychoanalytic attempt to construct a theory of early development and may be considered a more sophisticated version of Schaefer's book, *Aspects of Internalization* (1969), where Schafer attempts, with only partial success, to provide a model of early development in terms of processes of internalization. Bach is able to succeed in this in a much fuller way as he follows clinical leads and he is able to tie his clinical examples in a meaningful way to development. Not only does this paper make clinical material come alive, it is also a viable road map of early development that could profitably be further explored.

It may come as a surprise (perhaps not given the Marquis de Sade paper) that an author enmeshed in issues of self-esteem and oscillations of various elements of experience would be interested in issues of sadomasochism and perversion. However, in Chapters 7 and 8 one can see the extent that Bach is able to relate classical themes to his new implicit theory of object relations. He writes that in "one of the more philosophical passages of the Marquis de Sade's *The 120 Days of Sodom,* the Duke reflects with sadness and resignation that people are generally so difficult to comprehend" (p. 165). His friend replies, "That is why it is easier every time to fuck a man than to try to understand him" (p. 165). One might have seen comments like this in an earlier chapter (Bach and Schwartz, Chapter 6) but in Chapters 7, 8, and 9 Bach spells out the conditions that are dispositive for the development of perversions and how different types of narcissistic formations (overinflated–underinflated, as one example) are related to perverse states and tendencies.

Bach distinguishes neurotic perverse object relations that defend against anxieties about drive tendencies (unconscious), from perverse tendencies that occur instead of having a relationship. Another way of describing this distinction is to differentiate between those cases where parents condemn certain perverse behaviors but recognize the child as a separate entity, from those cases where the child is forced to flee "to the sadomasochistic drives in an effort to deny the (parental) loss and to buttress a failing sense of self" (p. 167). It is the latter type that Bach is concerned with in describing perverse and sadomasochistic tendencies and fantasies. It is his view that narcissistic personality types invariably have sadomasochistic tendencies or unconscious sadomasochistic fantasies. These perverse tendencies are part of the maintenance of a narcissistic balance and have a distinct object-relations function. In identifying this function Bach is placing the analyst in a position to empathically resonate with a person who is desperately struggling to keep a sense of self intact. He hypothesizes that narcissistic disorders have an origin "in what I have called the anal/depressive rapprochement/bisexual phase" of development (p. 202). In this newly named stage Bach combines a Freudian, Kleinian and Mahlerian perspective within what I have termed his own object relations identity. He is trying to show the impact of different elements during this crucial phase of early development, combining a variety of theories into an important new implicit theory. In all of his work, Bach is able to materialize a perspective implicit in Winnicott's essay of the capacity to be alone, illustrating how the type of internalization that is crucial to an individual's capacity to be alone is paradoxically dependent on the person experiencing a prolonged reciprocal relationship.

Perhaps one of the most vexing problems in the treatment situation as well as other avenues of life is the issue of how we communicate with one another. Clearly, Freud thought that a good deal of our communication occurred on an unconscious level. It is not unusual in a therapy session for a therapist (or patient) to have the sense of what is going on in the other person's mind even if it is not clear how or why the feeling/thought came to mind. Sometimes, it feels as if there are bits and pieces of the other that are present in our sense of self. We strangely sense what the other is feeling or what they will say or do. Bach in his chimera chapter (Chapter 1) asks the basic question how can an aspect of the other usefully become a part of the self. He notes that biologically some organ transplant patients learn to accept donor cells and treat the graft gradually as part of the "self". Bach notes that various narcissistic patients, or most patients to some extent, have difficulty in taking in the other. It is not unusual for an interpretation to be presented and then rejected by the patient only to reappear several months later as the patient's own creation. Bach in this paper traces how aspects of the other can be accepted as microchimeras if the therapist can tolerate how the other processes his interventions. Writing to the therapist, Bach states that in this circumstance; "The patient has taken a piece of you, a piece of otherness, which he initially rejected because it was experienced as an attack on his self and, through the process of chimerization or psychic metabolism, he has turned it into a usable form that now belongs to and strengthens his own sense of self" (p. 7). Bach then describes implicitly some of the difficulties in allowing the patient the process of chimerization. He quotes Winnicott who tells us, "The refusal of it [the good object] is part of the process of creating it" (p. 8). The chimera Chapter can be seen as a beginning sensitive understanding of how the patient can begin and continue to utilize the other in the analytic situation. Alternatively the chimera paper is an extension and clarification of Winnicott's view that the child does not passively receive reality but that the environment must provide the infant with the tools to create reality. Thus, for Winnicott and Bach the authentic self does not passively receive, but actively creates reality. The chimera Chapter then is a view of how the infant/developing child is able to experience the creation of reality. On both levels, the therapeutic and developmental, an important new concept is introduced allowing a new tolerance of the other's process in creating their reality.

Although I have only touched on some of Bach's more recent work, I will end this introduction by briefly noting one of his major contributions, his view of therapeutic processes. His therapeutic view is always implicitly present and is frequently explicitly present in all of his papers but it is highlighted in the last section of this volume, Holistic Clinical Management. There are many concepts that one might focus on but because of my own interest I will look at an aspect of his writings that is less well known. Bach gives us several ways (depending on the patient) of developing trust in the analytic situation. He first tells us of the importance of trust when he says that "without a certain degree of trust [a patient] can neither fully reveal himself nor truly engage the analytic process" (p. 43). He writes about trust when describing a patient who was so terrified of the return of his mental pain that he would flee the analysis. He also tells us that with sadomasochistic patients, trust is crucial for the analysis to survive. Thus, he says "before [these patients] become explosive, [hopefully] we will have built up enough analytic trust to enable the patient to talk…rather than to abandon the analysis or embroil it in perpetual enactments" (p. 195). More concretely, Bach provides a defining statement when he notes:

> Let me say immediately that I believe one of the most important factors in the cycling (between self and other transferences) is the sense of…analytic trust both on the part of the patient and on the part of the analyst. I…define trust as a continuing belief in the ability of the dyad to survive, to regulate each member of the dyad, and eventually to symbolize their experience together. Thus the waxing and waning of analytic trust in both patient and analyst is one major cause of cycle shifts between self trans- ference and object transferences. (p. 13)

Since I am an analyst who has helped develop the concept of analytic trust, I am particularly appreciative of one of the clearest and most useful statements about this concept. Of course in his typical manner, Bach clarifies the concept and relates the waxing and waning of trust to the type of transference one might see in the analytic situation.

Undoubtedly Bach is known for many other contributions to the analytic situation as compared to his statements about analytic trust. For example, he provides us with descriptions of several types of transference in the treatment of narcissistic patients. He features in- terventions to help bridge the various divides in narcissistic patients. He also points out that in the type of treatments he describes the "an- alyst's own narcissistic equilibrium is always strongly put to the test." Thus, while I have mentioned that in all of his papers he implicitly describes the therapeutic situation, one might more accurately state that he is always looking at the transference-countertransference balance that oscillates in the treatment of narcissistic patients. Of course, it is not surprising that he describes both sides of the analytic couch in sensitive detail. I venture that most (perhaps all) analysts will find important aspects of various patients exquisitely described and understood in this volume. In addition, they will find strong elements of themselves pictured and empathically brought to life.

Steven Ellman, Ph.D.

REFERENCES

Ellman, S.J. (2010). *When Theories Touch: A Historical and Theoretical Integration of Psychoanalytic Thought*. London: Karnac.

Sacks, O. (1973). *Awakenings*. New York: Random House

Sacks, O. (2015). *On the Move: A Life*. New York: Alfred Knopf

Schafer, R. (1968). *Aspects of Internalization*. New York: International Universities Press.

My Journey

The integration and disintegration of mind and body has fascinated me ever since I began to study psychology more than half a century ago. Even as a child I was curious about how it was that some people seemed so at home in their bodies while others seemed to inhabit their bodies with ill grace, as if they were on temporary loan.

As a young man I witnessed the devastation of minds and bodies and of bodies politic in Europe during World War II. After the war ended I lived, worked and studied in Paris for a number of years. My sense of my own unintegration that began in my childhood and my interest in altered states and transformations was compounded by my disruptive experiences as a GI: the sudden confrontation with life and death and the abrupt immersion in the strange and unfamiliar culture of a war-torn Europe.

I remember the culture shock that I experienced after the war when I was going to school on the GI Bill at the Sorbonne. In the United States, I had been given a taste of English literature from Beowulf to Thomas Wolfe in one crowded semester. In Paris, the professor wrote one line of poetry on the blackboard and this line, examined from many aspects, was our text for the year. As an impressionable young man, I was smitten by what I saw as the European outlook on life, and it took me a long time to integrate these two different perspectives.

But the existence of multiple perspectives became a given in my own life, and my thought was fueled by the postwar thinkers, political scientists, and poets who were each, in their own ways, trying to see if any sense could be made of the great psychological traumas of the war and the Holocaust. Thus I became interested not only in Freud, at a time in the 1950s when his presence dominated American psychiatry, but also in the great analytic traumatologists, such as Ferenczi and Winnicott, who seemed to me to be dealing with the very issues that I found so pressing.

When I returned to America I tried my hand at a number of pursuits, including writing, comparative literature and film making, all of which I found fascinating but at none of which I excelled. To help understand what was going on, I began my first analysis and this soon inflamed me to become a psychologist.

Luckily, my first analyst was not rigidly trained, so he neither interpreted this desire away nor dissuaded me from my ambition. I enquired and learned that the NYU Clinical Program was at that time considered tops in the country, so I applied there despite never having taken a course in psychology and despite assurances from the department secretary that my chances for admission were infinitesimal. I afterwards learned that in the end I had been accepted under their policy of admitting one "oddball" each year.

At NYU I happened by good luck to stumble into the Research Center for Mental Health where George Klein, Robert Holt, David Rapaport, and others were conducting cutting-edge research into psychoanalytic theory.

I was excited and fascinated by the ongoing studies of alternate states of consciousness, of dream imagery, of LSD trances and of subliminal stimulation. I was intrigued also by our ill-fated attempt to increase the sale of popcorn at movies by subliminally projecting EAT POPCORN! onto the screen. The atmosphere in which we all thrived was that of an academic, grant-supported, and research-oriented think-tank with a slightly nutty character, exemplified to my mind by a distinguished-looking Middle European psychiatrist who used to come to his laboratory cubicle on occasional afternoons, unpack an ancient violin, and dreamily play selected arias to experimental subjects while releasing vials of perfume in pursuit of his investigations into sensory synesthesia.

By contrast, the seminars that David Rapaport gave us on Freud's dream book were unparalleled examples of Old World scholarship. Rapaport would distribute two or three questions about the two pages of Chapter VII that were our text for the week. Although our small group was composed of some of the most distinguished scholars around, including George Klein and Robert Holt, to the best of my recollection hardly anyone every answered a question to the satisfaction of Rapaport, who would then bolster his arguments by quoting chapter, page and verse from memory. Two years later when I applied to be his research assistant at Austen Riggs and told him that I had spent a month reading Erickson's *Childhood and Society* with Robert Holt, he responded that he himself would read that book with his class at the New England Institute, but of course they spent a whole year reading it during which time they usually only finished the first chapter or two.

When in 1957 I interned at Jacobi Hospital in the Bronx, I had a chance to experience not only the immense variety of pathology on display in a city hospital, but also to encounter many of the greatest analysts of the day including Mahler, Greenacre, Jacobson and Hartman, some of whom would frequently come up to do Grand Rounds. The training I received at Jacobi and Einstein was first-rate and absolutely invaluable and I became best friends with two psychiatrists there, William Grossman and Lester Schwartz with whom I later wrote the paper on the Marquis de Sade. But I also had my first taste of discrimination against non-medical people there because of the rigid hierarchical system that then prevailed in most all hospitals and institutes. There were many restrictions on psychologists doing psychotherapy and even after I became licensed it took about two years of active politicking before I was given permission, as an exception only, to open a private practice while still at the hospital.

Working with the extraordinary analytic thinkers whom I met there was a heady experience. When I finished my doctorate I wanted to apply to the New York Psychoanalytic Institute for training but found that as a psychologist I could only be given "research" training and would have to sign a pledge never to actually practice psychoanalysis[1]. At that time a number of my colleagues went along with this requirement, received excellent training and are of course now practicing, but somehow I found this requirement unacceptable and instead enrolled in the NYU Postdoctoral Program in Psychoanalysis that was just opening. This was, I believe, the first University-based psychoanalytic program in the country. Its initial class enrolled some candidates who had been waiting for years for the opportunity to obtain this kind of official training in psychoanalysis; an historic event for psychologists.

The moving force behind NYU Postdoc was Bernie Kalinkowitz, although many others, including a number of medical analysts, worked very hard to make it happen. Many of these early candidates were more mature and experienced than typical postdoctoral students at the time and among them I was lucky enough to find my peer group, which has met once a month for over fifty years. We have voraciously consumed large tracts of the psychoanalytic literature and also discussed many of our own papers, for we turned out to be a productive group. Over the years we have also voraciously consumed large quantities of food and good wine for, as Heinz Hartmann noted in a letter to Kohut, one of the few compensations for the discomforts of aging is that the wines you drink tend to get better and better.

As for my personal views on psychoanalysis, I was trained in the Freudian tradition and still feel that my roots are there and that a dynamic way of thinking remains an underlying second nature for any analyst. If Freud were alive today he would be writing very differently than he wrote in 1939, for he understood the very provisional nature of his thinking better than most of his followers did. Some other great influences on my thinking and practice have been Ferenczi, Balint

---

[1] That was in 1960, but times have changed so that I was later awarded the Heinz Hartmann Scholar Prize for 2007 from this same Institute, which for many years now has welcomed psychologists for training without restrictions.

and Winnicott, many poets and artists of all descriptions, and the infant researchers and observers who have begun to discover the non-verbal rhythms of life and to translate them into ways of being with our patients.

When I first opened my private practice in 1962, I worked for a few hours into the night after a full day at the hospital. Naturally, my first referrals were recently-discharged patients so I found myself treating severely disturbed people before the advent of psychotropic drugs. Amazingly, these people appeared to get better at a rate that seems little different from what it is today, but of course I have not done a controlled study and perhaps my memory fails me here. We should recall, however, that there is now plenty of hard evidence that being with people and talking with them in the right way can change their brain chemistry and architecture in ways similar to psychotropic drugs, sometimes with fewer negative side effects.

My early experience with patients usually regarded as difficult or intractable influenced me enormously because I found that the model of classical psychotherapy I had been taught worked well enough with certain people but was ineffective or even downright harmful with others. Not wanting to be in the position of asserting that my treatment was correct and that it was the patient who was either at fault or untreatable, I began to explore different ways of viewing the therapeutic situation.

I was impressed primarily with my mishandling of narcissistic vulnerabilities and as I was trying to reflect on this I stumbled first upon Kohut and then upon Winnicott. Kohut's work was an immediately accessible revelation to me and seemed to spell out the direction my thoughts had been taking. I later had the privilege of meeting him and of speaking at some self-psychology conferences. When Mahler somehow heard that I was going to Chicago, she summoned me to her office to tell me to explain to "Heinz" that she, Margaret Mahler, thought he was wrong about separate lines of narcissistic development. She seemed convinced that if I reported to him what she thought, he would certainly change his mind!

As important as Kohut's writings were and still are, to me the picture always seemed a bit more complicated and eventually I turned to Winnicott for guidance. I was there in 1968 when he gave his famous talk at the New York Psychoanalytic Society on "The Use of an Object," a talk that was met with incomprehension and bewilderment, even by Edith Jacobson whom I so much admired. I also found the paper intriguing but confusing, primarily because I had not yet amassed enough experience of the way he was managing patients to fully comprehend his theory.

Eventually I tried to formulate my evolving understanding in the paper, "The Narcissistic State of Consciousness" included here, and in a book, *Narcissistic States and the Therapeutic Process* in 1985. I found that working with narcissism led inevitably to dealing with sadomasochism and perversions. After seeing many people with sadomasochistic leanings and perversions and thinking it over for a number of years I published my tentative views in *The Language of Perversion and the Language of Love* in 1995. While I have always been primarily interested in how one works with challenging patients in the clinical situation, treating sadomasochism and perversions unsurprisingly leads to questions about the nature of love and the particularly vexing question of love in the analytic situation. That is the subject matter of my later book, *Getting from Here to There: Analytic Love, Analytic Process*, from which some papers are included here.

All in all, I have been working in the area of psychology for almost sixty years now, and for more than 55 years as an analytic candidate or psychoanalyst. I continue to practice, teach and supervise because I find it utterly fascinating and, aside from plentiful vacations, I cannot imagine what else I could be doing with my time that would be more gratifying. I think that we in this field have very special obligations but also very special privileges, and that one of our privileges is the opportunity to obtain a unique view on the human mind at work, as well as the opportunity to further our own self-improvement while being paid for the privilege.

Although no longer involved in formal research, I have over the years retained a steadfast interest in the concept of states of consciousness because it seems to provide a conceptual crossroad where the body meets the mind to give us a view of the person as a functioning whole. This holistic viewpoint is one I have endeavored to maintain, with varying success, in the clinical situation. I am convinced that, to understand our patients well, we must learn to pay equal attention to both body and mind, to both process and content, and to encourage the integration of just those parameters whose dissociation often lies at the very heart of severe pathology. I have tried, as clearly as I can, to elaborate this view in these papers.

Contrary to the usual pessimism encountered these days, I am optimistic about the future of psychoanalysis because I cannot believe that our method of healing people by talking with them is ever going to disappear, notwithstanding the current co-optation of the field by the pharmaceutical-industrial complex. Psychoanalysis has long remained in a self-imposed isolation from which it now seems to be emerging. Today it is forging ties with neuroscience, academic attachment research, traumatology, early infancy programs and other real-world involvements. We have amassed over a hundred years of reflection, experience and research by some of the best scientists of the time on the subjective aspects of the human mind, and we have inherited an incomparably diverse literature. I believe that so long as people continue to think, this effort will not be lost.

Sheldon Bach, Ph.D.

ON NARCISSISM AND ALTERED STATES OF CONSCIOUSNESS

CHAPTER 1

Chimeras: Immunity, Interpenetration, and the True Self

In Greek mythology, the Chimera was an awesome fire-breathing monster with the head of a lion, the body of a goat, and the tail of a serpent, but in medicine, a chimera is a person composed of two genetically distinct types of cells. I learned from a fascinating article on immunity (Holloway, 2007) that human chimeras were first discovered when it was found that some people had more than one blood type. Most of them proved to be "blood chimeras," that is, nonidentical twins who shared a blood supply in the uterus. But many more people are microchimeras and carry smaller numbers of foreign blood cells that may have passed across the placenta from their mother, or persist from a blood transfusion or in vitro fertilization.

When patients need a new heart or other organ transplant, they are put on a lifelong regimen of drugs to suppress their immune system, because otherwise the immune system would reject the transplant as a foreign organism. But although these drugs permit transplants and save lives, they also have debilitating and sometimes deadly side effects, because the weakened immune system has trouble fighting off viruses and cancers.

Some years ago a well-known transplant surgeon named Thomas Starzl made an interesting discovery. He had brought together many of his former patients, including some he had operated on in the early 1960s. He learned that some of them had stopped taking their immunosuppressant drugs a long time ago, but were still in very good health. Starzl tested these patients and discovered that they were microchimeras, that is, that they had foreign donor cells in various tissues and blood.

For Starzl, these shared cells were the key to implant tolerance—acceptance of the graft by the host. His hypothesis, essentially, is that the body comes to terms with the "other" by dealing with it in an incremental way, by coming to see some circulating donor cells as "self" and paving the way for acceptance on a larger scale.

I hope that you are able to forgive this digression into the history of immune reactions because by now you can see that the transplant surgeons are dealing, at least metaphorically, with issues similar to those that face us analysts when we deal with the psyche of our patients. We too are faced with the mystery of how the other, or some part of the other, ultimately may or may not begin to feel like a part of the self. In our own language we talk about identification, introjection, identity, and so forth. By resistance we mean the patient's rejection of transplants, foreign cells, or foreign identities, and by projection we mean that the patient is trying to donate his or her cells that are foreign to us, a donation that we would normally reject with all the force that our own narcissistic defense immune system can muster.

But if, acting as psychoanalysts, we simply accept the patient's projections and try to metabolize them as they pass through us, then we too are engaging in our own process of chimerization, a process about which we probably know as much or as little as the surgeons.

We know, for example, that chimerization or the exchange of foreign cells sometimes occurs between a mother and her fetus. In our psychic analogy, it is most readily apparent between mothers and infants in the early dyad, and we have sometimes even given it the name of interpenetration, particularly emotional interpenetration. It is also a process we have studied at great length in the narcissistic disorders, which are characterized by immune reactions that are excessively strong or excessively weak. In a strong immune reaction the patient (whom I have called an inflated narcissist) is abnormally rejecting of whatever is experienced as other, whereas in a weakened immune reaction the patient (whom I have called a deflated narcissist) is abnormally accepting of whatever is experienced as other.

We have all had the personal experience of a narcissistic patient who seemingly rejects everything we say, only to see our rejected words reemerge weeks or months later as admired ideas, because this time the patient is the one who voices them. This is a typical example of chimerization at its most useful, and it occurs quite naturally in self-object transferences of various kinds.

We also know how to establish a self-object transference or, rather, how to encourage a self-object transference to establish itself. We do so by employing empathy and identification to minimize the differentiation between the patient and ourselves, and also by avoiding any interventions that the patient might experience as objectifying and that would tend to make the patient experience the analyst in the transference as adversarial or like a foreign body.

Thus we know that self-object transferences, in which mirroring, idealizing, empathy, and understanding have minimized the differentiation between patient and analyst, are the most fertile breeding grounds for chimerization. And in the simple example I gave of the patient who rejects the analyst's comment but later takes it over as his own, we have witnessed in vitro the process of chimerization, or the other turning into the self.

What else do we know about this process? Well, as I have suggested, we know that it works best when the differentiation between self and object is minimized, but only within a certain range. This range is what Gergely (2000) has characterized as "a high but imperfect degree of response-contingency" (p. 1205), that is, the object must feel similar to the self but must not feel identical to the self.

In Gergely's paradigm, the infant looks for perfect response contingency only in the earliest period when it is seeking to establish a sense of primary identity or absolute self-identity. Afterward, when primary identity has been established, the infant becomes more interested in new objects that display *similarities* rather than identities and that can be used for idealization, projection, and identification. For an adult, when the object feels *identical* to the self it usually evokes not identifications and chimerization, but rather fright, horror, or an uncanny feeling. We may recall that incident on the train when Freud saw his own reflection in the mirror of his traveling compartment and mistook it for a dirty old man whom he immediately wanted to eject. Typically, the identical self-object has often been regarded as a symbol of Death or other unpleasantness. The major exception that I am aware of involves the psychology of identical twins, which we know to be unusual in many ways.

Although the ancient myth of Narcissus tells of someone who falls in love with his own image, what we normally search for is someone similar to us in certain aspects but not identical. Freud has suggested that certain types of narcissistic choice make us seek someone who resembles what we actually are, or what we once were, or what we would like to become, or someone who was once part of ourselves, as a child to a mother or identical twins to each other.

Freud had also suggested that the search for an anaclitic object is always a re-finding of the original object. Thus, what a man looks for is someone who is similar to his mother, but if the resemblance were to become too close it might evoke the horror of incest.

Similarly, our children are loved and not rejected by us because generally they are experienced as a part of ourselves. In those cases where the mother rejects her child because it actually is defective or perceived as defective (for example—"You look like your father's no-good family"), we usually diagnose pathological narcissism, that is, an overreaction of the narcissistic defense system. The extremes of this syndrome might be postpartum depression, in which some mothers actually attempt to murder their children. But these are the exceptions, and in general our children are recognized by our narcissistic system as part of our self, and they enjoy all of the usual overvaluation, emotional rewards, and criticism that we normally reserve for ourselves and for our own accomplishments.

We have seen that in the process of the other becoming a part of the self, it usually helps if the distinction between the two is minimized, as in a self-object transference. Kohut (1971) gives the famous example of the Catholic patient who was searching for an idealized transference love similar to the one she had for her priest when she was a young girl. When the analyst pointed out to her that he was not Catholic, the treatment fell into a stalemate that necessitated a consultation. The analyst was unable to wear the suit that the patient had bought for him and, for reasons of his own, he felt obligated to make this clarification that the patient had not asked for and did not want to hear.

It seems important for many reasons that the patient be allowed to pursue the transference that she needs at the moment without interruption by reality confrontations or countertransference denials. This is easier said than done, as strong transference demands, whether positive and idealizing or negative and demonizing, place exceptional unconscious pressure on the analyst which, in my experience, no one, no matter how accomplished, has ever been able to completely resist.

But if we *can* allow the patient's transference to play itself out without undue interruption, the rewards can be immense. For one, this helps avoid stalemates and unending sadomasochistic battles but, even more importantly, it *strengthens* the patient's immune system and identity formation. When the typical narcissistic patient who may have rejected your comment six months earlier now "discovers" it for himself and presents it for your admiration, he has performed a piece of metabolic work similar to the work the analyst performs when he or she accepts an unbearable projection from the patient and metabolizes and returns it in some usable form. The patient has taken a piece of you, a piece of otherness, which he initially rejected because it was experienced as an attack on his self and, through the process of chimerization or psychic metabolism, he has turned it into a usable form that now belongs to and strengthens his own sense of self. Once this process gathers force, the patient usually becomes more and more able to hear your comments and to accept or reject them in a less allergic or dichotomous fashion. One might say that because he feels his immune system or identity to be stronger; he feels less threatened by otherness.

But the process of chimerization, or making a piece of the other into a part of the self, has other aspects as well. Let us imagine a situation where the analyst makes an interpretation and the narcissistic patient rejects it, but the analyst continues to insist on his or her interpretation and to analyze why the patient needs to reject it. If this scenario persists for a long time, certain narcissistic patients may withdraw from the treatment, that is, heighten their defenses and abandon the other, while others may masochistically surrender and accept the interpretation and thereby abandon their self.

But this piece of the other, accepted through surrender rather than through metabolization, will not have the same internal status as a piece of the other absorbed through chimerization within the self. I believe that it will remain isolated from what is experienced as a true self and exist as a separate, undigested introject in a separate self-state or as part of a false self. It will not belong to the true self in the same way it would have if the patient had processed it spontaneously.

To discover a part of the other in oneself and experience it as one's own, or to have a part of the other intrusively forced on oneself are of course extremes of a continuum, and intermediary cases could lead to other possible results. But it seems to me that at least in the extreme case, it might be wise to react to the patient's No! in the same way one reacts to a child who, in the process of forming his or her identity, goes through a period of saying No to everything, even to things he or she might very much desire. As Winnicott (1955) noted: "The refusal of it [the good object] is part of the process of creating it" (p. 182). That being said, the intermediary situations, between totally accepting the patient's rejection of your comment or totally insisting that he or she accept your comment, are of great interest. Freud advised us to wait before interpreting until something is just about to become conscious, but it has never been clear to me why in that case one should not wait until it does in fact become conscious. Ellman (2000) has characterized this continuum in terms of usability: That is, we wait to make an interpretation until we feel that the patient will be able to use it without rejecting it, which is a more patient-centered approach. What seems most important to me, rather than whether the patient ostensibly accepts or rejects the analyst's interpretation, is how the acceptance or rejection feels to the patient. I think it makes a critical difference whether the interpretation can be metabolized and can feel part of the true self, or whether it will continue to feel like an intrusion, like an introject of the other that can never become truly self, or whether it can only be accepted through compliance, in which case it may become part of some false self-state or -system. Developmentally, it seems crucial for the infant to feel that its actions are being propelled by his own energy, rather than coerced by outside impingements.

To quote Winnicott (1955) directly:

> In the early development of the human being the environment that behaves well enough enables personal growth to take place. The self processes then may continue active, in an unbroken line of living growth. If the environment behaves not well enough, then the individual is engaged in reactions to impingement, and the self processes are interrupted. If the state of affairs reaches a quantitative limit the core of the self begins to get protected; there is a hold-up, the self cannot make new processes unless and until the environment failure situation is corrected...With the true self there develops a false self built on a defence-compliance basis, the acceptance of reaction to impingement. The development of a false self is one of the most successful defence organisations designed for the protection of the true self's core, and its existence results in the sense of futility. (p. 25)

Often these self processes have been conceptualized by assuming a continuum of internalizations ranging from incorporation, through introjection, to identification, representing the analyst's view of increasingly complex levels of object relations. Most of the time these conceptualizations seem to have assumed a unified ego state, and have not sufficiently included the idea of multiple selves or of a true-to false-self continuum. This amplified conceptualization includes what I believe to be the very important parameter of just how the person *experiences* the internalizations. As Winnicott (1965) noted: "Compliance brings immediate rewards and adults only too easily mistake compliance for growth. The maturational processes can be by-passed by a series of identifications, so that what shows clinically is a false, acting self, a copy of someone perhaps; and what could be called a true or essential self becomes hidden, and become deprived of living experience" (p. 102).

It is this "living experience" that, to my mind, is one essential difference between the "true" and "false" self. I believe that is why Winnicott insisted on the "play" elements in psychoanalysis, because play is a *living* experience as opposed to compliance, which feels unspontaneous and deadening. In a *lived* or playful experience the psyche and soma are connected and communicating with each other in a fully symbolized way, whereas in the act of compliance psyche and soma become dissociated, with the body often feeling psychically surrendered to the other, and mind and body communicating primarily through concrete signaling (Bach, 1994; Ghent, 1990; Goldberg, 1995). For example, many complaints about boredom, emptiness, meaninglessness, and the like are complaints about experience that is not being owned and spontaneously lived, that is, complaints about a true self that has been surrendered or not yet found.

It seems to me that another aspect of true and false self experience is that living "true self" experiences occur in the context of an ongoing continuity of metabolization or chimerization. I mean by this that living experience occurs in the context of the self trying to deal with the other in an ongoing way, and not simply by rigidly applying the already learned formulaic rules of what pertains to self and to other. A personal example of what I mean occurred in the early years of my practice, when a young woman patient came into my office lugging a huge framed oil painting of her father and offered it to me. Because I had been taught to question enactments and never to quietly accept what was given to me, I asked her about this gift, whereupon she threw it out the window, where it narrowly missed killing a pedestrian seven floors below. If I had been alive instead of acting like a dead analyst, I might have recognized how important it was for *her* that I take this picture and preserve her father from her towering rage.

Because the environment, and this includes the cultural environment, is always diverse and continually in flux, the mental and physical immune systems must be constantly adapting, constantly sorting, filtering, and metabolizing to remain alive. It seems to me that one of the most prominent signs of both mental and physical aging in any organism is the slowing down of its ability to change and adapt, and the increasingly stereotyped responses it makes along older, nonadaptive neural pathways. One of the most obvious cultural examples is the difficulty that many older people have in adapting to the art, music, literature, and play behavior of the younger generations. Analogously, the immune system of older people has greater difficulty in coping with new challenges, toxins, and viruses.

It would seem that in the course of any analysis the patient's immune system and the analyst's immune system are engaged in intensive conversation. By this I mean that the patient's narcissistic defenses are interacting with the analyst's narcissistic defenses in a way designed to deal with each other's strangeness, improbability, and otherness, and to allow this otherness to be recognized, affirmed, and in good-enough instances somehow slowly metabolized. It is this process of recognition, interpenetration, metabolization, and reintegration that I have likened to chimerization, which also depends on the immune system's ability to change its classification of a foreign body from other to self, or depends on some change in the foreign body itself, or more likely both.

Our own thinking about the process of accepting a foreign body into the self has led to the idea that it can be accepted through interpenetration and metabolization, which makes it feel like part of the true self, or it can be accepted through psychic compliance, which makes it feel like part of the false self, or some varying position in between these two. Because any particular organ graft seems to be either totally accepted or totally rejected by the body, immune system reactions have usually been considered to be binary or dichotomous, but we have seen that they too can change over time. Furthermore, there remains that whole mysterious area of autoimmune reactions and diseases, suggesting that in some cases the immune reaction may not be as binary or as time-delimited as it appears to be.

I would now like to discuss some practical applications of this point of view in working with the more challenging patients. Let's begin by imagining that all transference paradigms in a psychoanalysis can be sorted into two categories: self-transferences and other-transferences. We have learned by now that transference goes both ways in an analysis, so that I mean to include both patient and analyst when I say that in a self-transference the other person feels preponderantly similar to oneself while in an other-transference the other person feels preponderantly different from oneself. In a self-transference the other member of the dyad is experienced as in some way belonging to or allied with the self; one could say that this includes varieties of positive identifications as well as various kinds of narcissistic, idealizing, mirroring, and other self-object transferences. I should add that in my experience one can be perfectly aware of the actual separateness of another person at one level while at another level still identifying with, idealizing, or holding him or her in a self-object transference.

In what I am calling an other-transference, the other member of the dyad is experienced not as allied with or wishfully belonging to the self, but rather as a frightening, uncanny, and potentially malevolent other. One might say that other-transferences include varieties of paranoid, projective, alien, and uncanny transferences along with some kind of negative identification or negative affect. Obviously, this distinction may not be as dichotomous as I am making it here, and one can easily imagine a continuum between self- and other-transferences. But because most thorough analyses seem to oscillate or cycle between self- and other-transferences, I am interested here in thinking about how to understand and manage these transference cycles.

Let me say immediately that I believe one of the most important factors in this cycling is the sense of dyadic or analytic trust (Ellman, 1998), both on the part of the patient and on the part of the analyst. I am going to define "trust" as a continuing belief in the ability of the dyad to survive, to regulate each member of the dyad, and eventually to symbolize their experience together. Thus the waxing and waning of analytic trust in both patient and analyst is one major cause of cycle shifts between self-transferences and other-transferences.

I should also mention that, while patient and analyst may both be in self- or other-transferences at the same time, that is, they may simultaneously be experiencing each other either as similar or as dissimilar, other combinations are possible. For example, it is possible for a patient to be in a self-transference with the analyst while the analyst has the patient in an other-transference, that is, the patient may experience the analyst as similar to himself or herself while the analyst may be experiencing the patient as dissimilar to himself or herself. This would be an example of what we commonly call countertransference on the analyst's part, and I will offer some illustrations later on.

It is by now commonplace in the infant observation literature to speak of dyadic regulation as being disrupted and then repaired. These cycles of rupture and repair occur regularly in ordinary good-enough mothering, and it is only when rupture in the dyad seems to have become irreparable that one begins to question the capacity of this particular mother and this particular infant to be regulated or to regulate each other. To the extent that these observations apply to the adult analytic dyad (Beebe & Lachmann, 2005), such a seemingly irreparable rupture can arouse the most intense feelings of anger, hopelessness, and despair in both patient and analyst.

It is, I believe, these seemingly irreparable ruptures in dyadic regulation that can transform a positive self-transference, whether in the patient or analyst, into a negative other-transference. It is when either patient or analyst or both lose hope in the ability of the dyad to survive, to regulate each other, and to symbolize their experience together that the opposite member of the dyad turns into a malevolent other. Likewise, it is when each member regains trust in the ability of the dyad to survive, to self-regulate, and to symbolize that the transference paradigm shifts from an other paradigm into some variety of a self paradigm.

Frequently the shift from a self-transference to an other-transference occurs when some traumatic failure, which occurred in the patient's or analyst's childhood, or perhaps both, gets reactivated in the transference. Often this is accompanied by some actual repetitive failure, by either patient or analyst, in the here and now. The analytic repair of this trauma can then transform a malevolent other-transference back into a positive self-transference.

Of course, patients and analysts may already have come with a preformed transference of some kind, as did a relatively new patient who one day, after carefully scrutinizing my bookshelves, turned to me and belligerently asked, "Why do you have all these foreign books here instead of regular books?" This took on added significance because the questioner was both a cultured and educated person. When I suggested that perhaps he felt that *I* was foreign to him, he agreed and added, "It feels to me that you're someone else, someone very different from me, someone observing me from far away and constantly disapproving." This other-transference grew increasingly more disturbing over time, and it took many years before we could transition into a mild variety of self-mirroring transference.

Because I believe that this sort of interaction is constantly operating on both sides of the couch, let me give you another example from an extended consultation with an *analyst* who brought this case because he "was having trouble with it." It took several interviews for this competent and experienced analyst to overcome his embarrassment and admit to me that he found the patient disgusting, that he could not wait until the patient left his office, and that this physical repulsion was so extreme that he used a special pillow only for this patient so that he would not "contaminate" the regular pillow. After ascertaining that the patient seemed objectively clean and not obviously repellent, we could agree that he presented some special issues for this analyst who, with only a little help from me, then began to seriously investigate his own feelings. It slowly became clear that the analyst was repulsed by the patient's utter self-absorption, his absolutely total involvement in his own eating, sleeping, excretions, and appearance, so that little room was left for the analyst. The patient was so intensely interested in his own appearance that, paradoxically, his appearance had become repulsive to the analyst; he was so involved in his own excretions that the analyst had begun to treat him as though he *were* an excretion. Thus the patient's self-transference, a mirroring transference in this case, was met with the analyst's other-transference, based on the analyst's own childhood fears of being taken over, a true countertransference reaction.

It was gratifying to watch how, as the analyst began to understand this and clear his other-transference feelings and lend himself more easily to what the patient needed, the course of the analysis changed dramatically. One day the analyst casually remarked, "You know, waiting for X the other day I began to realize how much I looked forward to seeing him!" Needless to say, in the interim the tone of the analytic work had changed from one of repetitive confrontations and defensiveness to one of greater collaboration.

Another constellation of cases that I commonly see are those that the analyst brings because he or she is afraid the patient is about to leave treatment. Sometimes the patient has openly declared that he or she is thinking of leaving or about to leave, and the analyst has tried various interventions that do not seem to work. The most striking cases are those where the analyst had felt that the treatment was going along well enough until suddenly one day the patient announces that he or she is terminating at the end of this session. Here we can note how the analyst's working self-transference can suddenly be turned into an other-transference—the patient who threatens to leave may immediately become an unknown stranger, often both feared and hated.

Usually there has been some disruption of trust, and the trick is to find and repair it before the patient actually leaves. Sometimes it can be something as obvious as the analyst's recent vacation, cancellation, or a change of appointment, a disruption to which the analyst has attached little significance, but which, in the transference, feels momentous to the patient. We can always get into the habit of taking a second look and trying to experience the transference from the patient's point of view.

Sometimes even the patient who continually talks about leaving may really be trying to send us a secret message. Perhaps when analysts are excessively anxious about a patient's leaving, they may be unaware or even defending against the realization of just how dependent the patient has become. And patients in turn may be speaking of leaving in order to reassure themselves that they are not really as dependent as they unconsciously feel or as they might like to become. The analyst can effectively reassure the patient simply by becoming cognizant of his own reluctance to permit a regression to dependency and of his own need to use an other-transference in order to keep the self-transference at bay.

I cannot sufficiently emphasize how important I feel it is for the analyst to trust or to become able to trust the analytic dyad. We talk a great deal about the patient's difficulties in trusting, but much less so about the analyst's. After all, we have invited a total stranger into our office, and we know enough to believe that anything is possible. I remember many years ago a new patient who arrived carrying a large gym bag, and my growing consternation listening to him as it slowly dawned on me that the bag contained a loaded assault rifle. As my office was then in my apartment and my family close by, I felt this was more than I could tolerate and that I would be unable to work with him in a useful manner. Probably sensing my discomfort, the young man didn't seem overly eager to work with me either, and we soon came to the mutual decision that the trip to my office was too far for him and that he should seek a therapist closer to home.

I also recall another young woman, badly scarred from a serious accident, who chose to sit down on the couch for the initial interview and began to tell me her story, oblivious to the fact that I was transfixed watching the cockroaches that were crawling out from under her coat onto my couch. In that case we actually did begin an analysis that turned out to be quite helpful to her, and probably an important part of it was the fact that I had not been disgusted or put off by her initial presentation.

The patient originally comes to us as a Stranger, just as we are a Stranger to him. Perhaps we tend to forget how difficult it was for some of us to get through the first session of our own analysis, and how difficult it also must be for each new patient. We are implicitly asking each of our patients to entrust their minds to a complete stranger. For my own part, I struggle in each analysis to reach a position where I feel I can trust the patient with my own mind and feel I have nothing to hide from him. This does not necessarily mean telling him about myself or engaging in what is known as self-disclosure, but rather allowing him to see the reasoning behind my thinking and allowing him to witness my mind at work in the process of free-associating or making formulations. I feel that at the appropriate time it is useful for most patients to experience the analyst as he tries to deal with doubts and ambiguities or to hold two ideas or two roles in mind at the same time, for it opens up the possibility of their doing the same. So these are some of the ways that analysts can work at trusting their patients and reducing their fear of the patient's otherness, a fear that the patient senses immediately and reacts to with mistrust.

For certain patients with extreme problems of object constancy and self-continuity, every time the analyst returns from a break it is like a return from the dead, both a feared and a wished- for state. It may be that one general function of a self-transference is to protect us, like a double does, from our archaic fears of separation and death, just as one aspect of an other-transference may be the breakthrough of these very fears and the unpleasant realization of the ultimate separation that awaits us all. For attachment and separation are two of the poles between which human beings oscillate, and to my mind one of the paradoxes in any treatment is the need to create a space for the patient without also creating a distance.

The person who has spoken most cogently about this problem is of course Winnicott, who has delineated the space that lies between and contains both self and other. This intermediate area seems to be peopled, in both sickness and health, by a variety of transitional phenomena ranging from security blankets, imaginary companions, doubles, vampires, ghosts, and other uncanny phenomena to gods, muses, and the artistic creation, all infused with various admixtures of self and other.

But these transitional products and the transitional area itself all depend on the maintenance of some form of trust and dialogue between self and other. When the dialogue fails or is traumatically disrupted, it can be disastrous or even deadly, as with hospitalism and marasmus. So the psychoanalytic process itself, as is true of most powerful therapies can, if it miscarries, be dangerous as well as helpful.

The derailment or failure of the dialogue is a subject of much interest these days and is being studied by infant researchers, attachment theorists, psychobiologists, sociologists, and others, as well as by psychoanalysts. Taken in its largest sense, it has the most profound implications, for war is of course the continuation of a failed dialogue by other means. So I feel that psychoanalytic research has the potential to teach us much about managing diverse situations, including wars, in which our fellow human beings are turned into or turn themselves into malevolent others.

I have suggested that most thorough analyses pass through cycles of both self- and other-transferences. Oscillations between these transferences are a normal part of the process, and these cycles are correlated with shifts in the analytic material and with different phases of the analysis, as well as with shifts in the degree of analytic trust experienced by both patient and analyst.

The evolution of these transferences may be aided by interpretations or other interventions, but they also have a life of their own, dependent as they are on shifts in analytic trust. I want to give an example drawn from early analytic history. In "Analysis Terminable and Interminable," Freud mentions that Ferenczi had at one time reproached him for not analyzing the latent negative transference in their short three-week analysis together. Freud maintained that in order to elicit this negative transference he would have had to deliberately offend Ferenczi. In my view, if one considers that the official three-week analysis in some sense unofficially stretched throughout their lifetime and was in fact interminable, the switch from self- to other-transference happened automatically as both Freud and Ferenczi became increasingly less trustful of each other. I think that Ferenczi, who felt just as alone as had Freud in his unprecedented endeavors, had always hoped that Freud would supervise or at least discuss Ferenczi's grand experiments, but they went beyond Freud's tolerance for narcissistic disequilibrium. Interestingly, in their last encounter Freud felt that Ferenczi "exuded an icy coldness," whereas Ferenczi noted that Freud had refused to shake his hand. Thus these two dearest and closest of friends had become others to each other and even related in an uncanny way: Freud felt that Ferenczi had become paranoiac and developed "uncanny" delusions, while Ferenczi felt completely misunderstood and rejected, and he developed a momentary walking paralysis (Bonomi, 1999).

As it happens, in the course of any analysis, the patient may present us with a picture of ourselves that we find unpleasant and can barely recognize, but as analysts we are obliged to "wear the suit" that the patient offers to us without too much protest, even though we find it uncomfortable and ill-fitting. This suit may feel terribly uncomfortable whether the patient has us in a positive self-transference, for example an idealizing transference, or in a negative other-transference, for example an "uncanny" stranger transference. In either case it upsets our narcissistic equilibrium because, in the idealizing transference, we know we are not as perfect as the patient believes and it leaves no space for our true feelings, whereas in the "uncanny" transference we know we are not as hostile and unfriendly as the patient believes and we feel unrecognized, also with no place for our true feelings.

In both cases we try to wear the uncomfortable suit without too much protest while we wait for the time when we can either make an interpretation that the patient will find "usable" (Ellman, 2007) or when the patient may arrive at this insight unaided. But, of course, in wearing the suit we begin to change its shape until it becomes a cocreation that is neither the suit the patient first gave us nor the one that we would have chosen for ourselves. Thus the resolution of the self-other dichotomy is built into the process if the analyst can only leave himself or herself open and trust the process enough to go along with it.

I have tried in this paper to make an analogy between the functioning of the immune system and the functioning of the narcissistic system both in keeping the other or non-self at bay and also in allow-ing for its eventual, gradual, and nonthreatening assimilation and metabolization. This led to a discussion of transferences where the other is experienced as either similar to or very foreign from the self, and the transformations and evolution of these transferences in the course of any analysis. I emphasized the importance of how the pa-tient actually experiences any intervention: whether he or she experiences it as being unusable because it feels like an intrusion of a foreign and untrustworthy body, or whether the patient feels it to be usable because it comes from a trustworthy source that feels connected to himself or herself, or some intermediate position. I speculated on the continuum of internalizations that range from feeling like part of the true self to feeling like part of the false self to areas in-between, all of which are subject to flux because of the influence of the present on memories of the past and vice versa, Freud's principle of *Nachtraglichkeit.* This led to the importance of establishing trust in the analysis, which is inevitably correlated with continuing attempts on the part of both patient and analyst to maintain their threatened self-esteem, to recover their narcissistic equilibrium, and to continue to survive as a dyad, to regulate each other, and to symbolize their experience together.

To some extent we are all chimeras, that is, an assemblage of dif-fering and sometimes incompatible needs, desires, fantasies, and self-representations, which we try to cobble together, more or less suc-cessfully, as best we can. We have now learned that an absolutely essential component of successful assemblage is another person who will allow himself or herself to be used by us in exactly the way that we need for the process to feel authentic and self-generated. I hope I have succeeded in sketching an overview of this process and convey-ing some sense of just how mutually gratifying it can be when it works successfully for both participants.

REFERENCES

Bach, S. (1994). *The Language of Perversion and the Language of Love.* Northvale, NJ: Aronson.

Beebe, B., & Lachmann, F. (2005). *Infant Research and Adult Treatment: Co-constructing Interactions.* London: Taylor and Francis.

Bonomi, C. (1999). Flight into sanity: Jones' allegation of Ferenzci's mental deterioration reconsidered. *International Journal of Psycho-Analysis* 80:507-542.

Ellman, S. (1998) Enactment, transference and analytic trust. In *Enactment: Toward a new approach to the therapeutic relationship*, eds. S. Ellman & M. Moskowitz. Northvale, NJ: Aronson, pp. 183-203.

Ellman, S.J. (2007). Analytic trust and transference: Love, healing ruptures and facilitating repair. *Psychoanalytic Inquiry* 27:246-263.

Gergely, G. (2000). Reapproaching Mahler: New perspectives on normal autism, symbiosis, splitting and libidinal object constancy from cognitive developmental theory. *Journal of the American Psychoanalytic Association* 48:1197-1228.

Ghent, E. (1990), Masochism, submission, surrender—Masochism as a perversion of surrender. *Contemporary Psychoanalysis* 26:108-136.

Goldberg, P. (1995). "Successful" dissociation, pseudovitality, and unauthentic use of the senses. *Psychoanalytic Dialogues* 5:493-510.

Holloway, M. (2007). Graft and host, together forever. *Scientific American* 296:32-33.

Kohut, H. (1971). *The Analysis of the Self.* New York: International Universities Press.

Winnicott, D.W. (1955). Metapsychological and clinical aspects of regression within the psycho-analytical set-up. *International Journal of Psycho-Analysis* 36:16-26.

Winnicott, D.W. (1965). The maturational processes and the facilitating environment: Studies in the theory of emotional development. *The International Psycho-Analytical Library* 64:1-276.

CHAPTER 2

On Being Forgotten and Forgetting One's Self

But were I granted time to accomplish my work, I would not fail to stamp it with the seal of that Time, now so forcibly present to my mind, and in it I would describe men, even at the risk of giving them the appearance of monstrous beings, as occupying in Time a much greater place than that so sparingly conceded to them in Space, a place indeed extended beyond measure, because, like giants plunged in the years, they touch at once those periods of their lives—separated by so many days—so far apart in Time.

Marcel Proust (1957), p. 2

Although in the real world, our experience of seeing, hearing, smelling, and touching people guarantees their existence for us, their continued existence when not within the grasp of our senses is guaranteed only by our memory of them. And just as we keep people alive by remembering them, so we sustain feelings of our own aliveness not only through the ongoing awareness of our actual physical beings, but also through feeling that we exist and are remembered in the minds of others (Stern, 1985; Winnicott, 1958). This paper deals with those who cannot feel continually alive in the present because, as children, they did not feel continually remembered and alive in the minds of their primary caretakers.

I first became interested in this topic when a patient, Jeffrey, told me that as a child, he was well known at Macy's Department Store because his mother would regularly come to the lost-and-found area to retrieve him after she had lost him while shopping. Although Jeffrey recounted this story in an amusing way, it turned out to be only the tip of an iceberg of isolation and despair, of which he had been largely unconscious.

From the beginning of the analysis, I had noted that, after mentioning some name or incident, Jeffrey would casually ask, "I've told you about him, haven't I?" or "Have I told you about that?" My countertransferential anxiety alerted me to the importance of these questions, but it was a while before we could discuss his expectation that I really would not remember what he had said yesterday or the day before. It took even longer to clarify that when he talked about something, he often unconsciously tried to remind me of what had happened, in a subtle way, so that I would be filled in even if I had forgotten it.

The *Oxford English Dictionary* (1989) defines forgetting as "to miss or lose one's hold" on something or someone (p. 70), and Jeffrey's conviction that he would be forgotten had led him to lose his hold on many things in his own life, most notably on a firm sense of himself. Jeffrey presented with many phobias, one of which was a fear of flying. Since his executive position required him to fly on a fairly regular basis, he was constantly living with anticipatory fear, which at times was so severe that he had walked off an already-boarded plane. After an appreciable time in analysis, when the transference had entered an early maternal phase, he began to get frightened on the couch, to feel that he was drifting, had no direction, and was unable to think or talk. As these moments increased in intensity, he would often feel the necessity to sit up and look at me, which usually relieved his anxiety. Eventually, it became clear that he was terrified of "losing his connection" with me, and that sitting up and looking at me reassured him that I was still there and thinking of him. For many months, we explored his anxiety about drifting without direction, and we learned that this anxiety culminated in a terrifying fantasy of falling endlessly into empty space. But we were still not sure what this was about.

When Jeffrey took business flights, he was usually accompanied by Matthew, a young assistant whose career he had mentored and to whom he had a close attachment. Jeffrey and I both assumed that being accompanied by someone helped to reduce his anxiety, and indeed, when frightened on the plane, he had often turned to Matthew for some kind of reassurance. But one day, Matthew suddenly became ill, and Jeffrey, on last-minute notice, was obliged to fly without him. Much to his surprise and my own, he discovered that he felt much better on the plane when Matthew was not with him, "because I suddenly realized that even if I died, there would be someone alive out there who would still remember me."

It thus became increasingly clear that at the center of Jeffrey's multiple phobias and anxieties lay a primary anxiety of being forgotten, a wordless fear of falling in an endless tumble out of his mother's mind and into the oblivion of nonremembrance. This primitive anxiety, which has been touched on in diverse ways in my work (Bach, 1985, 1995), as well as in that of Modell (1993), Ogden (1986), and Winnicott (1958), among others, seems to be related to a disturbance in the capacity for evocative constancy and a consequent difficulty in the establishment of stable representations and reliable self and object constancy (Auerbach, 1990, 1993). While the importance of a reliable maternal presence for the development of evocative constancy has often been noted, Jeffrey's case emphasizes the importance not only of the mother's physical presence, but especially of her psychic construction and holding of the child in memory. I have elsewhere reported from the other side, as it were, the case of a mother whose repeated suicidal threats and attempts were only finally resolved when she became able to retain the memory of her children-with-herself-as-mother as part of an enlarged state of consciousness (Bach, 1998). So this mutual holding in memory may well have life-and-death implications for both child and mother.

To return to Jeffrey's analysis, it became apparent in our work together that, in addition to his fear of flying, he also suffered from an elevator phobia, a claustrophobia associated particularly with bathrooms, a fear of public speaking, and a generalized social phobia. As we analyzed each of these phobias in detail, we learned that they formed an interconnected network centering on the same fear of being forgotten. Although we later began to use the concepts of *being forgotten* and of *not being remembered* interchangeably, the phenomenological experience of Jeffrey's fear was specifically of not being remembered, as if the act of being remembered by someone was very literally what was keeping him alive. And indeed this seemed accurate enough, because—at least for Jeffrey's mother—the state of not remembering her child seemed to be the more frequent and natural one, whereas forgetting him was often linked to a more deliberate but unacknowledged withdrawal, which served as a punishment when Jeffrey had crossed her in some way.

Who actually was this mother who appeared to be—both in Jeffrey's memory and in our analytic reconstructions—not remembering her own son? Here I should mention that I am not unaware of current controversies about childhood amnesia and reconstruction of the past (e.g., Fonagy, 1999), and I recognize that for a long time now, it has been out of fashion to attend to Freud's (1999) admonition that "analytic work deserves to be recognized as genuine psycho-analysis only when it has succeeded in removing the amnesia which conceals from the adult his knowledge of his childhood from its beginning" (p. 183). Nonetheless, my clinical experience has repeatedly led me to believe that in many cases, it is possible to reconstruct a patient's childhood with a reasonable degree of certainty, and moreover, that often the very process of this reconstruction is of great therapeutic importance.

In Jeffrey's case, his mother was someone he saw frequently as an adult, so that the material we worked on came from present-day telephone conversations or other interactions, often only a few hours or days old. Furthermore, Jeffrey's reports of his mother's current behavior and his recovered memories of her as a child retained a remarkable consistency over many years, and our eventual understanding of her behavior allowed us to consistently predict her actions in novel situations whose outcome would not be obvious. As is quite typical in such cases, Jeffrey's initial conviction was that he had experienced the most normal of childhoods, that his siblings were all wonderfully content, and that his own symptoms and emerging memories of early confusion, pain, and despair were proof that there was indeed something terribly wrong with him.

Over the course of the analysis, I developed a fantasy that I would be able to recognize Jeffrey's mother if I met her, and that I would understand her psychology. One of the many aspects of this fantasy was my growing confidence in the convergence of our two primary sources of information: Jeffrey's emerging memories of the interaction between his mother and himself, and our own reenactments in the transference and countertransference during the course of the analysis. I found it significant that I thought I would be able to recognize Jeffrey's mother, first because the analytic process involved a good deal of work by Jeffrey and me, and second, because a correlative was that Jeffrey now believed that he understood his mother's mind, which I took to be an essential part of his understanding his own mind. Before that point in the analysis, Jeffrey had usually felt confused by his mother's mental operations, and indeed quite hopeless about ever comprehending them. But I strongly believe that understanding how one's mother's or father's mind works is an important task of growing up, and one that has gone awry for many of our patients (Bach, 2002).

For example, when Jeffrey developed a serious medical condition that called for a complicated decision about whether to opt for drug treatment or surgery, his mother urged him to undergo surgery without even fully listening to an explanation of the issues. By this time, Jeffrey was able to see that she could not tolerate either complexity or ambiguity, and he could comment as follows: "That's the way she is—she just does things and doesn't think about them, and that way, she can actually deny that anything really bad has happened."

And indeed his mother, although an educated and intelligent woman, seemed to live in a world of superstitions, primitive beliefs, and magic, a world in which Jeffrey had been immersed to an extent that he had not fully comprehended. In his mother's either-or-world, things were either good or bad, right or wrong, smart or stupid, friendly or dangerous, and nothing existed between these extremes. Furthermore, her children could find themselves in the smart or good category one day, and in the stupid or bad category the next, without their having any idea what they might have done to warrant this shift. What Jeffrey had experienced throughout his childhood, and what he conveyed to me via transference enactments, was that *his mother had given him no real concept of process.* In practice, this meant to Jeffrey that if you let anything get even a little bit out of control, it could turn into its opposite—i.e., if you sneezed, that meant you were sick and going to die, or if you asked a question, that meant you were stupid and did not belong in the present company.

In paying attention to and reflecting on this world of superstition and magic that Jeffrey inhabited with his mother, we slowly came to realize that one of its main characteristics was this pervasive lack of a sense of process. One day, Jeffrey said, "It seems to me that each time I meet my mother, it's like having a new experience … as if we were starting afresh. I don't think I feel that way with most people…. Sometimes I have a good conversation with her and I feel connected, but then I'll meet her again and it's almost like meeting a different person. I think that it's very upsetting to me … there's no continuity…."

"When I was a kid, I used to take karate class," he continued, "and I liked it a lot. The instructors there thought I was very good, and they always picked me to demonstrate to the other kids. So I would be coming out of karate, where they thought I was wonderful, and then I would be expecting my mother to pick me up, and she didn't come, and I was waiting around, wondering if she would come or not. And then I would start to have these fantasies about meeting some big guy on the street who insulted me and said I was only a kid, and then I challenged him and used my karate, and he was really amazed when I laid him out flat!…I guess I must have been really angry at my mother, but that never even crossed my mind….

"And I used to dream about coming out of karate class, where everyone thought I was so wonderful, and my mother would be there, and I would jump into the car and tell her how great the class was, and she would be excited along with me. In my dreams, it would all come together: the excitement of the class, my mother's excitement, and everyone thinking I was great. But in reality, it was always split apart."

And it was in just this way that we learned the details of the discontinuities in Jeffrey's life that had never been repaired—the ruptures that had never been mended, the rents in the fabric of his ego that brought him to a halt in whatever he might undertake, whether in work or in love. It seemed that he could never count on feeling that the past was connected to the present and would flow into the future, or that each little fragment of daily experience fit into an overall pattern that gave a meaning to life. On the contrary, when he first came to analysis, Jeffrey lived his life in discrete and fragmented moments, which he experienced as unconnected to each other in any meaningful or unified way. Although he desperately felt the urge to contact other people, he could neither figure out how to do this, nor manage to pull together the scattered segments of his life experience. Thus, his memories of his life were split off from each other and stereotyped in such a way that living memories were shielded by a screen of words. Emotional memories from his early years were almost entirely absent. One could say with some legitimacy that Jeffrey had forgotten his childhood.

I puzzled over this to myself for many months, until one day when Jeffrey came in angry with himself. He began by saying, "I called my mother again...but why do I call her? Out of guilt or some other kind of obligation? She kept asking me if I had written a thank-you note to this person I hardly know who did something or other for my brother that has nothing to do with me....She's so concerned that I should do the right thing, but she doesn't seem to have any idea about who I actually am. I can't understand why I keep calling her!"

I commented, "You keep calling her to make sure that she doesn't forget you."

Jeffrey seemed taken aback. "That makes a lot of sense," he said. "I never thought of it that way, but it's true. Did I ever tell you that I always say, 'Mom, it's Jeffrey'—as if she wouldn't recognize my voice, wouldn't know who I am...?"

In fact, he had never told me this, but it dovetailed perfectly with his transference expectation that I would forget what he said, and also with his subtle attempts to remind me about what had happened in our previous sessions. So it made sense that Jeffrey would keep reminding his mother who he was—and, expectably enough, at the height of this transference paradigm, I occasionally found myself forgetting who my next patient was, when the next patient was Jeffrey, whom I had been seeing at the same hour for years.

It was at this point that I began to more fully realize how we are all bound together in time by a network of expectations, of which we are only dimly aware and which become clearly visible only when they are disrupted by dysfunction or pathology. I was reminded of a patient I had seen many years before who would constantly ask me, "When you come into the waiting room, how can you be so sure that it's me who will be there, and not another person, or some giant insect or a plant?" Although at that time, I had been able to respond in an appropriately analytic way, it now seemed to me that I had not fully appreciated the lived experience embedded in this poignant cry from the patient's heart.

While I had assumed from early on that there must be some kind of projective identification going on between Jeffrey and his mother that made her forget him, over time, we began to learn things about his mother that made her own part in this equation loom even larger than expected. For as Jeffrey began to feel less need to call his mother frequently, it became evident that she felt no need to call him at all. And so they went from having spoken to each other several times a week to not talking to each other for weeks on end—until Jeffrey called her, at which point she would reproach him for not having called earlier. Mother was apparently unable even to entertain the possibility that she could have called him.

I now learned that while Jeffrey was at college, his father had died, and his mother had not even notified him beforehand of his father's illness, in order "not to disturb his studies." Instead, she had notified him of the funeral at the last minute. In the period of mourning following his father's death, she had spoken only of her own loss, never once acknowledging that Jeffrey had lost someone important, too. And when it came time to distribute his father's legacy (which had been left entirely to her), she divided it in such a way that Jeffrey was objectively deprived of his fair share.

So it seemed that there were actual events in the past and particular attitudes of his mother's that formed an important part of the reasons why Jeffrey felt himself to be a forgotten person. Of course, the most significant result of his feeling not remembered by his mother was his pervasive sense that *he was a stupid and unmemorable person*, in addition to his total inability to vividly remember his childhood. For by not remembering it, he was forgetting a very important piece of himself—one that existed not only in the past, but that was also unconsciously affecting his every thought and action in the present, as well as his hopes and aspirations for the future.

In his repeated references to the concept of *Nachtraglichkeit*, Freud (1896) insisted on the ongoing two-way interaction between past and present. He noted not only the possible delayed effects of an earlier trauma, but also the mind's capacity to retrospectively attribute a causal meaning to an earlier event at a later time. In this way, both the past and the present are constantly rearranging or retranscribing each other in human memory, and this rearrangement affects our expectations for the future as well. Proust, also, showed how the human being is in a constant struggle to recapture his or her past, and emphasized that true memory is not merely a dry register of occurrences, but rather a total evocation of an experienced sensory and phenomenal world (Poland, 1992).

It was this submerged phenomenal and sensual world of his childhood with which Jeffrey was out of touch, and it only began to emerge in bits and fragments as the analysis proceeded. And in the course of our explorations, I repeatedly sensed that Jeffrey's lack of memories from the past was in some way connected in his mind to the experience of not being remembered by his mother, and, conversely, that the memories he was recovering in analysis—of both the past and the present—were continually rearranging themselves around his experience of being remembered by me.

It was then that I realized that a person's specific memories and experiences are like individual beads that can achieve continuity and gestalt form only when they are strung together to become a necklace. The string on which they are assembled is the child's continuous existence in the mind of the parent, which provides the continuity on which the beads of experiences are strung together and become the necklace of a connected life. We know, for example, that many people whose parents were actively involved with them, but took a primarily negative view of things, tend to string their experiences on a negative filament, so that each new event is assembled and viewed from its negative aspect—just as was the parents' habit. But the most difficult therapeutic issues arise in those cases in which the parent was emotionally absent or uninvolved, for then the string of continuity on which to assemble experience is missing, and the child is left clutching a handful of beads or memories that form no discernible pattern. This feels similar to the momentary experience many of us have had when a necklace or bracelet suddenly breaks, and what had been a coherent pattern or gestalt a moment before suddenly becomes a confusion of separate elements, rolling every which way on the floor.

This was the way that Jeffrey had consistently experienced his childhood, for he said about his mother: "It's not that she wasn't there, but I just couldn't feel any real connection to her." It then became clear to me that what was missing was the string of emotional connections and the continuity in time on which the beads of his experience could be strung.

So it seems that the mind creates our experiential world by both connecting and transforming stimuli across time. If, for example, we project a motion picture strip at ten frames per second, we see a series of static, disconnected images, but when we project it at twenty-four frames per second, these discrete images suddenly turn into a flow of continuous, connected movement. While this may tell us something about the processing speed of the brain center that establishes visual motion, it also suggests that a certain frequency over time is necessary for a visual sense of continuity to become established.

This phenomenon coincides with the experience of many analysts that a certain frequency of sessions is essential for the establishment of a deep transference, especially with those patients in whom problems of attachment, separation, and continuity are foremost. I have also come to believe that with such patients, it is primarily the analyst's faith, trust, hope, and expectations—that is, his or her emotionally charged remembering of the patient—that keeps the patient connected to the analyst. By this, I mean that in order for a dismembered life to come together, the analyst must keep the patient alive in his or her own mind in a continuous way, and the patient must believe that the analyst holds the patient and keeps him or her alive in memory. Reciprocally, of course, the patient must learn to keep the analyst consistently alive, and the analyst must feel that he or she remains alive in the mind of the patient.

Now, by reaffirming the importance of this mutual holding in memory, I do not mean to slight the importance of the multiplicity of defensive operations, denials, withdrawals, and attacks on linking that figure so prominently in all patients—and also, I believe, in all analysts. As I have discussed elsewhere (Bach, 1985), these defensive operations are often most clearly visible at times of separation or reattachment, such as at the end of a vacation, when the patient's reluctance to closely reengage may often be paralleled by the analyst's difficulties in doing the same. For it can also, among other things, be a burden and a worrisome responsibility for parent and child to hold each other closely in mind, as witnessed by the presence of not only pain, but also mutual liberation, when children finally do grow up and leave home.

For these and many other reasons, along with the need and desire to be remembered by the parent, there is also almost always a need to be left alone, to be disconnected, to soar into solitary freedom or sink into oblivious sleep. This need to be left alone was not absent in Jeffrey. His pervasive fear that I might forget him was, at another level, countered by the compulsive wish that I would completely forget him, leaving him alone and unencumbered by my insistent presence. In the first few years of treatment, he would sometimes sink into a state in which he would stop talking, responding to me by saying that there was nothing on his mind, unable as he was to locate any feeling except apathy and a painful sense that he was utterly disconnected from everyone. These silent and disconnected states persisted for a long time, and it was very difficult either to attach them to what had been going on moments before, or to otherwise help Jeffrey deal with them. Over time, they slowly began to shorten in duration, so that a silence that might have lasted fifteen minutes in the first year eventually became only a momentary lapse in the continual stream of consciousness.

During these silences, I at first experienced a kind of apathetic disconnection myself, so that it seemed that the countertransference was failing to provide its usual cues as to what might be going on. In the available time—of which I had plenty—I would force myself to entertain hypotheses about concealed rage, murderous intent, attacks on linking, reunion with the dead mother, and other interesting thoughts, but eventually I came to believe that I was simply trying to keep myself and Jeffrey artificially alive with these speculations, and that I might do better to join him in the land of the dead. This was not an easy task because it felt very uncomfortable there, but it gave me some experience of what it must have been like for Jeffrey to exist for most of his childhood in this desolate terrain of unconnected beings. Indeed, in this Dantesque landscape, momentary outbursts of anger seemed like a welcome relief, which led me to believe that Jeffrey's whole family system had achieved this degree of moribundity only by draining itself almost entirely of aggressive and libidinal energies.

So, although Jeffrey's stuporous states were in one way a simple repetition of the disconnection that had existed between his parents and himself, they were in another way a participatory re-enactment of the family defenses against the anger and violence that are necessary for separation and individuation. It seemed that, just as his mother had held the power of psychological life and death over Jeffrey throughout his childhood, he was now, through his silence, enacting that power of psychological life and death over me and over the analysis. But finally, and perhaps most important, these silences constituted an avoidance of the mourning and reparation that might have led to more mature and more real experiences of connection.

Thinking about all this, it seems to me that one way of summarizing what I learned is to say that *a parent may actually destroy a child, both psychically and even physically, by not constructing or holding that child's memory or representation in a particular way.* Conversely, as the child becomes an adult and the generational power reverses, the adult child may now destroy the parent by not carrying that parent's memory in a particular way. For while coming of age always involves some form of parental destruction, as Loewald (1980) has emphasized, it makes a huge difference to the parties concerned whether the parental psyche is left fragmented and dislocated in the universe, or whether the parent can mourn his or her own aging while nevertheless rejoicing in the string of continuity in which the parent's own life now finds a diminishing place.

So it seems that in normal development, there is, from the beginning, a kind of mutual holding in memory that is of greatest importance to both parent and child—as evidenced by the mother's jubilation when the child first seems to recognize her, and her disappointment when the child does not do so. We now know that a newborn infant can recognize the mother's smell within twenty-four hours of birth, so that this mutual recognition and holding seem to be in place from very early on. And we can imagine that, with a normal baby, the mother's *expectation* of being recognized and her ability to provide appropriate stimuli play an important role in bringing this about, and that an apathetic mother might take much longer to engage this mutual memory system. Somewhere along this continuum lie the intermittently engaged mother, the depressed mother, and, at the extreme, the missing mother and Spitz's (1965) marasmus and infant death.

Marasmus can be viewed as a demonstration that the infant's need to mutually hold and be held in memory can be life sustaining; and, with a stretch of the imagination, one might view Jeffrey's plight as an intermittent and very diminished kind of marasmus. But what I want to emphasize is that this mutual carrying and holding of memory representations is an important developmental function, and that impediments to this process can lead to psychical and even physical destruction.

Of course, even in normal development, a certain kind of destruction is not entirely avoided; such controlled, specific destruction must take place over and over on higher developmental levels for mature object relationships to develop. That is to say, connection cannot exist without the disconnection that destroys it, and normal remembering cannot exist without forgetting, as Borges (1962) so beautifully demonstrated in *Funes, the Memorius*, his story about a man who was unable to forget anything.

Cognitive researchers have recently begun to demonstrate a similar phenomenon (Nader, Schafe, & LeDoux, 2000). It has been known for some time that memory formation, which is fixed by protein synthesis, can be disrupted if a drug that inhibits protein synthesis is given within six hours of the memory stimulus. But apparently, even after a memory has become fixed, if the stimulus to recall it is reproduced and the memory reactivated, it returns to a malleable state and can once more be disrupted if protein synthesis is inhibited. What this seems to mean is that fixed memory is capable of becoming malleable again when exposed to the original memory stimulus, and thus events in the present can become capable of influencing even fixed memories of the past. Of course, this latest scientific discovery can be seen as a confirmation of Freud's (1896) concept of *Nachtraglichkeit*, and of the continual flux and interchange he postulated between the past, present, and future, and between remembering and forgetting. But how does this influence the problem of Jeffrey's difficulties with his sense of process, continuity, and being remembered?

We know that in normal development, the mother is the keeper of the child's memories, and that she normally inserts little bookmarks into the memory stream by making such remarks as "Yesterday we went to the playground and saw the little black dog," or "Do you remember last month when we went to Grandma's house? Well, tomorrow we're going again." Thus, she becomes the muse of the child's past, present, and future, helping to reintegrate memories at each higher level of development. By stringing these events on the filament of the mother's continuity, the child creates an ongoing sense of him- or herself as a continuing and expanding existence over time. Simultaneously, the child is influencing the mother's memory, quickening it with the vivid verbal and sensual details that are so characteristic of the normal mother—toddler dyad.

In this normal experience, the child is incidentally learning concepts such as the simultaneity of events and the succession and duration of time, which will form the very fabric of the child's working ego. The importance of this implicit knowledge is hard to overestimate, given that we take it so much for granted, but it becomes highlighted when we turn to pathology such as Jeffrey's in which the interaction with the mother, instead of having led to the synthesis and integration of events over time, has instead resulted in experiences of fragmentation. For example, Jeffrey was very prone to losing or misplacing things in everyday life. He would finish a report at work and then not be able to locate it, misplace his keys or his wallet, lose an important letter, or mislay the television remote control. His work assistant spent a considerable amount of time searching for the many things he had lost or forgotten. Repeated analyses of these parapraxes, as well as of similar ones in the transference, always brought us back to some real or fantasied lack of connection with his mother or me, thereby confirming Anna Freud's (1967) dictum that children who are chronic losers "live out a double identification, passively with the lost objects which symbolize themselves, actively with the parents whom they experience to be as neglectful, indifferent, and unconcerned toward them as they themselves are toward their possessions" (p. 16).

But this pattern of losing things and the experience of feeling lost were only the more visible aspects of a state of delimited inner fragmentation with which Jeffrey had lived from early childhood. I often puzzled about how he could have reached such a high executive position and achieved a certain maturity, while at the same time feeling so lost and experiencing himself as so insignificant. He was very intelligent, his chronic feelings of stupidity notwithstanding, but he was definitely an underachiever in many areas. He had successfully walked through all of his schooling in a state of mental fog, and had immediately forgotten most of what he had learned. He seemed to have excellent instincts for doing the right thing interpersonally and on the job, but he lived in constant terror of being asked to explain why he did what he did, for he could not seem to get an overview or to link things together in a logical or theoretical way. Thus, despite his intelligence, learning something new in any area filled him with dread because he lacked the ability to conceptualize it, to connect it with previously learned information, or to imagine a learning process over time.

What I came to realize about Jeffrey and the many other patients like him whom I have seen was that his sense of time had become fragmented, so that at certain moments or in certain states, the whole world was experienced as consisting of bits and pieces, none of which had any meaning. For such a sense of meaning arises out of the connectedness of things and their relationships to each other in time, and when the links of this connectedness in time are broken, we are left with only empty moments in a frightening and meaningless void. And I knew then that Jeffrey had been driven into his stuporous states as an escape from this terrifying sense of meaninglessness. A phrase from Shakespeare came to my mind, about Macbeth murdering sleep; and it occurred to me that, by not constructing or holding a child's memory or representation in a connected way, a parent can actually murder time for that child, with the resulting cognitive and emotional difficulties that I have tried to describe.

This particular story had a happy ending, for Jeffrey did eventually learn how to learn, how to connect without too much fear, and how to overcome certain of the deficits with which he had been left. And it is only as I write this that I realize the significance of the fact that, after many vicissitudes had taken place, when Jeffrey was engaged to be married, the first present he gave his fiancée was a watch—a significance that completely escaped me at the time.

REFERENCES

Auerbach, J. (1990). Narcissism: Reflections on others' images of an elusive concept. *Psychoanalytic Psychology* 7:545-564.

Auerbach, J. (1993). The origins of narcissism and narcissistic personality disorder: A theoretical and empirical reformulation. In *Empirical studies of psychoanalytic theories: Vol. 4. Psychoanalytic perspectives on psychopathology*, ed. J. M. Masling & R. F. Bornstein. Washington, DC: American Psychological Association, pp. 43-110.

Bach, S. (1985). *Narcissistic States and the Therapeutic Process.* Northvale, NJ: Aronson.

Bach, S. (1995). *The Language of Perversion and the Language of Love.* Northvale, NJ: Aronson.

Bach, S. (1998). Two ways of being. *Psychoanalytic Dialogues* 8:657-673.

Bach, S. (2002). A mind of one's own: Some observations on disorders of thinking. In *Symbolization and Desymbolization: Essays in Honor of Norbert Freedman*, ed. R. Lasky. New York: Other Press, pp. 387-406.

Borges, J. L. (1962). Funes, the memorius. In *Ficciones*, ed. A. Kerrigan. New York: Grove Press, pp. 107-115.

Fonagy, P. (1999). Memory and therapeutic action. *International Journal of Psycho-Analysis* 80:215-223.

Freud, A. (1967). About losing and being lost. *Psychoanalytic Study of the Child* 22:16-23.

Freud, S. (1896). Further remarks on the neuro-psychoses of defense. Standard Edition 3:159-185.

Freud, S. (1919). A child is being beaten. Standard Edition 17:177-204.

Loewald, H. (1980). The waning of the Oedipus complex. In *Papers on Psychoanalysis.* New Haven, CT: Yale University Press, pp. 384-404.

Modell, A. (1993). *The Private Self.* Cambridge, MA: Harvard University Press.

Nader, K., Schafe, G. E. & LeDoux, J. E. (2000). Fear memories require protein synthesis in the amygdala for reconsolidation after retrieval. *Nature* 406:722-726.

Ogden, T. (1986). *The Matrix of the Mind: Object Relations and the Psychoanalytic Dialogue.* Northvale, NJ: Aronson.

Oxford English Dictionary (1989). Oxford, England: Clarendon Press, Second Edition.

Poland, W. S. (1992). Transference: "An original creation." *Psychoanalytic Quarterly* 61:185-205.

Proust, M. (1957). Le temps retrouvé. In Proust, by S. Beckett. New York: Grove Press.

Spitz, R. (1965). *The First Year of Life.* New York: International University Press.

Stern, D. (1985). *The Interpersonal World of the Infant: A View from Psychoanalysis and Developmental Psychology.* New York: Basic Books.

Winnicott, D. W. (1958). *Collected Papers: Through Paediatrics to Psycho-Analysis.* New York: Basic Books.

CHAPTER 3

On Digital Consciousness and Psychic Death[1]

T his paper is about a particular class of states of consciousness that can be found to varying degrees in patients who seem challenging to treat and who might be classified as extremely narcissistic, borderline, or sometimes even psychotic. On occasion, however, they can form a part of anyone's repertoire of states of consciousness as, for example, in the traumatic moments after a car crash or some similar shocking event.

One of the distinctive parameters of this state is the experience of time, which in this state exists *only in the moment* so that the patient experiences neither his past nor his future but lives entirely in the present moment of the trauma. I refer to this as a digital state as opposed to the more usual analog log state in which experiences of the past as well as the potential for a future are felt to exist simultaneously, interpenetrating and affecting each other at every moment. As a consequence, people who are usually in the normal analog state experience a continuity in their life because at any given moment they know where they have come from and can imagine where they might

---

[1] This paper was the 2007 Heinz Hartmann Award Lecture given at the New York Psychoanalytic Institute on January 9, 2007.

be going, just as with an analog watch one can see the hour from which the hand has come and the hour to which it is going as well as its location at the present moment. Thus the analog state relies on reflective self-awareness so that consciousness is experienced as a "thick" time (Ludden, 2006) in which memories from the past and expectations for the future blend together with the experience of the current moment.

In the digital state, where time is "thin" rather than "thick," without past or future, patients lack this sense of continuity and consequently feel vulnerable and uprooted, as if they were constantly balancing on one foot. While in this state their experience of life is a succession of instantaneous digital moments, without connection to or even memory of where they have come from and where they are going. Each moment is split off from the previous or following moment so that a discursive account that links even the immediate past to the present and future is often not possible. Many of these patients, as competent as they might appear in real life, often live with an internal experience of not knowing how to get from one place to another or how to get from here to there. One consequence for the analysis is that their memory does not link past sessions to the present session and therefore learning from experience becomes difficult if not impossible.

But a far worse consequence for the patient's internal life is that the discontinuity between each digital moment and the next is sometimes experienced as a gap or a void or even a psychic "death of the self." Sometimes the patient may find himself abstracted or "spacey" or staring off into the void with a glazed look; sometimes someone in the room might ask him, "Are you all right?" These moments differ significantly from hysterical abstraction, where the continuity of thought is interrupted by unconscious repressed material and can be restored when the repressed or denied material is again made conscious. But in these digital states the gaps in consciousness feel like a void, empty of any material that feels alive, that can be thought about or verbalized. On the contrary, one might characterize them as the extinguishment of life, a psychic catastrophe or the "death of the self."

Thus, instead of the continual flow of life experienced in the analog state, there is an experience of a series of moments followed by little blanks or gaps or psychic deaths, keeping the patient in a continual state of anxiety, uncertainty, and mistrust. The patient distrusts this succession of labile, unfocused, and disconnected moments and cannot make them cohere into a unified narrative that might feel like a usable self or an identity that he can trust. Reciprocally, he finds it difficult to build trust in either the analyst or the analysis, and without a certain degree of trust he can neither fully reveal himself nor truly engage the analytic process[2].

Of course I am here emphasizing the parameter of time in this digital state, but there are many other parameters of states of consciousness that are also affected because they are all part of an interdependent system. For example, thought processes are usually linear, are concrete, and tend to be either/or, with little shading or gradation. The ability to symbolize and make playful transformations and the sense of agency and reflective self-awareness may also be severely diminished or absent. What people are nowadays calling triangularity or the analytic third may equally be absent or unavailable and the transitional area may be defective or entirely lacking. Another way of summarizing this is to say that the person's psychic space is severely constricted.

I want to make clear that I am using digital and analog as signposts for either end of what is in actuality a continuum of states of consciousness ranging from one extreme to the other. For example, a multiple personality disorder might be thought of as one extreme of digital consciousness because of the almost total lack of connectedness, integration and continuity between the various psychic nuclei.

It seems that in the development of the mother-infant dyad, the growing self and mutual regulation and the interpenetration of affects

---

[2] I should note here that I am writing about digital time, time without past or future, purely in its pathological aspects. There is another mythical or mystical time, the time of Eliade's in illo tempore, a magical reality that takes time out of history, but unfortunately I cannot go into that here.

and states of consciousness make for a continuity that the infant experiences as an ongoing sense of being. The child feels an elated sense of agency after experiencing his ability to make something happen, to have an effect on someone, or to make his mother enjoy him. But this continuity of being, this sense of agency and of the ongoing-ness of things, this feeling that we are living a connected analog experience rather than a series of disconnected digital moments, can be easily disrupted by trauma of any sort.

I will for the moment define trauma as a situation in which some new internal or external experience of the baby cannot be adequately held or contained by the environment and in which this disruption is not repaired.

When trauma occurs, then the experience of continuity becomes radically disrupted and the child or even the adult is suddenly thrown back upon his own resources to sustain life. That is to say that life, which up to that moment had been a collaborative effort between the child and his environment, now suddenly becomes a traumatic solitary endeavor. The child or adult, abruptly forced to manage things all on his own, can either sink or swim. Either he may survive and grow from this effort or else he may revert to the most primitive defenses such as denial, projective identification, or dissociation that will ultimately affect his reality testing. In either case, the child has been prematurely ejected from Eden, from a state of subjectivity in which he is being safely carried by an environment of which he may not even have been aware, in to an objective state where in order to save his life he must become prematurely aware and self-conscious, often with feelings of shame, guilt, and humiliation. These feelings arise because the traumatized child or adult so frequently blames himself for his predicament, and he usually does so in order to spare the person who has failed him and thus maintain his object tie.

While the continuous analog state I have been describing can be experienced as co-existing with the normal oscillations between subjectivity and objectivity that we all experience, the digital state entails either a frighteningly depersonalized objectivity that cuts the patient off almost entirely from his own feelings or else a total immersion in subjectivity that feels to the patient as if he is drowning in unbearable traumatic pain.

One man, who was so terrified of the return of his mental pain that he would put his fist through the window whenever this threatened, began slowly to find a space in which time was not so fragmented. He spoke in a highly intellectualized way in order to keep his emotions and pain at a distance. He said,

> I've had no appreciation for process. I've had a fundamentally skewed vision. Rather than freaking out because I don't have coffee and I have to go and get some or because I have to change some word for the third time—I don't realize that it's not about having written the book, it's about writing the book. I'm not willing to give myself five more minutes.
>
> It begins with memory. It's not about "what do I see?" It's about what I *do* see. Memory has always been a problem. I have an expectation of my ability to remember, a presumption that doesn't bend. I can't stand it when my daughter says: "I remember when we did that." I often say to you—I don't understand…I don't remember…I think all the details have to be right there, immediately.
>
> Yesterday you said something to me about continuity. I'm afraid to look in my notebooks, afraid that they'll be inaccessible. But then I thought—they're a part of me, my present. Like my school notes. I can go back to them. It has that time element. It can come alive to me again. I was leaving here thinking, feeling a sense of space. You could go back if you wanted to, if you gave it what it required, patience and time. I always wanted it to be done immediately.

This man, as he slowly found continuity in the analytic transference, began to connect process, time, and memory, and as his sense of time began to include a past and a future, he became more able to be patient with himself and with others.

A similar process occurred in a man whose clinical material I published many years ago (Bach, 1985) but whom I believe I now understand somewhat better than I did at that time. This young professional man had a severe narcissistic disorder that interfered with both his marriage and his work. After several years of analysis he had made considerable gains and was now terminating because of external circumstances, but not without ambivalence. As one expression of this conflict he had lost his old analog watch and replaced it with a digital watch. Reflecting on his new watch he said,

> Digital time is unyielding, it's absolute, but the hands on an analog watch never stop at any particular time, it's an unfolding...
>
> Digital time is the here and now; it allows for change from moment to moment but each reading is only itself. How can you be sure that the next reading will really be one second or one minute after that one? It requires a certain trust, a trust that something will remain the same even in the process of change, that there will be continuity behind or beneath the change. You remember how I used to feel that when I turned on the water tap, blood might come out? I used to marvel at how certain you seemed when you came into the waiting room that you would find *me* there and not someone else—a plant or a monster...Now I rarely think about those things...I guess I've developed some sense of trust that things will remain the same.

This sense of trust that things will remain the same even in the process of change, this feeling of self-continuity and of environmental continuity had been one of the major achievements of the analysis. At that time we had understood his losing his analog watch and replacing it with the newest digital variety as an attempt, in part, to make time stand still, to put off the termination and return to his earlier digital state of timelessness, particularly by eliminating the future without me. While this was undoubtedly true, I now feel that we slighted the importance of coming to terms not only with the separation but also with Death itself as a major unspoken component of separation, of process and even of the sense of time.

At that time when both the patient and I were younger, I was not so sensitive to the importance of Death as a component of life, although the patient had told me often enough of his discontinuous experiences and of his terror that he might not remain the same person or even remain the same species from one moment to the next. Where had I imagined that he existed in between these drastic transformations?

What I am trying to say is that the death of the self that occurs in between digital moments of consciousness, or the death of the self that a young child experiences after trauma or after the loss of a primary object, is an experience so frightening that for us it is almost unthinkable. Adults may describe it as imploding, or entering a black hole, or falling endlessly forever. In working with the most challenging patients, I have frequently observed an omnipresent fear of death or of dying, expressed either directly or indirectly through a complete avoidance of change, agency, initiative, or futurity. Eventually, following Winnicott's insight that a fear of breakdown might indicate that the breakdown had already occurred, I began to see that many cases of fear of death were indeed a fear of the psychic death that the patient had already experienced at earlier times in his life. This realization made it somewhat easier to understand and work with extreme disturbances.

I remember another patient, a talented and extremely suicidal young woman, who once wrote to me,

> When I was 10, I first tried to kill myself. This is a fact, although at that time I had no conscious idea that suicide was my aim. What I was trying to do was to reaffirm, or for once affirm, my own existence. I knew that whoever I was, was gone...I needed an explanation for the turmoil of sudden understanding that whoever I was had escaped and left me with no center...It isn't that I'm drifting or a chameleon, because then I could not have this dreadful detachment from my own feelings...When I was 10 and in the park and saw the broken green glass, all that went through my mind was that I wanted

to see if it could cut me, I wanted to see if I could feel pain. I wanted, in other words, to find out if at least the physical organism existed, if it still remained. I did not think of death.

This woman made a suicide attempt after her very first consultation with me, but fortunately she survived and the resulting analysis led to a rather successful outcome. At the time I wrote about her I spoke of the fantasy of "death of the self" (Bach, 1985), but I still had not understood clearly enough that for many patients this is a terrifying lived experience that can be repeated many times a day, and defended against with manic, schizoid or projective defenses. This patient, for example, would rent a room in a boarding house and late at night would start screaming uncontrollably. One of the reasons she screamed was that it made her feel for a moment that she really existed. After a few weeks she would be evicted and then repeat the incident in yet another rented room. She was struggling against the overwhelming trauma of re-experiencing her earlier psychic death.

Today we know somewhat more about the infant's reaction to catastrophic trauma both from infant observation and from neurobiological research. In a review article on the subject, Allan Schore (2002) noted that,

> The infant's psychobiological response to trauma is comprised of two separate response patterns, hyperarousal and dissociation. In the initial stage of threat, a startle or an alarm reaction is initiated, in which the sympathetic component of the autonomic nervous system is suddenly and significantly activated, resulting in increased heart rate, blood pressure, and respiration. Distress is expressed in crying and then screaming...
>
> But a second later forming reaction to infant trauma is seen in dissociation, in which the child disengages from stimuli in the external world and attends to an 'internal' world. The child's dissociation in the midst of terror involves numbing, avoidance, compliance and restricted affect (the same pattern as adult post-traumatic stress disorder). Traumatized infants

are observed to be 'staring off into space with a glazed look.'
This behavioral strategy is described by Tronick and Weinberg
[137, p. 66]:

> When infants' attempts fail to repair the interaction, infants
> often lose postural control, withdraw, and self-comfort.
> The disengagement is profound even with this short dis-
> ruption of the mutual regulatory process and break in
> intersubjectivity. The infant's reaction is reminiscent of the
> withdrawal of Harlow's isolated monkey or of the infants in
> institutions observed by Bowlby and Spitz.

> This parasympathetic dominant state of conservation-
> withdrawal occurs in helpless and hopeless stressful situations
> in which the individual becomes inhibited and strives to avoid
> attention in order to become 'unseen'. This metabolic shut-
> down state is a primary regulatory process, used throughout
> the life span, in which the stressed individual passively disen-
> gages in order 'to conserve energies...to foster survival by the
> risky posture of feigning death, to allow healing of wounds and
> restitution of depleted resources by immobility' [150, p.
> 213]...This elevated parasympathetic arousal, a survival strate-
> gy, allows the infant to maintain homeostasis in the face of the
> internal state of sympathetic hyperarousal. (pp. 15-16)

Schore's description of the neurobiological and behavioral consequences of trauma, which he has synthesized from many sources,
seems to be linked to the phenomenological experience I have been
calling "death of the self." While my own clinical material is largely
derived from psychoanalytic work and reconstructions in patients
with severe childhood trauma, the phenomenological descriptions
are fairly consistent across a large number of patients. Usually a current trauma, and most particularly a traumatic repetition in the
current transference, triggers a remembered or repressed incident or
an accumulation of incidents from childhood. The patient experiences a dramatic shock and a generalized hyperarousal, followed by a

disorganization that is often described as a kind of "splintering," "disintegrating," or "falling apart," often accompanied by intense feelings of shame. The content is variously described as a kind of "void," an "emptiness," a "disappearance," a "death," or a "black hole," and it seems as if the humiliated person's wish to become "unseen" or to disappear off the face of the earth had actually been realized.

What ensues in reaction to this trauma is often a series of digital states of the kind I have been describing. In certain cases where some degree of trust remains, a healthy reaction of rage can emerge and then the sense of time and of agency may begin to expand again. But with the most severely traumatized patients the rage never develops, the experience remains purely in the moment, the sense of agency is diminished and the regression to what Schore has called "dissociation" and what feels like a "death of the self" may continue unabated unless the patient encounters some kind of healing environment.

I mentioned earlier that one way to conceptualize trauma is as a situation in which some new internal or external experience of the child cannot be adequately contained by the environment and cannot be repaired. It implies a breakdown of the system and a failure of the continuity of symbolization. Conversely, healing or repair may be thought of as beginning with the re-provision of just those elements of the environmental system that had been so dramatically lost or disconnected by the trauma. This would then permit the reworking of inner psychic conflict within the context of a more benevolent environment. I believe this is some part of what we mean when we speak of holding, containing, or helping to regulate the traumatized patient.

In an extraordinary series of experiments, Myron Hofer (2003) has begun to explore precisely what this might entail by analyzing catastrophic separation into its component parts. He has noted that every separation or transition means the "loss of a number of individual regulatory processes that were hidden within the interactions of the previous relationship, with individual components of the interaction regulating specific physiological and behavioral systems" (pp. 194-195).

†

Fortunately, this research also suggests that the catastrophic depressive reactions resulting from the simultaneous loss of multiple "hidden" regulators may sometimes be partially reversed by re-providing some of the individual regulatory components such as the mother's warmth and stimulation that were offered by the lost relationship. Hofer went on to say,

> The discovery of regulatory interactions and the effects of their withdrawal allow us to understand not only the responses to separation in young organisms of limited cognitive-emotional capacity, but also the familiar experienced emotions and memories that can be verbally described to us by older children and adults. It is not that rat pups respond to loss of regulatory processes, while human infants respond with emotions of love, sadness, anger and grief. Human infants, as they mature, can respond at the symbolic level *as well as* at the level of the behavioral and physiological processes of the regulatory interactions. The two levels appear to be organized as parallel and complementary response systems. Even *adult* humans continue to respond in important ways at the sensorimotor-physiologic level in their social interactions, separations and losses, continuing a process begun in infancy. A good example of this is the mutual regulation of menstrual synchrony among close female friends, an effect that takes place out of conscious awareness and has recently been found to be mediated at least in part by a pheromonal cue (Stern and McClintock 1998). Other examples may well include the role of social interactions in entraining circadian physiological rhythms, the disorganizing effects of sensory deprivation and the remarkable therapeutic effects of social support on the course of medical illness (reviewed in Hofer 1984). In this way, adult love, grief and bereavement may well contain elements of the simpler regulatory processes that we can clearly see in the attachment responses of infant animals to separation from their social companions. (pp. 204-205)

Personally, I have found this point of view remarkably useful in the clinical situation. For example, I have come to understand that certain patients who arrive for analysis bringing along a retinue of physical therapists, personal trainers, yoga teachers, Pilates instructors, and massage therapists may very well be attempting to do for themselves the same thing that Myron Hofer did for his deprived rat pups. Here we are again dealing on a more sophisticated level with issues similar to those that Groddeck was discussing with Freud in the early years of psychoanalysis.

I have tried in this paper to delineate a class of states of consciousness that seem to arise as a reaction to trauma and may continue thereafter either sporadically or on a regular basis. I have called this class digital states of consciousness because one prominent feature is the experienced sense that time exists only in the here-and-now of the trauma, as opposed to analog states of consciousness in which present, past, and future are experienced as connected and interpenetrating. This lack of a *feeling* for the past and the future profoundly affects the person's sense of continuity and the ongoingness of his being, as well as affecting his object attachments including the treatment relationship. The fragmented and digitalized nature of this experience interferes with symbolization and with the formation of a continuous self-identity and the consolidation of a sense of agency. The profound feelings of loneliness, guilt, and shame that often accompany this state were viewed as part of a narcissistic reaction to trauma in which the victim feels responsible for his mishap and believes that the trauma has revealed some unspeakable defect in his very being.

I have also tried to suggest that a healing response is possible if the regulatory environmental interactions that were so shockingly disrupted by the trauma can somehow be reinstated. With challenging patients, the trauma has usually been reenacted in the transference, and if this rupture can be somehow repaired then the possibility is reopened for working through psychic conflicts and disturbed relationships. One way of repairing these disturbed interactions in analysis is through the creation or recreation of a shared, mutual, or

dyadic state of consciousness, that is, a regulatory state of consciousness created and shared by analyst and analysand, which bears some
relationship to Winnicott's (1953/1958) transitional area, and which
is often referred to nowadays as an analytic third (Aron, 2006). There
may also be other ways of doing this, as suggested by Hofer's remarks
about menstrual synchrony, social interactions, and social support.
This is a huge area about which we know very little and which is now
potentially ripe for psychoanalytic research. But I hope I have raised
some questions worth thinking about the next time that we see a patient
in what seems to be a traumatized or unusual state of consciousness.

REFERENCES

Aron, L. (2006). Analytic impasse and the third: Clinical implications
of intersubjectivity theory. *International Journal of Psycho-Analysis*
87:1-19.

Bach, S. (1985). *Narcissistic States and the Therapeutic Process*. Northvale, NJ: Aronson.

Hofer, M. (2003). The emerging neurobiology of attachment and separa-
tion: How parents shape their infant's brain and behavior. In
September 11: Trauma and human bonds, eds. S. Coates, J. Rosenthal,
& D. Schechter. Hillsdale, NJ: The Analytic Press, pp. 191-209.

Ludden, D. (2006, August 9). PsyCritique, 51(32), Article 2.

Schore, A. (2002). Dysregulation of the right brain: A fundamental
mechanism of traumatic attachment and the psychopathogenesis
of posttraumatic stress disorder. *Australian and New Zealand
Journal of Psychiatry* 36:9-30.

Winnicott, D.W. (1958) Transitional objects and transitional phenomena. In *Collected papers*. London: Tavistock. (Original work
published 1953)

CHAPTER 4

Two Ways of Being

> We do not know the Hells and Heavens of people we pass in the street. There are two possible perspectives. According to the first, on a miniscule ball of earth, in a smudge of mold called a city, some microorganisms move around, less durable than mayflies. And the internal states of [such] beings, deprived of any reason for their existence, perfectly interchangeable, what importance can they have? According to the second perspective, that of a reversed telescope, every one of these beings grows up to the size of a cathedral and surpasses in its complexity any nature, living or inert. Only in the second case can we see that no two persons are identical and that we may at best try to guess what is going on inside our fellow men.
>
> *Milosz, 1986, p. 120*

In this article, I suggest that a pervasive distinction exists between two different ways of knowing or thinking or of being in the world. I trust that this will not remain a purely poetic or philosophical concept, because in the end I hope to demonstrate its clinical importance and to show that this is a phenomenon we struggle with in every analytic hour.

These two states of being in the world or of perceiving it are familiar to everyone but perhaps under different categories or with very different names. I am talking about what some people have called the Apollonian mode and the Dionysian mode[1], or the Classical and Romantic points of

---

[1] Unlike Nietzsche's (1872) usage, *Apollonian* is used here to mean serene,

view, but I could equally well have called them the tragic or pessimistic and the enthusiastic or optimistic points of view, the obsessive and hysterical points of view, or even the secondary process and primary process points of view.

I could have pointed to the distinction that Winnicott makes between doing and being, or, had I wanted to run the risk of being politically incorrect, I might have said that the distinction is between the masculine and feminine points of view. Those of you interested in physics might think of Einstein's deterministic model of consistency versus Bohr's relativistic model of complementarity; those interested in philosophy might compare the correspondence theory of truth with the coherence theory of truth; those interested in poetics or theology might think of the profane as opposed to the sacred; those with a literary bent might recall Coleridge's discrimination between primary and secondary imagination; and those with a sociological interest might remember Foucault's distinction between cognition and experience. I could lengthen this list indefinitely, because a similar dichotomy can be found in almost every field of human endeavor, but I will make my point immediately and suggest that all these contrasting points of view are complex transformations of our two primary states of consciousness, subjectivity and objectivity.

Subjective awareness, as I call it, is a state in which we are totally into ourselves and our feelings while the rest of the world is in the background—that is, a Romantic or Dionysian state of mind. This was presumed to be the original conscious state of the neonate, like the noble savage of Rousseau, but the baby watchers tell us that within 24 hours the infant can discriminate its mother's odor, so that the precursors of objective awareness also begin to emerge very early. But, usually objective self-awareness is dated from the ability to recognize oneself in the mirror, at one and one-half to two years of age. Self-recognition is the precursor of *self-reflection,* the ability to view oneself objectively from the outside as if looking at another person—that is, the

---

rational, self-disciplined; *Dionysian* is used here to mean ecstatic, sensual, self-abandoned.

Classical or Apollonian state of mind. I need hardly remind you that, in psychoanalysis, we expend an enormous amount of effort trying to get our patients to reflect on themselves, to entertain a state of objective self-awareness, and that the success or failure of the treatment often depends on their ability to do this.

My favorite illustration of these two states comes from a young woman who, complaining of her inability to have a mutual orgasm with her lover, once said, "I can't make the smooth transition...I'm either *me*, totally me, and so excited that nothing else exists, or else I'm Tony's lover, and I can give him pleasure, but then I don't have it myself." When she was totally into her own sexual excitement, she was in a state of subjective awareness; when she was Tony's lover, she was observing herself from the outside, objectively aware of herself, as if she were standing on the ceiling or on Mars, watching herself.

But I also have reports from a mother about her seven-year-old son, who, when in a state of subjective awareness, was heard to remark, "This world terrifies me sometimes...it seems to be all me!" That is, he was frightened that his subjectivity, overburdened with narcissistic grandiosity, had encompassed everything and left him feeling enormously terrified and yet all alone in the world. Conversely, when in a state of objective self-awareness, he once asked, "Is this world a *dreaming*, or is it real?"—thereby expressing his feeling that he was standing outside of his experience, observing it like a dream, as if it were happening to someone else.

Of course, most of us oscillate between these two states, at times being unself-consciously lost in what we are doing and at other times being very self-conscious, as if we were viewing ourselves from the outside, as others might see us. So, in effect, we are all both Dionysians and Apollonians, Romantics and Classicists, but one difference lies in our preferred mode of being and also in our abilities to make the transition or oscillate back and forth, flexibly and appropriately, between these two states. Another important difference lies in the degree to which these two states have been integrated. In pathology, they are radically dichotomous—"I'm either all me, or else I'm someone else's object"—whereas more normally we can be in a subjective state, centered on ourselves, and nevertheless still experience the world as participatory. We have to remember that the grandiose self or object and the mirroring self or object, although extremely valuable clinical concepts, were derived from pathology and that their normal analogues are in fact far more subtle and complexly integrated states.

But, if you allow me a bit of poetic leeway, I could say that hysterics, extroverts, and acter-outers tend to prefer the Romantic mode of being—that is, they are in unreflective communion with their nature and doing their own thing without taking too much perspective on their actions. In this way, they resemble the Romantic writers and poets, who disdained and outraged social conventions, sought ecstasy in drugs, and were ready, in Baudelaire's language, to voyage "anywhere out of this world." On the other hand, obsessives, introverts, and schizoid types prefer the Classical mode, in which they reflect on their own thoughts and actions, appreciate and conform to social conventions, and seek their pleasure in more meditative and durable pursuits rather than in the throes of ecstasy. In this way, they resemble the Enlightenment thinkers and writers, who set so much store on calm and measured objectivity, valuing cognition and the intellect above experience and the flesh. Thus, subjectivity has been more highly prized in periods such as the Romantic era and by the more hysterical psychological types, whereas objectivity has been more highly valued in periods such as the Classical era or Enlightenment and by the more obsessive psychological types.

Of course, married couples often tend to be of complementary types, so that the predominant subjectivity of one is offset by the predominant objectivity of the other. In this way, the couple tends both to self-regulate and to have a built-in Other from which each can distinguish himself or herself. We can easily think of friends, relatives, and even members of our psychoanalytic societies who fall into one camp or the other, but we hope that our own regulatory processes are sufficiently integrated so that most of the time we can make the transitions between subjectivity and objectivity in a way that seems appropriate to the task at hand.

Unfortunately, there are many who cannot do so, and this brings us into the realm of psychopathology. A good analytic patient, for example, is expected to be able to free-associate—that is, to enter a state of subjective awareness and, eventually, to make the transition to objective self-awareness by pausing to reflect on his free associations. But, even the best of analytic patients will occasionally be unable to associate subjectively or else unable to objectively reflect on his associations for dynamic reasons that can then be analyzed. More disturbed patients may hardly ever be able to free-associate, either because they cannot enter a state of subjective awareness or because they cannot verbalize it. Others may hardly ever be able to reflect on their associations, either because they are unable to view themselves objectively or because it feels unbearably painful to share this with someone else. Indeed, it may take years before some patients can trust us enough to free-associate and even more years before they can allow themselves or us to make objective comments about these associations.

The pathology that we are dealing with involves the regulation and homeostasis of these two states of consciousness and of the dialectic between them. For example, some years ago, I tried to show that there are two kinds of narcissistic patients—the inflated sadistic type who presents with open grandiosity and an unconscious sense of worthlessness and the deflated masochistic type who presents with open feelings of worthlessness and an unconscious sense of grandiosity (Bach, 1994). The inflated type with open grandiosity exists primarily in a state of subjectivity, concerned only with himself and unable to be objective about his aspirations, but unconsciously he feels worthless and self-critical. The deflated type with open feelings of worthlessness exists primarily in a state of objective self-awareness, masochistically denigrating and criticizing himself as if he were some hostile outside observer, but unconsciously he may feel quite special or grandiose.

In both cases, the smooth continuum of states of consciousness is sharply split or dichotomized, and neither type is able to flexibly make the transition from viewing himself subjectively to viewing himself objectively, as we normally do. Their difficulties with emotional control are also connected to this pathology of dysregulation because, rather than making smooth transitions, they flip back and forth between Apollonian and Dionysian affect states, between overinhibition and overexcitement, both of which are frightening because the person feels helpless to regulate the transitions. The extreme forms of this pathology are manic-depressive disorders and especially multiple personalities, where all attempts at integrating the subjective and the objective into the same self have finally been abandoned. I am going to suggest that all disorders of self-regulation are also disorders of subjective and objective awareness and the somatic processes in which they are embedded. But, before I proceed with this line of thought, let me descend from the gray heights of theory to the golden tree of life by presenting some clinical material.

Some years ago, a woman painter named Julia, with whom I had never discussed the subject, began an analytic session by saying, "I've just begun to see very clearly that I switch back and forth between two perspectives on myself, or two ways of looking at things, and the way that I look at what's happening seems almost more important than what's actually happening. In the first way, which I'll call Column A, I have an absolute belief that the importance of living lies in using my creative juices in whatever way I can...that's what living is about. I don't have to figure out why it is, it just feels that way, and it doesn't matter what the outcome is 'cause the important thing is the act of doing it—the creation or nurturing of it—the important thing is just to paint, and I believe that...but when I switch to Column B, I don't believe it, and I don't believe the importance of it, and it's only significant if it has a meaning for somebody else—I have to know that it has a meaning for somebody else in contrast to Column A. [What about Column B?] It's a sort of reflection of how I grew up...in a totally communal life where nothing that I did was confirmed or appreciated and what was valuable was what other people valued...and it's always a problem for me, because I may look at something I paint and think it's quite good, but then it always feels solipsistic and arrogant to feel that way..."

In the next hour, Julia continued talking about this and mentioned that the switches from Column A to Column B occur so abruptly, uncontrollably, and unpredictably in her mind that, when she is in one state, she can hardly imagine that the other state exists. [Does anything come to mind about these abrupt switches?]

After a long time, she said, "I hadn't thought of this in many years, but, when I was a little girl, my father used to tell me stories about all the places we would travel to…we could go to France, and he would draw up pictures of the bridges over the river and the Eiffel Tower, how we would sit in the cafe and drink hot chocolate, and watch the people and the organ grinders with their monkeys…I was transported, and I would sit there drinking all this in and then ask, When are we going? And he would answer that he couldn't say exactly when we were going, but that we would go sometime…It was only much later that I slowly realized we weren't going anyplace, that we would never go anywhere…I can't remember the actual effect that it had on me at the time….

"But it's the same effect now—an idea comes to me, and I think it through, and I'm going to do it, and I love it, and then comes the darkness…Not that it won't happen but that that it won't go anywhere…just be what it was…that moment of excitement and anticipation and those mental images…that had a profound effect on me actually…[I said, "That's what triggers the switch from Column A to Column B!"]

"Yes, it's all fantasy and imagination…like in the room where my father took me and spun these images, and I was completely enthralled, and then he'd say it was time to go, and the door would close, and that was okay for him, but for me it was a terrible disillusionment because the evocation was so powerful…

"It's an abrupt switch between A and B, but my father often switched like that, and so did my mother…it was confusing to me when I remembered this other stuff, because most of the time my father was totally disinterested in me, didn't know I existed, and he let my mother beat me and abuse me every single day…maybe if I could find a way I could bring him back into Column A…How could I feel that he was a cold, indifferent, and distant man when he was sharing this beautiful world with me?"

If we remember that these incidents took place in a poor immigrant family living in near-poverty in the Chicago slums, we can imagine how poignant the situation was for this little girl to be cast from the very heights of Romantic illusion to the depths of Classical tragedy, and how painful, sudden, and abrupt was the transition from the participatory subjective awareness of her mutual fantasies with her father to the coldly objective realization that in fact she had been duped, that he was indifferent to her and it had all been nothing but fantasy.

Later, Julia described the physical manifestations of this abrupt shift from one state of consciousness to another by saying:

"It's all very visceral...When I'm in Column A, I feel it in my body like waves...It's a joyous state like a warmth, a surge. It comes from the bottom of my being, and, when I'm in Column B, it's not like waves—it's like claws that grip me, and, when they grip, there's a nauseous feeling like I'm screaming from the impact of the feeling...Column A is like music...[and B?]...is like cruelty, and chills and tears come to my eyes."

Elsewhere, I have connected the origins of what Julia called Column A (i.e., subjective awareness, with the extreme excitement of the practicing period and the hyperarousal of the sympathetic nervous system) and the origins of what she called Column B (i.e., objective self-awareness, with the low-keyedness or mild depression of the rapprochement child and the activation of the parasympathetic or inhibitory system). Listening to her father's stories, she is in a state of subjective awareness and of hyperarousal of the sympathetic system, manifested by waves of joyous warmth and sexuality and a surge of good feelings about herself and her objects. The sudden realization that this is all an illusion abruptly terminates sympathetic arousal, cuts short these good feelings, and instantly initiates the onset of inhibitory parasympathetic tone, bringing with it bad feelings, like claws that grip, and the nausea that is characteristic of sudden parasympathetic tonus. When these alternations occur abruptly and frequently enough, they become a cumulative trauma, so that joyful arousal carries with it the threat of a precipitous fall into despair. And we now have learned (Schore, 1994) that, in response to repeated traumas of this kind, the autonomic and limbic systems become modified in such a way as to increase the probability that such shifts will feel abrupt, extreme, and out of control.

Now, of course, we cannot hope to remain in a permanent state of joyful arousal or euphoria, as the lotus-eaters do, for it is our destiny to shift between happiness and sadness, between arousal and inhibition, between the world of joyful subjectivity and the world of objective assessment of our subjectivity, between fantasy and reality. What was traumatic for Julia was not that her father had told her romantic fairy tales that would never be realized but rather the abrupt disconnection between this world of fantasy and the harsh world of her everyday reality—to which he provided absolutely no bridge or transitional space. Of course, one might wonder whether these fantasies nevertheless nourished some positive force in her creative life as a painter.

But, let me contrast this with a more normal everyday incident—a charming story told to me recently by a mother whose five-year-old daughter one day demanded to know if there really was a tooth fairy and would not be put off by evasions. The mother finally admitted that the tooth fairy was only a story invented by adults, and her daughter seemed satisfied with this explanation.

This little girl had recently experienced the death of a grandparent but had seemed to be tolerating it in a relatively unremarkable way. Yet for the three nights following this discussion about the tooth fairy, she was unable to sleep well and expressed fears that she might die and that her mother wouldn't live forever. And, when the mother explained that we live on in our children, the little girl was worried that she might not be able to have children of her own.

This very sophisticated mother had the distinct impression that, in addition to the grandmother's death, the tooth fairy was somehow involved in all this and that her husband would have handled it in a better way. When I inquired how her husband might have handled it, she said without hesitation, "Oh! He would have answered, 'Of course there's a tooth fairy!' but with a big smile that would have left plenty of room for ambiguity...I suppose that this must be a reaction to some loss of illusion or faith, the first doubt that things aren't necessarily permanent or continuous or replaceable."

Now whether one prefers the mother's method of handling this incident or the father's, what is important is the care and concern that each parent showed in handling what for this little girl was a very important part of her mourning and of the transition between illusion and disillusion and between subjectivity and objectivity.

I have noted that in self-pathology we are dealing with problems of the dialectic between subjective and objective self-awareness, and in these two examples we can contrast the responses of loving parents, different as they might be, with the response of a parent who showed no concern and no ability to help his child grapple with these issues.

So we see that normally there is a slow process of disillusionment that occurs, preferably at the child's own pace. Objectivity and reality enter the child's subjective world in a nontraumatic way, within the area of the child's omnipotence. The tooth fairy, for example, comes to populate a transitional world that forms the fabric of our ego and allows us to face the brutal objective fact that we are now alive but will eventually be dead with the thought that we may perhaps live on in our children. But, reality also entails the loss of illusion, and that loss always involves some depression or inhibition of affective arousal.

Let me remind you that Mahler, as well as Klein and others, have regarded depression as a developmental achievement because it is only in reaching this stage of separation-individuation that the child is able to view himself from the outside in objective self-awareness, as another person would see him. Characteristically, he finds this a sobering and somewhat depressing experience because it illuminates his own insignificance and dependence on parental care. Although infants in the first year of life typically respond to their mirror image with unrestrained joy and enthusiasm, they start to withdraw as soon as they begin to recognize themselves in the mirror and they become wary and self-conscious of their image.

Interestingly, there is often a phase of a few months after self-recognition when little Johnny points to himself and denotes himself as "me" but continues to point to and denote his mirror image as "Johnny." Looking through this little window in time, I imagine the child has realized that, for others, "Johnny" and "me" refer to the same thing but that he himself is not quite ready to metamorphose his subjective, somatic awareness of himself into its invariant transformation as seen by an objective observer in the mirror.

This initial hesitation and perhaps disappointment at transforming "me" into "Johnny" continue to some degree throughout life, as evidenced by the common observation that many people are shocked and disappointed by photographs or tape recordings of themselves or even by prolonged self-observations in a three-way mirror. We seem to have stumbled on some basic ontological gap in the world, because "me" feels very real and undeniably alive in our flesh, whereas Johnny-in-the-mirror or the Other is always more of a mental construction and a stranger. "Me" feels like a "who" with whom we are intimately, proprioceptively acquainted, whereas Johnny-in-the-mirror or other people feel more like a "what," the existence of which we have cognitively constructed but can never quite apprehend with the same certainty.

I hope that by now I have given you a sense of the dichotomy between states of excited, subjective bodily awareness, for which the developmental model is the practicing child, and states of inhibited, objective, more cognitive self-awareness, as typically seen emerging in the rapprochement child. I have also, in a far-ranging leap of speculative play, related this to the many dichotomies that have so often engaged people in pitched battles, such as Classical versus Romantic and Apollonian versus Dionysian, correspondence theory versus coherence theory or, in our own field, conflict versus deficit, reality versus hermeneutics, and so forth. I have suggested that, from one perspective, these may all be related to complex derivatives of the basic states of subjectivity and objectivity. And I have implied that, just as we oscillate between subjective and objective awareness, with some inclined more in one direction and some more in the other, we may also view different conflicts, cultures, and periods of history in a similar way.

But, let me now descend from this grand overview and return to its developmental origins in each of us as I understand them (Bach, 1985, 1995). We remember that the height of subjective awareness is in practicing and that rapprochement is characterized by the achievement of an objective perspective on the whole self and, in the process, by oscillations between subjectivity and objectivity, between centering on the self and centering on the other, and between elation and despair, which is why it is known as the "terrible twos." In psychopathology, a fixation or regression to this phase is characterized by sadomasochistic interactions between an omnipotent, sadistic, and idealized self and a masochistic and denigrated other, or vice versa.

Normally, it is the caretaker who helps the child regulate between the extremes of elation and despair, between self and other, and between the subjective and objective states of consciousness. But, what occurs, as the child matures, is not just better regulated and more appropriate oscillations between subjectivity and objectivity or between self and other but rather a more complex synthesis, a blending and interpenetration of the two in the transitional area so that they are no longer simply dichotomous. Thus, the infant experiences the mother's thinking and feeling about himself, and then the mother experiences the infant's experiencing her, which the infant in turn reexperiences. Through projection and introjection, subjectivity and objectivity become infiltrated and informed by each other; the inner world becomes penetrated and suffused by the outer world, and the outer world in its turn becomes permeated by the inner world. Opposing qualities become reconciled into a higher unity, and relatively simple states of consciousness are continually reorganized into increasingly more complex networks of interactive states that feed back into each other. The present is continuously interacting with the past, and the past is continually being retranscribed back onto the present.

You may recall that, in Winnicott's original description of the transitional object such as a piece of blanket, it is literally permeated and suffused with the handling and odor of both caretaker and child. Thus, at one and the same time, it provides both a safe haven of attachment to the object and a means of separation from that very object. It is both a link to the past as it was and a way of carrying and transforming this past into the emerging future. It is a way of remaining immersed in subjectivity and also a path toward objectifying the world as the transitional object expands into the world of culture while at the same time losing its magical qualities so that in time it becomes simply a torn piece of blanket.

It is only when this does not occur, as in pathology, that one finds an obsessive alternation between frozen dichotomies of subjectivity and objectivity, of self and other, which seem unable to fluidly fluctuate, to reconcile, or to reach some homeostasis. Thus the subjectivity of the manic or narcissistic patient differs from normal subjectivity not only quantitatively, in its extravagant intensity and unregulated swings between extremes, but also qualitatively, in its not being permeated with otherness—that is, in its not having reached a higher level of self-representation and object representation. Reaching these more complex levels of synthesis changes the nature of dichotomies, diminishes the splitting, and, at each successive level, changes our vision of and relationship with the world. Let me now give some examples of how dichotomous concepts move to higher levels of integration and how thought processes and states of consciousness become more complex in the process.

I start with a woman I once knew who suffered from a multiple personality disorder and whose treatment I was rash enough to undertake in a classical psychoanalysis. After several hectic years characterized by multiple enactments, desperate transference and countertransference crises, and repeated suicide threats and enactments, she one day left this message on my answering machine:

Dr. Bach, I just wanted to keep you informed that, in addition to the many other things that psychoanalysis has deprived me of, I now seem to have lost the ability to commit suicide. I can never be positive that I had it, but I certainly scared myself a great number of times and was convinced that I was about to suicide. But yesterday, I had probably the most painful day of my life, but I never seriously considered suicide—that is, I never even for a moment flipped out or, as you call it, split off…I never seemed able to forget that I was the mother of little children and other things as well, and this was something that formerly didn't seem relevant to me and would never even have come into my mind.

Here we have a simple example of what I mean by the self-representation becoming suffused and permeated with important object representations and raised to a different level of integration so that what the patient calls "forgetting" that she was a mother was no longer possible. Of course, for her this was far from an unmixed blessing, and for a very long time thereafter she was furious at me for the many losses and deprivations that this process entailed.

Let me reiterate that what is at issue here is not just a simple shift from subjective to objective self-awareness, because, even when suicidal, she was always able, if reminded, to make this shift and objectively realize that she was in fact a mother. But this fact simply did not *mean* anything to her or was immediately forgotten until the enlargement of her subjectivity included her children within the sphere of her normal narcissistic omnipotence. Thus, what was required was an interactive change in her ability both to make a transition between subjective and objective awareness and to change the organization of her representational processes—two of the more important factors in a complex state of consciousness.

Now let me give you a sequence of dreams from a young woman who had been raised by a disturbed mother. One of Sara's most traumatic memories was of a night alone with her mother, who had become quite psychotic and was insisting that Sara's hair was on fire. When she came for analysis, Sara was unable to maintain an objective view of her mother and would either fall completely under her spell or else be obliged to physically escape in order to view her objectively. After about three years of analysis, she dreamed that she had a twin and that she and the twin were struggling for her mother's attention. After various competitive maneuvers, she suddenly said to her twin, "This is ridiculous!" and they embraced and walked off together holding hands, leaving her mother behind.

A few days later, she had the following dream:

"It's about my mother…she told me my hair was on fire and I look in the mirror, and it is! She said, "See it's burning" and I couldn't believe it, but it was true, and then I looked again, and I saw that it wasn't true."

To this, she associated: "There are two realities…there's the feeling of being swept up in what's going on with my mother…I want so much to be close to her, and it's impossible…part of me believing what my mother tells me…that's the first time I actually dreamed about that memory, when I was a little girl…one of my scariest memories…unacknowledged by her, she doesn't remember anything of it, it's all gone… I didn't expect her to remember it…everything she was doing was weird and crazy.

One of my biggest fears is that she tells me something, and it's true…the scary thing is that she's right…the worst thing that comes to mind is maybe it's not them, it's me! In the dream of the two Saras, one believes and the other doesn't believe my mother…I can't work this through with my mother because she doesn't remember anything."

A week later she had another dream:

"I let my cat out of the house, and she died…she was running around, crashing into walls, and finally just collapsed…there was a horrifying moment when I picked her up, and I thought she was dead, but then I looked again, and she was okay, and she started to walk around again."

Her associations: "After my disappointment about not getting the job, I wanted to call my boyfriend and be with him, but then I went home and went to bed by myself and had this dream about the cat…All of these dreams I had…it's still new for me to feel different things at the same time…it used to be that, if I focused on one thing, then another thing would get blocked out and pushed away…It's a very new experience for me…something that's definitely changed…I can do more than one thing at a time...I can feel upset about something and still manage to get pleasure out of something else...I know that today I feel sad, but that doesn't blot out the other things that I've been feeling...I'm so used to things being black and white in my family...that's the way we always operated...So I'm uncomfortable with this because it's still new...but I'm beginning to see that it's okay to miss my boyfriend and feel sad about it but still feel angry at him and not have to go back to him...it feels weird."

What Sara is describing is that she no longer feels engulfed by her subjectivity but has become able to sustain an objective point of view and to make the transition more appropriately between subjectivity and objectivity. Furthermore, she is able to encompass these multiple points of view and contrary affects within an enlarged self-representation that is part of an emergent and more complex state of consciousness. One might say that she is beginning to create a psychic space within which her subjective experiences of herself and her experiences of herself as seen by others are beginning to coalesce. In terms of our mirror analogy, "Johnny" and "me" are beginning to feel more like the same person, a person who has an ongoing continuity of existence across diverse times, places, and states of consciousness.

In conclusion, let me turn once more from this microanalysis of a self-representation to macroanalysis of a cultural representation and try to show that analogous forces are at work. I had planned to conclude this article with some recent literary research demonstrating that "the 18th century, so renowned for its rationality and objectivity, in a certain sense also invented the uncanny. Thus, "the very psychic and cultural transformations that led to the...glorification of the period as an age of reason or enlightenment...also produced, like a kind of toxic side effect, a new human experience of strangeness, anxiety, bafflement and intellectual impasse" (Castle, 1985, p. 8) that we call an uncanny experience.

This was to demonstrate my thesis that extreme cultural objectivity seems to create the conditions for a reversion to subjectivity and vice versa. But, just as I had finished writing, I came across this half-page article in *The New York Times*, which I cite in somewhat condensed form:

Paris, April 29, 1996—The French see themselves as a people who appreciate method and logic. Their teenagers are taught logic and philosophy in school. Intricate discourse fills as much television time as any national sport. And this year the country is making a fuss over Rene Descartes, France's emblem of rational thought, who was born 400 years ago.

Yet a contradiction arises that the great philosopher himself might have liked to consider: Why are the French spending so much time these days with psychics and seers?

A recent poll showed that more French men and women believe in the devil today than a decade ago. The French are reportedly consulting clairvoyants and numerologists in greater numbers than ever. Demand is also up for people who seek underground water with a dowsing rod, heal the sick by telephone and interpret handwriting.

"It's bizarre, but it's very clear that the more machines we build, the less we know how to live and the more we are all searching," said Ange d'Orment, a psychic.

The Government has evidence that magic is thriving. Last year, the tax authorities said that close to 50,000 taxpayers, the highest number ever, had declared income from their work as stargazers, healers, mediums and similar occupations. By comparison, the country had fewer than 36,000 Roman Catholic priests and some 6000 psychiatrists...

Some say all this activity shows the great fear of the end of the millennium. Others see it as a result of the erosion of other systems like institutional religion, Marxist ideology and psychoanalysis.

"My clients think that psychoanalysis is very exotic," said Alain Beunard, a self-styled druid who keeps a discreet office above the Paris wax museum. The place was hard to find, he explained, because his clients—"businessmen, politicians and so on"—do not like to be seen there.

"We've become too scientific, too intellectual," Mr. Beunard said. "People want something direct, something simple."

I hope that by now I have demonstrated that every turn toward objectivity carries within it the seeds of a reversion to subjectivity and vice versa. Although we might hope that each reversion would lead to some higher level of integration, this is unfortunately not always the case. Progression to higher levels of synthesis is not only difficult to achieve but always bought at something of a price. My suicidal patient experienced it as a loss that she was now no longer able to commit suicide but had, by incorporating her children into her subjectivity, become more firmly anchored to reality and given hostages to fortune.

I imagine it as a loss in some ways that men in Western cultures are no longer able to achieve that cosmic state of consciousness that must have been the everyday experience of the Paleolithic hunter, for whom the animal was a miraculous totem and the hunt a sacred encounter between the ecstatic hunter's endangered body and the awesome yet terrifying animal-god made visible. Bodily yearnings from this time may still surface in a degenerate way in the rituals of a bullfight; in the annual deer-hunting season, when bearded men in totemic costumes slaughter animals with automatic weapons; or perhaps even in certain seemingly inexplicable atrocities and wars.

I have tried to sketch a sweeping overview of one aspect of psychic change as it emerges on both individual and cultural levels. On either level, it always seems difficult for us to pay the price of loss and mourning to abandon a familiar dichotomy for the uncertainties of arriving at a higher synthesis. I hope, nevertheless, to have encouraged you all in the ongoing attempt to do just that.

REFERENCES

Bach, S. (1985). *Narcissistic States and the Therapeutic Process.* Northvale, NJ: Aronson.

Bach, S. (1995). *The Language of Perversion and the Language of Love.* Northvale, NJ: Aronson.

Castle, T. (1995). *The Female Thermometer: Eighteenth-Century Culture and the Invention of the Uncanny.* New York: Oxford University Press.

Milosz, C. (1986), *Unattainable Earth*, trans. C. Milosz & R. Hass. Hopewell, NJ: Ecco Press.

New York Times (1996), April 29, Section 1, p. 1.

Nietzsche, F. (1872), The birth of tragedy. In *The Birth of Tragedy and the Genealogy of Morals*, trans. F. Golffins. New York: Doubleday Anchor, 1972.

Schore, A. N. (1994), *Affect Regulation and the Origin of the Self: The Neurobiology of Emotional Development.* Hillsdale, NJ: Lawrence Erlbaum Associates.

CHAPTER 5

On The Narcissistic State of Consciousness

I

Our present ego-feeling is, therefore, only a shrunken residue of a much more inclusive—indeed, an all-embracing—feeling which corresponded to a more intimate bond between the ego and the world about it. If we may assume that there are many people in whose mental life this primary ego-feeling has persisted to a greater or lesser degree, it would exist in them side by side with the narrower and more sharply demarcated ego-feeling of maturity, like a kind of counterpart to it. In that case, the ideational contents appropriate to it would be precisely those of limitlessness and of a bond with the universe...

Freud, 1930, p. 68

Analysts who work with narcissistic patients frequently complain of the difficulty they experience in 'getting through' to the patient and 'making themselves heard', or, with growing irritation, they speak of 'making a dent' in the patient or 'cracking the narcissistic shell'. They sometimes develop an intense feeling of frustration about the impermanence of even their effective interpretations and compare it with talking into the wind or writing on the sand, only to have one's words effaced moments later by the waves.

And indeed one of the characteristics of the narcissistic transference is that the patient either welcomes or resents the analyst's words, experiences them as an anodyne or as an intrusive, officious imposition, and frequently does not even register the actual content of what is said but rather reduces it to a jumble of words, sounds, noises or tones. He may experience the intervention as comforting or soothing, or may react to his impression that *something* was being said in a friendly or angry tone, in the wrong way, at the wrong time or, simply, by the wrong person. Thus, the reaction is to the physiognomic or formal quality of the interpretation rather than to its communicative content which is either not heard or, if heard, is not registered or, if registered, is not understood, remembered or acted upon.

This incidentally, adds to the problem of the 'negative therapeutic reaction' so common with these patients, for the sudden or premature disruption of the narcissistic transference which causes this reaction can be brought about not only by making a 'correct' interpretation at the wrong level or wrong time, but also by making it in the wrong context, with the wrong words, in the wrong tone, etc.

At other times these patients themselves complain of their difficulty in understanding what is said to them or in remembering it. A common experience, irritating to the analyst and ultimately also to the patient, is that a session which seems to have led to a certain understanding, affective development or *experience* of some kind may, 24 hours later, be either totally forgotten or no longer retain the *meaning* which had been attributed to it.

I have discussed in another context the lack of continuity which these patients experience in their lives and related this to the 'uncanny' experiences from which they frequently suffer (Bach, 1975). This lack of continuity or, rather, the presence of discontinuous and 'uncanny' self-experiences was viewed as both a developmental interference, which is the emphasis that Kohut (1971) gives, and also as a defensive operation, which is the emphasis that Kernberg (1975) gives. In this paper, I shall try to describe some further characteristics of what I have come to regard as the narcissistic thought disorder or, more inclusively, the narcissistic state of consciousness.

My interest in this was sharpened by a particularly difficult narcissistic patient, a wealthy and successful man who had improved behaviorally in a lengthy prior analysis, but whose subjective experiences had remained relatively untouched. After several months of analysis, he admitted that, although the previous treatment had enabled him to marry, he had 'never really loved anyone' in his entire life.

This admission came after a chance meeting on the street with his previous analyst, where the primary content of consciousness was an observation of almost hallucinatory clarity that the analyst's white shirt collar was frayed and somewhat dirty, an observation accompanied by intense feelings of superiority and contempt. It was difficult for him to report this incident, which was connected with considerable guilt at having 'murdered' so many people in his life who had tried to love him.

In the transference regression the patient would at times become confused, drowsy and dazed, unable to focus on his own thoughts or to understand what I said and would eventually fall asleep, awakening after a few minutes, suddenly, and with total amnesia for what had occurred. In other sessions he would be rational, hyper-alert and talkative, but the content of consciousness would typically be filled with excited self-aggrandizement. In either state, it became extremely difficult to do analytic work. Sometimes, in moods of despair, he would complain that I was not helping him 'to get an overview' of things, but the meaning of the complaint remained unclear.

From time to time there were periods when the patient's state of consciousness appeared more normal and during these times some good work was done. But after a while I began to wonder if this man had at any time in his life enjoyed a relatively stable and integrated 'normal' state of consciousness. This puzzlement was useful if only in reducing the counter-transference, but it also led me to understand his complaint about lacking an 'overview' and it raised other questions as well.

It seems that while 'syndrome' and 'phenomena' refer to both objective behavior and subjective states, a 'state of consciousness' is an organizing notion which emphasizes the primacy of subjective experience. Yet it differs from Escalona's (1968) 'experience' construct in being dimensional, ranging from less to more, from non-conscious to highly conscious, with a particular emphasis on the vicissitudes of self-awareness. The underlying assumption is that there is a dimension of subjective awareness which has its roots in diurnal variation—Lewin's (1968) sleep-waking ratio—and which fluctuates both developmentally, with clinical state, and with clinical diagnosis.

Rapaport (1951) discerns 'the following groups of variants of the state of consciousness':

    a.   a continuum of normal states of consciousness ranging from the waking to the dream;

    b.   special states of normal consciousness, such as absorption, hypnosis, boredom;

    c.   developmental states of consciousness, such as those of children of various ages, and of preliterates; and

    d.   pathological states of consciousness.

Each of these appears to be characterized by:

    a.   a specific form of thought-organization;

    b.   specific forms—including absence—of reflective awareness;

    c.   specific limitations of voluntary effort and/or spontaneity; and

    d.   underlying the others, a specific quality (degree of binding), quantity, and organization of available cathexes (pp. 707–708).

Klein (1970) speaks of consciousness as

a conceptual convenience referring to the existence of a structural means of dispensing attention cathexis in varying amounts, giving rise to a pattern of awareness—the available parameters in which experience can occur, the distinctive ways in which it is possible to experience an idea. Awareness, in this view, is no unimportant epiphenomenon but has an adaptive import defined by the controlling structures that affect the deployment of cathexis. One cannot speak of *a* 'consciousness' or even, strictly speaking, of *a* 'preconscious,' without keeping in mind its context of ego organization and the particular parameters of awareness that distinguish it. (p. 248)

At this point I began to feel that my patient's 'normal' state of consciousness was habitually different from the theoretically normal state on many parameters, and that this might have consequences for both theory and technique. It seemed that the 'normal' adult waking state of consciousness was a developmental achievement which certain patients never completely attained or from which they were in a chronic state of regression. For example, although my patient's speech appeared to be predominantly in the secondary process mode, he frequently used language not for its communicative function but rather to establish a sense of well-being or avoid a loss of self-esteem. In most instances his reflective awareness seemed to be disturbed, that is, his awareness of himself as thinker of his thoughts or executor of his actions appeared at times to be overly acute and at other times to be diminished or non-existent[1]. Indeed, he had been correct in asserting that he lacked an 'overview,' for he suffered wide fluctuations of reflective self-awareness and a consequent difficulty in properly evaluating and integrating the relationships of this self to the object world.

Rapaport (1951) has emphasized the importance of reflective awareness in consciousness and its relation to the process of socialization:

---

[1] Schafer (1968) presents an illuminating discussion of this point in which he proposes the term *reflective self-representation* for the representation of oneself as thinker of the thought. For various reasons, I prefer Rapaport's conceptualization, with the understanding that what is meant is the awareness not only of awareness, but of the 'I' or self as originator of the thought or action, which might more fully be called reflective self-awareness. Such reflective self-awareness exists, by definition, in the context of object-world relationship.

We know from Piaget's studies that the transition from 'egocentric' thinking and its naive absolute realism, to a higher level of thinking which recognizes the relativity of qualities, is dependent upon the discovery of the relativity of the 'me'. Motility, by drawing a line between the excitations from which we can withdraw by motor action and those we cannot, draws the line between the 'me' and 'not-me': but self-awareness so achieved is quite incomplete...Only the implicit reactions and explicit communications of a variety of other 'me's' can free the 'me' from its solipsism (autism), by providing mirrors to reflect various sides of the 'me'. The experience of these variations replaces the autistic *naive realism* of the sensory-motor 'me, ' by a relativism of self-awareness. (p. 724)

Thus reflective self-awareness rests on socialization processes in which the relativity of the self and its experiences is established by experiencing how others see the world and ourselves, within a maturational framework. Piaget & Inhelder (1948), for example, have demonstrated the inability of children to understand that an object might look different when viewed from a position other than their own, that is, a lack of 'empathy' with the differently-situated observer. Piaget & Inhelder (1966) emphasize:

...the transition from an initial state in which everything is centered on the child's own body and actions to a 'decentered' state in which his body and actions assume their objective relationships with reference to all the other objects and events registered in the universe. This decentering, laborious enough on the level of action (where it takes at least eighteen months), is even more difficult on the level of representation, because the preschool child is involved in a much larger and more complex universe than the infant...As soon as language and the semiotic function permit not only evocation but also communication with other people...the universe to be represented is no longer formed exclusively of objects (or of persons as objects), as at the sensori-motor level, but contains also sub-jects who have their own views of the situation that must be reconciled with those of the child, with all that this situation involves in terms of separate and multiple perspectives to be differentiated and coordinated. (pp. 94–95)

This differentiation and coordination of separate and multiple perspectives necessitates a higher order of abstract conceptualization and, consequently, of reflective awareness.

Rapaport (1951) states:

It is as though every set of abstractions amounts to a hypercathectic organization in which, at a lesser expenditure of cathectic energy but presumably on a higher level of potential, a broad system of objects or relationships is integrated...We may assume that a similar pattern of hierarchic progression of hypercathectic organizations is experienced in the varieties of reflective awareness. The lower orders of reflective awareness are mirrored in the higher. Like higher-order abstractions, reflective awareness also suffers when tiredness or other normal or patho-logical conditions sap the available amount of hypercathexis. (pp. 706–707)

Thus, it seems that, when as a result of tolerable frustrations or disadaptation, self and object representations are brought into aware-ness, the relativity of the self is experienced, the nature of these representations is changed, and a higher-order conceptualization of the dyadic relationship eventually integrated. There would then be a series of ascending orders of awareness, from primitive sensori-motor non-awareness through elementary self-awareness with perception of the other as 'not-me', up to and including those higher orders of re-flective awareness which we call empathy, concern and mature love.

Having arrived at this understanding, I realized that I had become overconcerned with my patient's primitive defenses against envy, rage and object longing, and that I had lost my perspective as well. I was then able to share with him the simple observation that he seemed to have some particular difficulty in keeping both of us in awareness or in perspective at the same time. This formulation captured his interest and led to some fruitful self-observation and collaboration in the course of which the fluctuating states of consciousness, along with their idealizing and grandiose content and self-esteem variations, gradually integrated into a cognitively and affectively more stable state. We eventually learned that falling asleep represented his need to trust someone to care for him, the 'rude awakening' expressed his discovery of maternal unreliability when he awoke one night to find his mother gone and discovered her in another part of the hotel, *in flagrante* with a stranger, and the hyper-alert grandiosity his precocious proclamation that he must henceforth care for himself to avoid a repetition of this trauma. But the trauma itself was the crystallization of a defective mother–child interaction which had persisted throughout childhood and adversely affected his awareness of himself and others.

The capacity for mature reflective self-awareness is of complex origin and involves ego-ideal and superego issues which are here neglected, but in at least one respect it is similar to the related 'capacity to be alone' (Winnicott, 1958): it develops only in the presence of another who is capable of nurturing it. In principle, it is the mother or mirroring 'other' who focuses, integrates and interprets the child's experience and gives this experience human meaning. The good-enough mother confirms and integrates the child-initiated appetitive behavior, cues and partial actions, and by doing so shows the child that he is alive and can have a positive effect on the object world (Winnicott, 1965; Escalona & Corman, 1974). She is, thus, instrumental in the development of the child's theory about himself, that is, in developing his sense of self which is built around the experience of the action-self, the 'I' as thinker and doer in relation to an object.

This experience first culminates in the rapprochement phase (Mahler, 1965) where the child, among other things, is working through the issue of his place in the object world, that is, the relativity of his primitive self-awareness which had burgeoned in the practicing period. Severe defects of self-awareness and the sense of self seem particularly related to these early periods and are contributed to by both child and mother, although I here emphasize the latter's role in this dialogue.

For example, the mother who imposes her own initiatives upon the child may promulgate a self-experience of the 'I' as being lived by forces external to the self. Conversely, the mother who is unavailable for 'emotional refuelling' (Mahler, 1968) may lead the child to feel that he has no recourse other than himself. Reflective self-awareness may then move out of the optimal range and fluctuate between the two extremes of the child who reactively sustains himself, with overcathected self-awareness, or the child who fails at sustaining himself and seeks the mother, with undercathected self-awareness. Let me cite, as an example, the remarks of a 7-year-old, recorded by his mother:

a. 'Is this world a *dreaming*, or is it real?'—illustrating a pathological undercathexis of self-awareness.
b. 'This world terrifies me sometimes. It seems to be all me!'—illustrating a pathological overcathexis of reflective self-awareness.

Thirty years later, this man presented himself for analysis suffering from a narcissistic disorder. As might be expected, one of his main complaints was that he experienced his thoughts and actions either as terrifyingly omnipotent or else as involuntary, that is, as being coerced by people, situations or uncontrollable internal forces which made the decisions, as it were, without his participation.

In general, the broadest statement I can make about the 'narcissistic state of consciousness' is that it attempts, either through selective alterations of reflective awareness or through an earlier interference with the development of such awareness, to establish or recapture an ego state of physical and mental wholeness, well-being and self-esteem, either alone or with the help of some object used primarily for this purpose (Sandler & Joffe, 1965).

These alterations of reflective self-awareness may fluctuate from absence through under-emphasis to a gross overemphasis on the self as thinker and doer. They may therefore result in a de-automatization or overautomatization of function (Hartmann, 1958) which distorts the means–end relationship so that the multifaceted awareness of the goal or 'meaning' of an action and one's relationship to it is never completely experienced. From the defensive viewpoint, one might speak of a regressive de-automatization or overautomatization whose purpose is to obscure the 'meaning' of an experience so that the responsibility for decision, choice and action, with the inevitable narcissistic injuries these incur, may be avoided[2].

As a function of his effort to establish or recapture an ego state of physical and mental wholeness, well-being and self-esteem, an effort which has both defensive and maturational aspects, the narcissistic patient seems to show a characteristic altered state of consciousness. This altered ego state involves disturbances of self and body-self, language and thought, voluntary effort, mood arousal and time sense, which I discuss under separate headings. These observations are of clinical value to the extent that they increase our empathy with these patients, by alerting us to certain parameters which we normally assume but which in these patients cannot be taken for granted.

II. Self and Body-Self

Nobody is my name. My father and mother call me Nobody, as do all the others who are my companions.

Homer, Odyssey 9: 366

---

[2] I am of course discussing this from the viewpoint of normal and abnormal psychology. A regressive deautomatization which obscures the 'usual' or 'ordinary' meaning of experience is also a feature of the narcissistic creative and mystical states (Deikman, 1966).

There is no word for 'self' or 'oneself' in Homer...The 'self' or the identity is defined concretely and specifically in terms of 'Who is your father?' 'Whence do you come?' Further, one's identity is largely couched in terms of the story, or *stories*, of one's life...If the version of events is different, then the identity is different...What develops in later Greek thought, is that the definition of self and of identity becomes contingent upon an *active* process of examining, sorting out, and scrutinizing the 'events' and 'adventures' of one's own life...

Simon & Weiner, 1966, p. 308

The discovery of the self, or the ontogenetic development from the narcissistic state of consciousness to the adult waking state of consciousness, seems to show interesting phylogenetic parallels with the development of early Greek thought[3]. Dodds (1951), Snell (1953) and others have shown that Homer's people lacked an integrated concept of both 'mind' and 'body', that their self-esteem regulation was predominantly external and that they viewed internal tensions as concrete, anthropomorphized and instigated by the actions of the gods. In general, their thought processes appear to be more concrete than abstract, more passively experienced than actively instigated and, as one of the pre-Socratics from the vantage point of his later mode of thinking remarked, they seemed to be more 'asleep' or dreaming than 'awake' (Simon, 1972). These attributes are, of course, also characteristic of narcissistic states, so that studies of the later discovery of the self by the Greek lyricists and pre-Socratics may illuminate and be illumined by what we know about the discovery of the self in childhood and in the course of psychoanalytic treatment of the narcissistic disorders. Here, I shall use this material merely to highlight certain features of the narcissistic state of consciousness.

---

[3] These generalizations are merely suggestive and should be taken in the light of the considerable qualifications advanced in a somewhat different context by Simon *et al.* in a series of scholarly and fascinating papers (Simon & Weiner, 1966; Russo & Simon, 1968; Simon, 1972, 1973a, 1973b).

Let me begin by noting that I use the word 'self' to refer to a mental content rather than a psychic structure, that is, a content having to do with people's theories about themselves including their fantasies, both conscious and unconscious, about self-integration and self-disruption[4]. These theories, which have both conscious and unconscious aspects, also include to varying degrees contents which on a theoretical level may be classified as belonging to id, ego and superego or to other theoretical entities which may perhaps better fit earlier hierarchical developmental organization (Gedo & Goldberg, 1973). I shall have more to say about the development of these self theories, but for the moment let me simply note that when a patient says that he is 'falling apart', feels 'like two people', has 'no willpower', no 'identity', or feels that his body 'is in pieces', we are under no compulsion to translate this directly and anthropomorphically into its (apparent) metapsychologically structural equivalent.

But to return to our beginnings. Snell (1953) convincingly demonstrates that Homer does not have a word for the body and 'does not even have any words for the arms and legs', nor for the trunk. 'He speaks of hands, lower arms, upper arms, feet, calves and thighs' (p. 310). Snell believes that in early Greek epic and art

> the physical body of man was comprehended, not as a unit but as an aggregate. Not until the classical art of the fifth century do we find attempts to depict the body as an organic unit whose parts are mutually correlated. In the preceding period the body is a mere construct of independent parts variously put together. (p. 6)

> Thus, the early Greeks did not, either in their language or in the visual arts, grasp the body as a unit. The phenomenon is the same as with the verbs denoting sight; in the latter, the activity is at first understood in terms of its conspicuous modes, of the various attitudes and sentiments connected with it, and it is a long time before

---

[4] I am deeply indebted to Dr William Grossman for his help in clarifying my thinking on this point as well as on many others.

speech begins to address itself to the essential function of this activity. It seems, then, as if language aims progressively to express the essence of an act, but is at first unable to comprehend it because it is a function, and as such neither tangibly apparent nor associated with certain unambiguous emotions. As soon, however, as it is recognized and has received a name, it has come into existence, and with the knowledge of its existence quickly becomes common property...With the discovery of this hidden unity, of course, it is at once appreciated as an immediate and self-explanatory truth.

This objective truth, it must be admitted, does not exist for man until it is seen and known and designated by a word; until, thereby, it has become an object of thought. (pp. 7–8)

Thus the concepts of 'body' and 'self' apparently did not exist in early Greek thought and came into being only when the body and the self became objects of thought or, more primitively, objects of perception. And it is precisely to this point that Lacan (1949) addresses himself in his important paper on the mirror-phase.

This phase, according to Lacan, occurs between the sixth and eighteenth months, when the child, while still in a state of powerlessness and motor incoordination, anticipates on an imaginary level the acquisition and mastery of his bodily integrity. This imaginary integrity is accomplished through identification with the image of another similar human being perceived as a Gestalt; it is illustrated and actualized by the concrete experience in which the child sees his own image in the mirror. Laplanche and Pontalis (1968) note,

> Lacan draws attention to 'the triumphant assumption of the image, with the accompanying jubilant mimicry and the playful complacency with which the specular identification is controlled'....What happens is that the infant perceives in the image of its counterpart—or its own mirror image—a form (*Gestalt*) in which it anticipates a bodily unity which it still objectively lacks (whence its 'jubilation'); in other words, it identifies with this image. (p. 251)

We may note in passing that this phase is apparently contemporaneous with Spitz's (1965) second organizer of the psyche, the 'eight-month' anxiety (Ajuriaguerra, Diatkine, & Badaracco, 1956; Dixon, 1957), and an early stage of Mahler's (1968) 'practicing' period. For Lacan, incidentally, it is this phase which gives rise retroactively to the disintegrative fantasy of the 'corps morcelé' or 'body in pieces', that phase of autoerotic body fragmentation which precedes the establishment of the narcissistic object.

More concretely, the infant, faced with the mirror, discovers that he can act and thereby directly influence that which he sees at a distance. He suddenly realizes that that which he can see at a distance and can also influence completely is—himself! This is the reverse of another kind of experience, where what is *not* me moves exactly *like* me, uncannily, as with a double, or comically, as in a Marx Brothers routine (Bach, 1975). Thus proximal cues are connected with a distal perception and an affective state correlated with a cognitive organization, culminating in an 'aha! experience'.

Something of the process involved was described to me by a patient, who remembered trying to defend himself against reflective self-awareness as a child, a process which he was in fact repeating in the transference.

> You keep telling me that I should become aware of myself, that I should live in reality, that I should take account of death and loss and time and work....Not that you ever actually say that, but I think that that's what you really mean....
>
> One time I lived without being aware of myself and that was just fine....I didn't know about death and frustration and disappointment....I didn't think about them. ...
>
> If you become self-conscious, it's intensely embarrassing because it means that you see yourself as an object...[?] I would become an object, objectified, someone who wasn't worth considering any more. I could be told something that would objectify me...[?] I mean I'm becoming aware that I'm mortal....I'll go to the doctor and he tells me I'm dead....I'll go to work and they'll

tell me I'm fired. ...I'll go to you and you'll tell me I'm crazy....Once there's the other one then you become an object also, because you become someone else's other....

I remember when my sister was born, driving home from the hospital, my mother kept saying, 'Why don't you turn around and look at your sister?'...I wouldn't turn around, I withdrew into myself...[?] A mystery takes place at birth...I didn't really think that I was born...And then suddenly there are two, and you become alienated and self-conscious....If you give objectivity to another person—names, sexes, personalities, favorite flavors (that's contemptible—I prefer butter pecan to vanilla!) then you become the same thing as they are....I'm not a magical being, I was born like her, we drove home from the hospital in an old Plymouth, they probably showed me to someone else just like they showed her to me...Big deal!...Why couldn't you just be a person...generic, like a human...not to have a name or dress...I hate my name!...[!] Yes...I should be amorphous—like a god—Look at this horrible thing I'm forced to wear now...[?] My body! It's not an abode fit for a person.

This struggle against the diminishment of the self and its fantasied omnipotence may often be seen most clearly in the concrete fantasies of body imagery. It is known that amputees tend to dream of themselves as whole, that is, to regain their bodily integrity by means of a diminished or altered state of consciousness. From this point of view, phantom limbs could be seen as narcissistic restitution phenomena, and the observation that postmastectomy phantoms are accentuated during menstruation, pregnancy and sexual excitement would be consistent with their correlation to alterations in the state of consciousness. Fischer (1969) regards 'the loss of limb as a distortion of corporeal awareness and the phantom limb as a readaptation phenomenon to correct the distortion in physical space-time'. Similarly, narcissistic 'phantoms' such as transitional objects, imaginary companions, doubles, vampires, ghosts, muses and the creative product itself may be regarded as readaptation phenomena to correct distortions in the sense of mental and physical well-being, particularly when these distortions have occurred before the establishment of a firm sense of self (Bach, 1971, 1975; Bach & Schwartz, 1972).

Freud (1933) takes pains to point out that we must deal, not with a simple theory of 'organ inferiority', but with a more complex issue of values. In his view, it is erroneous to relate the personality of Wilhelm II to his withered arm, without noting that *his* mother, unlike some other mothers of handicapped children, rejected him for this infirmity (p. 66). Thus, the sense of physical and mental well-being is dependent not only on the cognitive facts of physical spacetime, but on these facts as embedded in a set of values and meanings with which they mutually interact. The loss of the foreskin may enhance or diminish self-esteem, depending on a large variety of other circumstances.

But to return to the narcissistic conditions. Although many of these patients may function at a high level of professional competence in the outside world, in the chronic or transference regression one is frequently confronted with disturbances of the body image, hypochondriacal preoccupations and difficulties with eating and weight regulation. There may be a split-off self representation which shows a mirror complementarity with the conscious presenting complaints, so that someone who feels physically weak and powerless may harbor a grandiose and dangerously powerful split-off image, while someone who presents with arrogance and grandiosity may be fearful of the dangerously vulnerable and dependent little-child self. Although in some instances this is purely defensive, in others it seems as if the child had never achieved and stabilized the transition from the self experienced as fragmented and uncontrolled to the self seen as integrated and controllable in the mirror. The analyst may then become the enticing or frightening 'other half', and continual attempts will be made to hold him, repel him and control him, primarily through denial, splitting and projective identification (Kernberg, 1975). Just as the central phenomenon in the mirror stage is the recognition of the self in the mirror or in the mother's face, with the bridge from the proximal cues of the 'body in pieces' to an integrated distal percept of the body self as whole, so in the narcissistic regression one finds the distal percept being lost and the proximal cues once again becoming salient. A patient who had recently developed a reliable sense of self and could clearly remember what it was like before, reminisced:

> It used to be that I would look in the mirror and see the individual features but not my face....I would run my fingers over my face, count the hairs that I'd lost and inspect the pores...but I really couldn't even see what I looked like....
>
> In reading I would become overly concerned with the individual words and even the letters, their shape, peculiarity...and I totally lost the sense of what I was reading....When I couldn't read I would masturbate...it was a way of putting myself together when I felt I was falling apart....
>
> My whole adolescence was just a total blur...I recently passed the 'Y' building which I used to go by every day of my life, and I think I saw what it looked like for the first time.

This change from a fragmented, peripheral, auto-erotic, self-oriented and proximally dominated perception to an integrated, focally organized, object-oriented and distally dominated perception has been beautifully described by Schachtel (1959) as the genetic development from 'autocentric' to 'allocentric' perception. When it occurs in patients as the indirect result of psychoanalytic therapy, it frequently gives rise to the same sense of discovery and triumphant exhilaration as seen in the child before the mirror, the experience celebrated by the early Greek lyricists such as Archilochos and Sappho, who were just awakening to the value of the self-experience and Ich-Gefühlung which had for so long been embedded in the communal and archetypal inheritance.

A relevant contribution is the ongoing research of Escalona & Corman (1971, 1973, 1974), which suggests that a style of maternal care focused on proximal, interpersonal mother-initiated interactions produces a very different kind of child than a style focused on pre-dominantly distal, not exclusively interpersonal, infant-initiated interactions. I shall discuss these findings later but here I would emphasize the relative predominance of the proximal mode in narcissistic patients and their use of self-stimulation in the form of libidinized thinking, self-touching, masturbation, transitional phenomena and acting out as a substitute for stimulation by the object in the maintenance of their precarious sense of mental and physical existence and well-being.

A professional woman came for treatment when, as the result of her husband's sudden business failure, she had become catastrophically disillusioned with her hitherto idealized marriage. Refusing him sex, she had continual fantasies of affairs with other men who represented her idealized, boyish, competent self, a derivative from her early idealization of an older brother. She would lie on the couch stroking her face, a gesture first traced to her desire to be stroked by the fantasied lover or analyst, then to her need to be reassured that her face could be seen or actually existed, and finally to a transitional habit of early childhood which was confirmed by her mother. Musing about playing out her fantasy, she said:

> There's a feeling of mystery about myself...that I'm not a woman...that other women have something or know something that I don't know....If Arnold [the lover] had raped me, then, it would clarify my confusion of identity...If he goes inside me then that proves there's an inside...that's what bothers me when my climax comes from cunnilingus rather than intercourse....I'm thinking about that English writer who changed his sex...about Aschenbach in *Death in Venice*....He was fixated on that child's beauty like I was fixated on Arnold's beauty....Why don't you ever talk to me?...I need a man to make me feel like a woman...to make me feel alive.

While not neglecting the obvious phallic fantasies and oedipal issues, it became clear in the course of this analysis that we were dealing not only with a defensive regression and narcissistic identification, but also with some early developmental disturbance of the body image. One frequently finds with narcissistic patients an early history of head-banging, skin masochism, vestibular disturbances or hypochondriasis as restitutive attempts to recathect the self-boundaries. Often in the course of analysis such odd feelings as wanting 'to whirl like a dervish' or 'to hang with my head over the couch' are signs that the area of the early splitting is being approached.

A patient who for years had been grossly overweight was able to begin reducing when his overeating and sleep phobias were connected with a fear of death. He then reported the following memory which I was unfortunately unable to record verbatim:

> I was about six years old when I developed a severe pneumonia. The family doctor missed the diagnosis, and for about ten days I became sicker and sicker. They finally called in a German specialist who examined me and told my parents at the bedside that I was very ill and might possibly die. I was running a high fever. I remember flying up to the ceiling and looking down on the scene: my parents, all frightened and agitated; the doctor, who I think had a white beard and spoke with an accent, and somebody lying on the bed, covered with blankets. But I was up on the ceiling and I remember thinking: 'Those idiots! They think I'm going to die but *I know better.*'...I've been up on the ceiling ever since.

This patient had indeed been 'up on the ceiling', having been hospitalized in his twenties after hearing voices which urged him to jump from the window. This memory was both a screen for a primal scene in which he had identified with a sick mother, as well as the locus of a chronic alteration of consciousness carrying multiple body representations. A propensity to such altered states has been related by Stein (1965) to the defensive regression following traumatic events, in particular childhood illnesses where the fever and altered body perceptions provide an open channel to changes of consciousness.

Sometimes the split-off self appears to have a psychophysical embodiment, like a phantom limb or imaginary companion.

After many months of analysis I discovered that a 45-year-old engineer was accompanied on the couch by his fantasied eight-year-old self, nicknamed Pepe, who lay parallel, about a foot to the left, and was mocking the whole procedure. At a later date the patient said about him:

> He was my other self…a Siamese twin…after screwing off all day I said to him: 'What do they expect of you? You're just an eight year old kid!'…I have no attachment to anything else except to that little boy, and through him to a world that's no longer there.…I was trying to control and stop things that I couldn't control in the real world…keeping my parents alive forever and making sure they took care of me…denying the fact that this little boy would grow up and suffer dangers and some day, eventually, die.…I couldn't manage the world so I just stepped away from it.…Like when a camera pulls you away from the image on the screen…it becomes a pattern of lights and shadows or little dots on a film screen and you're outside of it.…
>
> There's a real fear that this other person which I should stop pretending I am…that killing that off is as dangerous as cutting off a Siamese twin…and you as the doctor and me as the one who's talking to you and is going to survive…I kept saying I must make that decision, but the kid was in control. …
>
> This man who created a sham world, a sham marriage, a sham business, a sham life—where is he? What am I doing? I like this little boy but he doesn't belong in a commissioner's seat or an engineering office.…Yet I can't kill him off, he's the most resilient thing in me.…
>
> Sometimes I measure how far I can walk out of this door before he takes over.…To get rid of him would be like amputating a part of myself.…I would have wanted to be more than what's left…more than you see of me.

This fragment illustrates several points worth noting: the coexistence of contradictory theories about the self, their incarnation as alter egos or narcissistically prized body parts, the regression involving destruction of the Gestalt so that it becomes only a pattern of lights and shadows and, finally, the 'Peter Pan' dynamic for warding off narcissistic injury, which, here, includes loss of control, loss of parental care, loss of the idealized self, loss of body parts and, ultimately, loss of life. The final words, 'I would have wanted to be more than what's left' (after the amputation of Pepe), poignantly illustrates the transference conflict at that time when the analyst was seen as demanding total surrender of the child's autonomy under threat of abandonment. Shortly afterwards we discovered that the patient had made two suicide attempts in childhood as a final, desperate assertion of this autonomy.

I conclude this section with an example of the thermal sensitivity so commonly found in narcissistic patients for whom chill often represents the coldness of non-recognition and death, as opposed to the warmth of adequate reflection which may evoke its own danger of self-incineration.

This patient, a 45-year-old actress, presented with a history of multiple analytic failures extending over 25 years, extreme hypochondriasis and acute shame reactions. An unusually diligent and talented woman, she would fill her calendar to overflow, become agitated with her growing excitation and confusion, begin desperately to cancel appearances or make excuses, become terrified that she would be isolated and forgotten, start accepting all bookings indiscriminately and repeat the cycle over again. She began the session with a tale of her visit that morning to the most recent doctor, an unusually patient man who carefully examined her pains and paraesthesias, allayed her fears of rheumatism, sciatica and cancer, and demonstrated a vascular hypersensitivity, which he suggested was inherited. She told of having sex with her lover the day before and feeling an unusual closeness, but then suddenly becoming chilled which necessitated her sleeping alone under the covers although it was a hot night in July. She dreamed that she was in the back seat of a car, engaging in exciting sexual play with an unknown man, when the driver who was going too fast, lost the brakes. The car went out of control, crashed through the wall of a house and into the kitchen, passing through EITHER THE STOVE OR THE REFRIGERATOR, *then out of the house and, all unhurt, back on to the same street, but now it was snowing.*

She wondered whether sexual excitement and closeness frightened her...but if excitement frightens her, then coolness isolates and terrifies her—like the doctor said, her sensitivity is too extreme. For 15 years now, ever since her first analyst had unilaterally terminated treatment, she had suffered from an inability to completely empty her bladder and bowels which forced her to spend as much as several hours a day in the bathroom. Up to now no doctor had ever been able to help her. That was a question of self-regulation, wasn't it?

She remembered that she had almost quit analysis with me because of her insistence on being hypnotized. She knew now that I wouldn't tell her what to do nor stop her from doing anything—she would have to regulate herself. She had stayed up worrying about an appearance tomorrow—it was too much work, she was not prepared, it was beyond her ability, etc. But it was also a great honor to be asked. Throughout the evening she had felt hot and cold flushes, but her lover had comforted her. He seems to get less enthusiastic than she does, but he is also less frightened. He is really like a thermostat for her...the first person she has ever really loved because she neither submits to him completely nor controls him completely. Before this she never believed it possible that she would ever be able to live together with another human being.

Although this dream was later pursued in another direction, I cite it as a typical example of temperature and boundary sensitivity, obviously related to Kohut's (1971) discussion of blushing and the work of Hermann (1929) and Bak (1939) on thermal sensitivity. It also nicely illustrates the homeostatic function of hypochondriasis in the maintenance of self-esteem and a sense of well-being.

The acceptance of mental and physical imperfections without the need for compensatory alterations of awareness is a particularly difficult task for those with narcissistic problems. A patient who, in filling out a passport application, had at first responded 'no' to a question about identifying scars, later erased this response and enumerated some body stigmata of which she had always been ashamed. She remarked the next day: 'I have just begun to realize that you can't have an identity without having identifying scars.'

III. Language and Thought Organization

> That the topless towers be burnt
> And men recall that face,
> Move most gently if move you must
> In this lonely place.
> She thinks, part woman, three parts a child,
> That nobody looks; her feet
> Practise a tinker shuffle
> Picked up on a street.
> *Like a long-legged fly upon the stream*
> *Her mind moves upon silence.*
>
> W. B. Yeats, *Long-legged fly*

"The fact is that the speech of subjects between four and six (observed in situations in which children work, play, and speak freely) is not intended to provide information, ask questions, etc. (that is, it is not socialized language), but consists rather of monologues or 'collective monologues' in the course of which everyone talks to himself without listening to the others (that is, egocentric language)....It is only after long training that the child reaches the point (at the operatory stage) where he speaks no longer for himself but from the point of view of the other" (Piaget & Inhelder, 1966, pp. 120-3).

As noted earlier, in the narcissistic state, language is used predominantly in an autocentric manner to regulate well-being or self-esteem, rather than in an allocentric manner for purposes of communicating with or understanding an object. Thus the emphasis is less on the communicative function and more on the genetically earlier manipulative function of words, which may be used to frighten or to soothe, to distance or to merge, to control or to be controlled.

A patient whose mother was dying of cancer, overwhelmed by feelings of fear, rage and impotence, began to have sadomasochistic fantasies whenever he visited her in the hospital. The fantasies were of hanging women upside down, giving them enemas, raping them and of having the same done to him. In the context of discussing this, he replied to a simple question:

> You're very impatient with me....I'm very upset with your voice....You seem to be talking louder than usual which to my mind means that you're shouting.... [shouts] YOU'RE KILLING ME....Then I seem to be shrinking from you....You've been shrunk and now you're shrinking me....When you talk to me it's always an attack or intrusion....I fasten on one word and forget what you're saying...I hear my mother telling my father: 'You'll have to talk to him!'....I DON'T WANT TO BE TALKED TO! [?] Your voice became like thunder....[?] I resent that you don't tell me your fantasies....You're fine and clean and I'm dirty....[?] I want to be hugged by you....Talking doesn't count for anything— what counts is being hugged.

Because language is used more manipulatively or as a substitute for more primitive, proximal and autocentric modalities, such as touch, taste and smell, one has the overall sense that the language is impoverished, although at times it may be rhetorically brilliant. Frequently patients themselves complain that the words are 'empty' or 'without meaning'.

A 20-year-old student said: 'I left the University because it became only words—all words. There was a separation between words and actions or words and things, and the words began to have less and less meaning...Only the student revolt was real!'

Another patient, a writer by profession, complained that in the narcissistic transference it seemed 'as if we are in a space capsule floating in air, and I am filling up all the inside with words. My words feel empty, false; they have no meaning.'

Although on the extremes of the continuum narcissistic language and thought may merge into primary process, one more typically sees apparent secondary process functioning which lacks the truly integrated quality to be expected in the normal state of awareness. Frequently, for example, there is a lack of free communication between the various modes of thought representation (Horowitz, 1972), so that images or enactive gestures appear but are untranslatable into the lexical mode, or vice versa. This blocking or absence of the bridge between words and percept (image), contributes to the impression that the patient is talking to himself, or that his words are circling endlessly and leading nowhere.

The patient quoted above, whose mother was dying, had accused me interminably of wanting him to spill out all his feelings which would certainly drive him insane. After his mother's death, unable to experience his grief, he began to accuse me of being wordy, intellectual and rejecting his feelings. I pointed this out and remarked that, since his feelings were not in his words, they must be somewhere else. He began to cry and told me that ever since his mother's death he had been haunted by an image of himself 'dancing with her corpse as I saw it in the coffin, dressed in a white shroud, like a bride.'

Another patient with a persistent learning difficulty, who had just begun to make some headway with this problem said:

> I used to read without images, just words with no referent, and
> if things got very abstract then it was difficult to conjure up
> some personal experience, something that I've seen in some-
> one else, something I've thought or know about....Then it all
> begins to have a sterile quality and it gets harder and harder to
> remember....But this morning when I was reading I found lots
> of imagery that was cogent and and it helped enormously.

Here one could clearly see that the loss of the integrated meaning-quality of the experience was correlated with a decrease of reflective self-awareness. Generally, one finds a loss of flexibility in perspective, leading to overabstractness, overconcreteness or fluctuations between these extremes. As one patient remarked:

> I seem to have no sense of humor....I'm anybody's straight man....I can't tell when anybody's kidding or not....When Lois came into my office where the plants were dying from lack of light, she just put them in between the window and the screen.
>
> It was a good idea but I never would have thought of that....I'm upset because my period has been increasing....I can't control when I'm going to have a baby, or that I'm getting older....I can't control when people are making a joke or when they're serious....Flower pots are supposed to go only in one place—on the desk or on the ledge, not in between the window and the screen...if you don't have to see other things then you don't have to manage them...if things can have many meanings then you can be in trouble....It's a way of avoiding a multiplicity of meanings because a single meaning is more manageable.

When multiple meanings are avoided, then indeed the patient may become literal, humorless and aesthetically insensitive. On the other hand, when the focal meaning of an experience is denied, then the component parts may become ludicrous, empty, bizarre and, in the extreme, 'uncanny'. A patient who watched a violinist rosin his bow, tune his instrument and prepare to play, found himself thinking: 'A cat died and a tree was cut down to produce *this*?' In this case his attacks on the meaningful links between the actions had helped him to avoid his envy of the musical performance (Bion, 1959).

Concurrent with the changes mentioned above, one generally finds a syncretism of both thought and affect which is one of the hallmarks of the narcissistic state of consciousness and has been described by Freud (1913, 1930) and Ferenczi (1913). I shall give two examples, one chronic and one situational.

An extremely narcissistic man who for years was secretly convinced that I used the same Kleenex all day long for each patient, and who himself picked discarded objects off the street, was unable to boil water without anxiety because of his excessive 'empathy' with the overheated bottom of the kettle. Although his sympathy for the inflamed bottom and the discarded object was traceable to his having been beaten and discarded as a child, the mutative determinant was an 'oceanic' consciousness about which he said:

'I feel that the world is seamless...that we're all connected by a sticky ocean of glue, and I cannot allow any cracks or ruptures or breaks in this medium which holds us all together'.

While this man, from all that we learned in a lengthy analysis, had apparently never fully attained a normal state of consciousness, the following incident is more typical of the situational regressions that one sees daily.

A middle-aged woman came in complaining of constipation and a swollen stomach. She feels dizzy, strange and 'discombobulated', her brain is scrambled; she has a strong urge to jump out of the window. She is leaving on a trip tomorrow and she feels confused...she is so stupid that in planning her itinerary she thought that Frankfurt was in France and Strasbourg in Germany. This morning she wasn't sure whether today was Wednesday, Thursday or Friday.... She is bothered that the next patient has come early...it seems to cut into her session, as if warning of the end....Today she found herself unable to transcribe some Old English into Modern English, although this is her area of expertise...it seemed as if she couldn't clearly see that there were any differences between the two...She has also been regretting that she can't take a favorite old dress along on the trip...but it's just become too worn out.

Here the denial of differences, boundaries and temporal-spatial limitations is clearly in the service of denying the loss of the analyst in an as yet unresolved narcissistic transference. The urge to jump through the window, which had at one time gotten her hospitalized, was part of a fantasy of returning to the womb where she might avoid the separations and limitations of ordinary life.

Coincident with these changes in the thought processes, one finds that sentence structure tends to shift from a syntactical to a more psychological mode, while at the same time the 'I' as subject or doer begins to drop out and be replaced by more impersonal language: 'it's a feeling of resentment'; 'there was a dream last night'; 'the thought occurred that,' etc. Ultimately, the 'I' gives way to a polyphony of voices representing multiple facets of the personality experienced as coming from outside or not belonging to the self (Rapaport, 1951). The patient whose mother had recently died reported:

> When I come here I hear your voice telling me that I haven't grieved enough—that if I really cared I would kill myself on the grave. But Aunt Agnes is saying: 'Stop grieving—you must go on living.' It all sounds like clichés. People become tokens on a game-board and you move them around to represent feelings and play with your feelings and control them that way....Like the Everyman plays—all parts of his mind out there and they talk to him and to others...none of the parts are me....
>
> I hear voices in my head...they make the feelings real but they don't possess it, or let it possess you....Let them fight it out!...it sounds like some child's view of a family squabble....I hear the voice but it's not me, and then there's always another voice to oppose it, also not me...let them fight it out....I always thought that that's the way everybody thought.
>
> My mind was like a collection of little people...stereotyped... so there was a rude person, a courageous person, a fool, a villain...none of them were really you. They were like vectors...one would pull this way and another the other way, and the strongest would win.

In this instance, so characteristic of narcissistic regressions, the 'I' as decider and actor is decomposed into idealized objects, each representing a different side of the conflict. Sometimes also the instinctual urge is represented as one side of the conflict and an external object as the other; or two conflicting instincts, both experienced as alienated from and stronger than the self, are left to fight it out while the self observes the outcome. The conflict can then be experienced as external and the decision as coerced, leaving the observing self passive, not responsible and therefore still omnipotent.

There is also a particular type of memory deficit to be observed in these cases, but I have discussed this elsewhere (Bach, 1975) in connection with the startling deficiency they show in a consistent and continuous experience of the self.

The memory deficit, however, is related to the question of educability, since many of these patients present with a mild to moderately severe learning disability of long-standing. Normal narcissism, which ordinarily furnishes a motive for educability, in its pathological form often makes the learning process all but impossible. The narcissistic child or adult, unable to admit that there is something he does not know or must slowly and painfully learn, often cannot tolerate the learning process which by its mere existence becomes a narcissistic injury. This fact, of course, has well-known implications for the technique of psychoanalysis which is, after all, a learning experience. How many of our patients have insisted, like Ferenczi's (1923) 'clever baby', on being born or reborn 'knowing it all'.

Finally, I would repeat my impression that the 'thought disorder' described may be attributable to a developmental interference, to a defensive regression or, frequently, to both. Sometimes, indeed, it may be more accurately called a 'value disorder', in that the person may be capable of both ways of thinking but chooses the narcissistic mode as a preferred way of dealing with the world. The literature on psychological testing occasionally refers to such patients as 'lazy', which may sometimes be true, but I hope to show that the often immense efforts required to pursue such a radical 'Oblomovism' have other determinants.

IV. Voluntary Effort and Spontaneity

Further, the development of what one calls "intentionality"—the child's capacity to direct himself toward something, to aim at something, in perception, attention, action, etc., a process that according to Freud probably presupposes hypercathexis—could be viewed as one ego aspect of developing object relations. Actually, intentionality is among the first achievements of the child we would not hesitate to characterize as true ego functions.

Hartmann, 1952, p. 173

As long as the schemata are not intercoordinated but function each for itself, the child's judgments of value (desirability) are almost entirely confused with his judgments of reality. More precisely, they are one with the activity inherent in the schema....On the other hand, an object in the behaviour patterns of the present stage is no longer characterized by one value only;.... it can be considered either as an obstacle, or as a useful intermediate, or else as an end in itself....It thus assumes a series of different values according to the way in which it is utilized as a means in view of different ends.

Piaget, 1936, p. 173

The good-enough mother meets the omnipotence of the infant and to some extent makes sense of it. She does this repeatedly. A True Self begins to have life, through the strength given to the infant's weak ego by the mother's implementation of the infant's omnipotent expressions. The mother who is not good-enough is not able to implement the infant's omnipotence, and so she repeatedly fails to meet the infant gesture; instead she substitutes her own gesture which is to be given sense by the compliance of the infant. This compliance on the part of the infant is the earliest stage of the False Self, and belongs to the mother's inability to sense her infant's needs.

Winnicott, 1960, p. 145

One of the major characteristics of the narcissistic state of consciousness consists in limitations of voluntary effort and spontaneity in the areas of perception, attention, will, action, etc. The areas of perception, attention and action have been documented by Schachtel (1959), Spitz (1965), Piaget (1936), Mahler, (1968) and others, and I shall confine my observations to the limitation of choice, will and intentionality which are most strikingly manifested in narcissistic patients. Let me begin with two mundane examples:

A narcissistic patient complained that she had the urge to sneeze while putting her hair up in curlers and was unable to decide whether to give in to the urge or to finish placing the last curler. In the same hour she mentioned that, on her way to the bank, she had the urge to urinate and felt uncertain whether to stop and relieve herself or to complete her business first.

In analysis we learned that the mother had trained her to a strict schedule and taught her to urinate, even when she felt no urge, by imitating the trickle from an open water faucet. This practice the patient continued as an adult, thereby perpetuating her preference for physiognomic and syncretic perception and thinking, as well as for other-initiated rather than self-initiated behavior. At the time of beginning analysis, this patient was living with a man whom she was unable to decide to marry, in an apartment which she had been unable to decide to furnish.

Lest I give the wrong impression, let me add that she was a very competent and intelligent professional woman who made daily decisions of considerable import, but always with the sense that she was playing at a role which did not seem *real*. When I asked how she had decided on her career, she responded:

I just happened to be standing on the street corner....I applied to professional school as a joke and was astonished that I was accepted at all....I decided to go to Florida on vacation, and if I still had nothing better to do when I returned, then I would go....I think there are very few times when I actively *want* to do something...make love or anything....Most of the time I feel: 'Well, I'll do it if you want, or I just don't want to but maybe you can convince me, or, recently, sometimes I just don't want to'.

This latter was a reference to the early stages of treatment in which she had begun to exercise her will through a peremptory 'No!' (Spitz, 1957), by refusing sex with her lover, coming late for sessions and asserting herself at work. In the course of investigating those incidents which aroused an initially faint and timid 'No!' reaction, we uncovered much historical data relating to an early split between mother and nursemaid, both of whom were competing over the child's early training. The result was that this otherwise competent woman at the age of 32 still disposed of a pantheon of idealized objects to decide her every action: her mother to tell her when she ought to want to urinate, her nursemaid to tell her when she ought to feel hungry, her lover to tell her when she ought to feel sexually aroused, her boss to decide how she ought to spend her free time, and her analyst to tell her how she ought to feel about it all.

In more regressed cases all decisions may rest, not with a pantheon of god-like objects but with an omen or portent of some sort: if he calls on Sunday I'll say yes, but on Monday I'll say no.

Often the inability or refusal to make decisions is rationalized. As one patient said: 'If this were something I were destined to do, I would have noticed myself doing it.' Frequently the importance of the choice or decision is denigrated: 'The idea of trying to make myself better than I am doesn't seem worth it. How much better could I become anyway? Not much...just a little better.' Ultimately, this reduces to the absurd, as in a borderline patient who said: 'I was thinking of not showing up and I decided that it really wouldn't make any difference, because I knew that I wasn't going to be cured today anyhow!'—To which the analyst responded that he had discovered the therapeutic Zeno's paradox[5].

---

[5] I am indebted to Dr William Grossman for this anecdote.

The patient quoted above, who was not satisfied with getting only a little better, had carried his theory to the extreme of not answering phone calls or opening his mail, but one can see a similar dynamic in apparently energetic and decisive people who either feel that the decision is forced upon them or that it is not really they who are making it. One such patient dreamed that

> he was called to a conference of heads of state. Seven black limousines drew up, out of which emerged seven identical selves. He was not sure which one was really himself, but he knew that the other six were doubles, intended to frustrate a possible assassination.

Sometimes the issue is handled by waiting for the choice to become either perfect or hopeless, as with the patient who wanted a divorce because her husband was not ideal, but could not go through with it because he was not all bad either. It was difficult to show her that if he were either all bad or all good, no real choice would be involved.

At other times there is a smokescreen of frenetic activity which upon examination is seen to be disorganized, counter-productive, and self-contradictory, leading nowhere. This pseudo-activity has precisely the point of not committing the patient to any definitive choice or course of action while making him appear to be very active and productive. The grandiose fantasy behind this became very clear to me in the case of a busy professional man who was constantly losing his appointment book. One day, having lost it again, he came in bemoaning his worthlessness and inefficiency. He fantasied that I had been chasing the previous patient around the desk and that she had jumped out the window. When we saw this as a compensatory denigration of me, he became quite suspicious and felt that I had found the appointment book and was hiding it to teach him a lesson. When I persisted in enquiring, despite repeated rationalizations, why he hadn't replaced the book in his pocket, he became increasingly angry and finally shouted: 'A stupid idiot like you may have to put everything back in the same place, but I can put things wherever I goddam please and find them anyhow!' He was shocked and frightened at hearing his own words, but finally began to laugh at the ridiculousness of his statement.

In this case, which was mentioned earlier in connection with the imaginary companion Pepe, an apparent success neurosis concealed early narcissistic distortions, with a crushing sense of oedipal guilt and responsibility covering primitive shame reactions and an archaic grandiosity. One might easily apply to these patients Sartre's (1960) dictum that: "People who do nothing feel responsible for everything."

And indeed, true choice and real action, whether successful or a failure, have a beneficial effect in helping to define one's place in the world, sharpen one's sense of self and limit the area of personal responsibility appropriately. The narcissistic patient who cannot accept the limitations of choice and action is in the unfortunate position of having either to play God himself or to find someone who will, often with disastrous consequences. How does this come about?

In an elegant series of papers exploring the development of competency and the sense of self in infancy, Escalona & Corman (1971, 1973, 1974) have followed two infants intensively and demonstrated the intimate links between the mother's ministrations and early ego development. Although both mothers were attentive and affectionate, Mary's mother, from a conventional authoritarian background, felt that "the baby needed to be taught not only what to do and what not to do, but even each step on the developmental ladder" (Escalona & Corman, 1974, p. 152). Spontaneous impulses arising from within the child were felt by the mother "as a sort of dangerous wildness that needed to be tamed" (p. 152). The early mother–child interactions were characterized by a preference for the proximal systems of touch, temperature, pain and kinesthesis, a restriction to essentially direct person-to-person contacts, a general containment of 'floor freedom' and a predominance of mother-initiated interchanges.

John's parents, on the other hand, felt that "their primary responsibility was to nurture 'the miracle of growth' and to protect it against 'unnatural' constraint. Every effort was made to accommodate to the baby's needs and impulses and to acquaint him with all that is good in the natural and social environment" (p. 153). John's early interactions were characterized by a growing preference for the distal systems of sight and sound, a greater emphasis on the inanimate environment along with social contacts, more spatial freedom, and a relative predominance of child-initiated interchanges.

In the first year, John was *more* active when the mother was *not* there, "sought out opportunities for exploration and activity, showed vivid affect, and engaged in many of his most complex and mature activities in her absence" (p. 164). In the second year "he spent an increasing proportion of time in pursuit of relatively independent play activity....Yet, during these long spells of self-directed play, he never lost contact with the mother. He frequently called out to her phrases relevant to what he was doing (apparently expecting her to understand), went to show her something only to at once depart contentedly, and often, as he worked quietly and intensively...he whispered 'mommy' as if to evoke her image, clearly not addressing himself to her or to anybody else" (p. 164).

In the first year, Mary "demonstrated her most complex and most mature developmental accomplishments chiefly in mother's presence. By contrast, her behaviour, when mother was not close by, showed a degree of stereotyping and emptiness, less affective modulation, and, frequently, something akin to boredom" (p. 164). In the second year, "Mary became increasingly dependent upon the presence and responsiveness of other people for pleasure and interest in activity...She constantly sought out other persons and it was as though even preferred toys...gave pleasure to the degree that others acknowledged and participated in what she was doing. If such response was not forthcoming, she called for mother or whoever was at home, roamed restlessly and carried things about (p. 164).

There is no need to elaborate here on the relevance of these findings to Winnicott's (1958) ideas about the development of the capacity to be alone or the 'true' and 'false' self (Winnicott, 1960), to Spitz's (1963) concept of the 'dialogue', or to Kohut's (1971) descriptions of the narcissistic patient's reactions to the presence or absence of an empathic self-object.

Of course we cannot predict with any assurance how Mary will eventually develop, nor whether that development will be experienced *by her* as troublesome in the context of her own milieu and values. Nevertheless, it is worth noting that the disturbances of voluntary action and spontaneity described above, as well as the disturbances of self-continuity discussed in an earlier paper (Bach, 1975), seem historically linked with disturbances of the mother-child 'dialogue', either through its absence or through a maternal monologue or pseudo-dialogue, characterized by a predominance of non-empathic interactions initiated, imposed or controlled by the mother.

Rapaport (1957) has shown that the ego's autonomies from the environment and from the drives are interdependent, i.e. that, within certain limits, these autonomies guarantee each other. Thus, the intrusive mother, by limiting the field to the interpersonal environment and decreasing autonomy from it, is also decreasing her child's autonomy from the drives. I shall illustrate one of the consequences of this in the next section.

V. Mood Disturbances

The early Greeks, newer philological studies show, did not clearly distinguish semantically between perception, knowledge, feeling, and action. The word that later meant to fear originally (perhaps also) meant 'to be put to flight'; the word for *I know* originally meant 'I have seen'—or rather, there was no differentiation between flight and fear, sight and knowledge....From these and similar comments, particularly if we give words to implications, it appears that the subjective experiences of early life become split up only with the development and education of the ego. Then, the holistic mass-event becomes conceptually differentiated into cognitive, affective, and motor elements....Of Homer's heroes it suffices to say that *I know* means 'I have seen' and *I fear* means 'I am fleeing.'...If there were no concept of the independent observing cognitive self, we should have no corresponding concept of the independent feeling or the independent action. The growing, intellectually developing, ego recapitulates the history of philosophy.

Lewin, 1965

L'action de vivre m'agite trop.

Unknown 17th-century aesthete

The narcissistic state of consciousness is characterized by mood swings which patients variously describe as feeling 'manic' or 'depressed'; 'up' or 'down'; 'alive' or 'dead'; 'together' or 'disorganized'; 'excited' or 'dull'; 'interesting' or 'boring', etc. Although patients may talk about these mood swings as either depressions or elations, they in fact bear a qualified resemblance to the classic cyclothymic states both descriptively and dynamically, being characterized by limited duration and rapid vacillations, with relative maintenance of insight and the general integrity of the personality. Typically, the depressions follow a narcissistic loss or defeat, have a primary quality of apathy and show a predominance of shame over guilt, without the necessity for the usual introjective processes found in melancholia (Bibring, 1953). Similar manifestations have been discussed by Reich (1960) as pathologic forms of self-esteem regulation, by Jacobson (1957, 1964) as related to archaic superego structures, and by Kohut (1971) as faulty discharge patterns of narcissistic libido. These states appear to be the extremes on a continuum from apathy to arousal, and seem to be related to the loss or recapture of an ideal state of psycho-physical well-being (Sandler & Joffe, 1965), with accompanying feelings of helplessness and annihilation or of omnipotence and exhilaration. The precise role of aggression or rage in these mood swings seems to be a debatable point, further complicated by the innumerable defensive vicissitudes which these moods can undergo such as regressions, reversals of affect, psychosomatic equivalents, etc.

A patient who had just come from the gym was exultant over the 'perfect' game of squash he had played:

There are some sleeps, some games, some analytic hours where everything goes just perfectly and I experience a kind of rejuvenation...but if I anticipate it or make an effort towards it, then it will certainly never happen...When I anticipate it I get excited and then I become afraid...[?] I don't know...maybe of getting excited...so I have to short-circuit it...the only way it really works is if it catches me unplanned...

I was reading this book yesterday and I got so excited that I was reading too quickly and I had the feeling of being consumed by my excitement...really... while at the same time fearing that if I continued to read I would finish it and then it would be over...I wouldn't have that kind of excitement available tomorrow.... I wanted to stop because I was feeling consumed and also because the pages would run out on me...and then I couldn't fall asleep...

I tried to slow down but I couldn't...the only way to slow down was to stop reading...it would be a good time to die...[?] to die in a state of ecstasy...if things had to end it would be nice to end on a high note....Somewhere there's the feeling that if I allow the excitement to continue, I will die...a sense of getting so wrapped up in the book that I'll lose contact...not exactly...a sense of becoming monomaniacal and reading nothing but books forever without stopping....

There's a difficulty making the transition from reading something exciting to going out and socializing...it seems irrelevant and mundane...I have a sense of superiority, an arrogant attitude....I don't want to get involved in small talk that bores me....I'm uncomfortable saying that but it's true....When I'm feeling good what accompanies it is a sense of not really needing anybody...there's no single person in the world I couldn't live without....

When I'm excited and feel superior and don't need anyone...I'm alone and there's nobody around to keep me from being consumed...to say, 'If you don't stop eating ice cream, you'll turn into ice cream'...monomaniacal...I would be consumed by my masturbation...I wouldn't be able to stop and I'd go crazy...I used to feel that way as an adolescent.

The danger of gratifying yourself completely is that not needing anybody you can become crazy all by yourself...but on the other hand, running out of pages is being at the mercy of the rest of the world....There's two states...when I'm depressed and can't find personal gratification and am at the mercy of the rest of the world for support and gratification...and the other end is not needing anyone at all....

Either I'm in danger of being consumed by myself or consumed by someone else—I keep trying to find some balance between them...and I think I'm on the verge of finding one that I'm comfortable with...weighted more on the side of being alone...although, of course, I'm married now and really less alone than I've ever been before in my life....

In this excerpt from the third year of treatment, the patient, who had originally presented with panic and 'depression', had now begun to stabilize and was occasionally experiencing 'highs'. Stimulated by a faultless game of squash that afternoon, he begins to describe an ideal state of psycho-physical well-being which he desires but only rarely attains. This state is a balanced state, and he is reluctant to strive for it directly out of fear that he may overshoot the mark and become 'too excited', lose contact, be unable to stop, be consumed and die. This *hyper* -arousal is associated with physical transcendence, grandiosity and megalomania.

On the other extreme of the continuum, although here mentioned only in passing, is the state of hypoarousal, associated with physical debility, worthlessness and 'depression', leading to fears of loss of self and identity, 'melting into a puddle', disappearing, becoming ill and dying. Both the hyperarousal and the hypoarousal, seen as deviations on either extreme from the state of well-being, are related to early undifferentiated ego states and are experienced as mentally and physically painful because of excessive or insufficient stimulation, whether internal or external in origin. Both states are connected to actual or threatened narcissistic-object loss, because the object is experienced as a regulating mechanism essential for maintaining the ideal state of arousal and well-being.

Brazelton et al. (1974) who have studied the development of attention and reciprocity in the early mother–infant dyad, describe a typical cycle of alternating attention and withdrawal which appears as early as the fourth week of life:

> Thus it appears that an infant withdraws and even invests energy in the negative part of the cycle—that of turning away and looking away—just as he does when he is attending to his mother....He can use the period of looking away as if he were attempting to reduce the intensity of the interaction, to recover from the excitement it engenders in him, and to digest what he has taken in during the interaction. These perhaps represent a necessary recovery phase in maintaining homeostasis at a time in infancy when constant stimulation without relief could overwhelm the baby's immature systems....
>
> This homeostatic model, which underlies all the physiological reactions of the neonate, might also represent the immature organism's capacity to attend to the messages in a communication system....Unless she responded appropriately to these variations in his behaviour it appeared to us that his span of attention did not increase, and the quality of his attention was less than optimal....For example, in the case of two similarly tense, overreactive infants, the mothers responded very differently. One mother responded with increased activity and stimulation to her baby's turning her off; another maintained a steady level of activity which gradually modulated her baby's overreactivity. The end result was powerfully in favour of the latter dyad....[In the former dyad the] baby has learned 'rules' about managing his own needs in the face of an insensitive mother. He has learned to turn her off, to decrease his receptivity to information from her. (pp. 59–60)

These sorts of observations are the early components of our clinical stereotypes of the seductive or intrusive mother, who induces hyperarousal or some compensation or defense against it, or the depressed or neglectful mother, who induces hypoarousal, or some compensation or defense against it.

The normal process of internalizing a well-functioning homeostatic mechanism is complex in the extreme, culminating in superego integration in the oedipal period and perhaps again in adolescence. It involves all areas of affect, action and cognition, and includes such apparently simple things as the mother teaching the child to discriminate among the discomforts of fatigue, hunger, excretory needs, affective states, etc. Because of interferences with this normal process, the patient in the narcissistic state of consciousness sometimes cannot make even such elementary discriminations, and may consequently feel powerless to regulate his own state of physical and mental well-being. He then uses his objects or the analyst, not primarily as libidinal objects, but as 'thermostats' to regulate the primitive holistic ego states of hyperarousal and hypoarousal. Failure of the analyst or object to perform this function successfully revives the original trauma experienced with the mother or father, and gives rise to primitive rage reactions with fantasies of vengeance and retaliation (Kohut, 1972; Bach & Schwartz, 1972).

A patient who sought analysis because of inability to write his doctoral thesis had made no progress in this area after three years despite extensive analysis of the oedipal and anal dynamics. He decided to change analysts, began treatment with me, rapidly moved into an idealizing transference and, without any extensive discussion of the problem, was able to complete his thesis within a few months.

On the night he passed his oral exams, he dreamed that he was a member of a secret cabbalistic Jewish sect which had just elected him the Chief Rabbi. There was an older man, a cantor, who was standing by, watching approvingly. ('That must be you—the Cantor of Leipzig!') *Afterwards he began to feel as if he had to vomit and tried to control himself. He walked out of the synagogue quickly, but finally vomited on the steps. All the congregation and the other rabbis ran out crying: 'The Great Rabbi has thrown up!' and they rolled deliriously over the steps, wallowing around in his vomit.*

This was followed by a dream of a flood, which rose to the second story of the house where he lived. He was frightened, but found the courage to walk out the front door, when it changed to just a trickle of water —'like Moses cleaving the Red Sea'.

He went on to talk about his fear that he would

blow a gasket...there's too much pressure...everything will explode inside...it's all connected, one thing to another...like the great chain of being...we're like microbes on the thumb of a cosmic giant...like ants in the universe....As a child, when I went fishing, I thought that I would be fished up by giants who used chocolate bars for bait....I would listen to the ocean, the waves crashing, thinking that it would drown me....I threw up meat and milk as a child the first time I mixed them.... In the dream I try to control the vomiting but it came up the wrong way....

I have a fantasy that my chest is rotting...the inside is falling off like scabs, falling into the stomach...it's all foam and crust...decaying gas develops...it will erupt out of my mouth...my lungs blow up, the plumbing is all gone wrong...the faucets...the valves...they used to say to me, 'Don't blow your gasket!' whenever I got angry....

I've been staying up too late, till four in the morning....I do it in order to feel tired...to be stupid...I feel bright and happy now but I'm afraid of it...maybe that's not what's wanted—I shouldn't be here if I'm too smart....

I keep thinking that I'm smarter than you....I'm afraid that when I make you laugh—you should be wiser than that. I'm taking you in...controlling you....I'm forcing your mind to follow my mind....I used to go along with whatever my students wanted of me....Lately I'm asserting myself more....I know I'm good 'cause my students laugh and enjoy the class....

I'm getting the last laugh...the rabbis are lying on the steps...no reason why they should make me Chief Rabbi or roll around in my vomit....They've made a mistake and when they find out, they'll chase me down the street like the pussycat in the cartoons....(Maybe you'd rather be a pussycat than a Chief Rabbi?) [He laughs]—No one can be that important— everyone can be found out! That was my mother's philosophy. She used to satirize people and say—Although he's a famous neurosurgeon, he's still a schlepp —and he doesn't even know it! I want to be a pompous ass and I have enormous tendencies that way that I have to guard against....I felt that my father was a sententious fool—you always knew what he said before he opened his mouth....[Section omitted]...Tell me something about yourself...what have you been doing? [At this point I explained my understanding of his anxiety in the transference that had led to this question.]

He began the next session by telling me that I was solid, in control, that my voice over the phone was the same as in the sessions, and compared this to his own fears of losing control. He fantasied that I was obliged to act in a measured way with him because—' I'm so attractive and sweet that you have to be careful not to lose your wits and give me a big hug!'

He told me of a talk with his father who counselled him to lie: 'Say something nice to your mother, even if it's not true, ' and of his recurrent disappointment with father.

Suddenly I feel as if I'm falling...down the rabbit hole...I'm dizzy... vertigo...like on a swing...a see-saw...I need you to balance me...and you could do it if we weighed about the same....[I made some comment about how he needed me to reflect his feelings honestly—to help him balance so that he would neither blow up in the air nor fall through the ground...a function which he couldn't trust his father to perform.] He began to cry....

At this point we could begin the analysis of the work inhibition, which extended to other areas as well and required many months of effort. It seemed to me that the previous analyst had neglected this crucial area of tension management and that his oedipal interpretations, while 'true', were premature and had only served to enrage and frighten the patient who, like an overexcited child, needed to be calmed before he could be reasoned with. This tension regulation was achieved, not by 'gratification', but by the provision of the specific type of narcissistic object relationship needed at that time to enable the analysis to proceed.

The use of objects for the regulation of primitive ego states, tensions and moods, is paralleled by a use of the environment for the same purpose. I have, for example, seen several patients who were perfectly able to drive in the city when regulated by traffic lights and level ground, but who became terrified of the open highway or hilly terrain; a form of agoraphobia.

With these patients, who might have been called 'oral hysterics', but who formed clearly narcissistic transferences (Kohut, 1971), the early interpretive work turned out to relate to the generalized tension and mood-regulating functions of the reassuring narcissistic object or environment, rather than to specific libidinal or aggressive dynamics. These latter seemed to differentiate out, as it were, only much later in the treatment, coincident with the establishment of a less narcissistic and more object-related transference.

In summary, the patient in the narcissistic state of consciousness shows problems of mood, self-esteem and tension regulation, with roots that may go back to deficiencies in the early mother–child homeostasis, or to later interactions where either parent serves a tension-regulating function. The narcissistic patient uses objects and the environment to help achieve a steady state of psycho-physical well-being. He displays a dread of either hyperarousal, which elicits fears of excitement, explosion, loss of contact, insanity and death, or of hypoarousal, which elicits fears of depression, powerlessness, loss of self, annihilation and death. One might say that the failure of the encircling membrane to adequately regulate internal and external pressure threatens either explosion or implosion of the narcissistic bubble.

This failure of the object in its compensating function is typically responded to with narcissistic rage. More primitive mechanisms may then be employed to counter hyperarousal, such as denial, sleep, depressant drugs, etc., or to counter hypoarousal, such as self-stimulation, acting out, stimulant drugs, etc.

It is interesting to note that the state of well-being may be threatened either by an inordinate increase or decrease of environmental stimulation, or by an inordinate increase or decrease of internal stimulation, following Rapaport's (1958) formulations for ego autonomy. These are, of course, the four principal ways of *producing* altered states of consciousness, as with sensory overload, sensory deprivation, stimulants and depressants. Fischer (1971) has offered a thought-provoking classification of altered states of consciousness on a continuum of ergotropic and trophotropic arousal, but the relationships between this essentially neurophysiological theory and a psychological theory are as yet unclear.

VI. Time, Space, Causality

Homeric epic is informed of time as duration, as before and after, life and death, as fate, youth and aging, and as day following day but not of time as some ongoing universal process or abstract property of the world at large. Roughly, this corresponds to the preoperational level in the cognitive development of the child in genetic epistemology. And, just as in the language of children, in Homer we never find "time" as the subject of a verb.

Frasier, 1975, p. 12

Carried to their extreme, all the rites and all the behaviour patterns that we have so far mentioned would be comprised in the following statement: "If we pay no attention to it, time does not exist; furthermore, where it becomes perceptible—because of man's 'sins,' i.e. when man departs from the archetype and falls into duration—time can be annulled". ...Like the mystic, like the religious man in general, the primitive lives in a continual present.

Eliade, 1954, pp. 85-6

Westerners measure time by action and outstanding events are recorded as history. In contrast, India has never produced a written history. ... [For Indians] personal life is only a sample of a succession of lives, repeating themselves endlessly. Transmigration of souls and perpetual rebirth make meaningless any quantitative view of a particular period of time. Life, infinitely recycled, makes history less significant, and an individual's biography is merely a transient moment in the process.

Luce, 1973, p. 19

Although the notes I had been taking during several years of sessions with narcissistic patients sorted themselves quite naturally into categories of body-self, cognition, volition and affection, I was left with an ambiguous grouping which ultimately seemed related to orientation in the world[6]. Some of this material has been previously published (Bach, 1975), with an emphasis on experiences of discontinuity and the depersonalized, 'uncanny' feelings which result. An example of the kind of material to which I refer is this excerpt from a woman who was three months pregnant with a planned and essentially desired child:

My stomach is sticking out a little and I don't know why...[?] Well, I know it's probably because I'm pregnant but it's only sticking out a little, not a lot....If it were a lot, I'd *know* I was pregnant....I have this very odd sense of time, I feel sort of confused about how much time has gone by or what happened

---

[6] There were other modalities such as perception which seemed significantly different for these patients, but the analytic situation was less than ideal for eliciting them. A provocative study along related lines is Schachtel's (1959), developed from Rorschach perceptual psychology.

when...but I keep track of how pregnant I am, not in terms of the condition but how many weeks I'm pregnant, how many weeks to go, what proportion of time is over, what proportion is left...that's how I deal with changes, try to get a hold of them by making them concrete or turning them into a ritual...try to abracadabra them away or to make them happen faster....There's no sense that what's happening is going to lead to a baby at the end....I notice I'm getting fat but maybe I'm just overeating...and I keep having to go to the bathroom but maybe it's just cystitis. ...I know that when you're pregnant it generally leads to having a baby but at one level I don't know that at all...it's so mysterious to me....I see schematic drawings of fertilization and implantation, the fetus at all the different ages. That's a very tangible reality, but inside me personally it doesn't seem like such a reality. I know that David is much better at imagining what's happening than I am....It would be helpful if there were some kind of pain or signal or something that indicated what *would* happen or *had* happened....Maybe *it* should say: O.K. now, I'm 3½ inches long and weigh 12 ounces....What I need is an announcement—somebody should send me something written on a little card.

This young woman, who had come into analysis with a chronic sense of disorientation and discontinuity of the self, had improved considerably in three years and had married, gained a profession and, most importantly, begun to feel that her cognitive and affective life was at one with her behavior. This temporary regression, initiated by the pregnancy and a reality-based fear of miscarriage, could now be handled by an analysis of the conflicts and fantasies evident from this excerpt. Nevertheless, it is worth noting how this temporary loss of her normal reflective awareness directly affects not only the parameters discussed above, but also her sense of the reality of time and causality. Time loses its abstract, impersonal quality and is reckoned by internal duration, the number of weeks of the pregnancy; causality loses its long-term, abstract, inferential quality and regresses to temporal and spatial contiguity. Thus, the fantasies of oral impregnation, phallic-baby and annunciation are supported not only motivationally, but also cognitively, since they are phenomenally concrete and make more sense to a regressed adult as to a child.

Such regressive phenomena seem to accord with our knowledge of the development or 'construction' of reality in the child. Piaget (1954) says:

> In general, it may be said that during the first months of life, as long as assimilation remains centered on the organic activity of the subject, the universe presents neither permanent objects, nor objective space, nor time interconnecting events as such, nor causality external to the personal actions....At the other extreme, at the moment when sensorimotor intelligence has sufficiently elaborated understanding to make language and reflective thought possible, the universe is, on the contrary, formed into a structure at once substantial and spatial, causal and temporal. This organization of reality occurs, as we shall see, to the extent that the self is freed from itself by finding itself and so assigns itself a place as a thing among other things, an event among other events. (p. xii-xiii)

Piaget has often compared this egocentrism of the child, its inability to "assign itself a place as a thing among other things," to the Ptolemaic or pre-Copernican view of the universe, and has noted the increase of egocentrism whenever the child copes with new levels of cognitive functioning, as in the preschool years and adolescence. The concept of reflective self-awareness in its broadened sense is related to Piaget's *prise de conscience*, the development from 'egocentrism' without awareness to 'decentration' with awareness of the self and its relativity. There are, however, differences in emphasis necessitated by considerations of adult pathology, and particularly the psychoanalytic understanding of the unconscious and the mechanisms of defense.

Defects of reflective awareness always include a defect, developmentally inappropriate in the adult, in the construction of the object, i.e., a defect in object relations. Since the patient is to some degree unable to assess the contribution of his own perspective to the way things appear, objects are always, to a greater or lesser degree, narcissistic self-objects. As Kohut (1971) has emphasized, this means that *experientially* the subject may be all-important (mirroring transference), or the self-object may be all important (idealizing transference), but that the normal perspective of equilibrated reflective awareness is seldom achieved. While this process of constructing reality and finding one's place in it is, according to Piaget, fully achieved only after adolescence, it seems to have gone awry for the narcissistic patient, who not only lives with the defect but defends against a resumption of the process. Thus, in these cases, the analysis of character and defense seems most effective in conjunction with an understanding of the developmental block and an engagement in the narcissistic transference which permits the experiential resumption of the process.

In the following example, the patient's real inability to see the analyst as a center of initiative independent of her own desires, leads to distortions in the sense of time and reality. I should emphasize again the selective nature of these defects which become caricatured in the transference, for the patient is simultaneously a person who functions at a high level in her profession.

Some time ago an analytic colleague who was moving to the West Coast called to ask if I would see a narcissistic patient who had been in analysis with him for two years. After waiting a month and not hearing from her, I called my colleague to enquire. He told me that, although the impending transfer had been the subject of persistent analysis for the last year, the patient still couldn't really believe it was going to happen and had not asked for a referral or made any other plans!

She in fact called the week before his departure, and arranged to continue analysis with me. Although obviously other issues were prominent as well, she herself never ceased to marvel, in an awed tone, at her absolute inability to believe that the treatment would end.

After a brief 'honeymoon' period, she relapsed once more into her habit of coming 15–40 minutes late for most sessions, a practice which had been extensively discussed by the previous analyst with only sporadic improvements. She could remember little or nothing of the content of these discussions, yet felt that the analysis had been of considerable help to her; she was terrified at the thought of alienating the analyst and would conform whenever she felt the threat of termination.

This patient, whose dilemma over sneezing and urinating was discussed in Section IV, had a fear of hyperarousal which was manifested both sexually and in a phobia of driving on open highways. She had an analogous fear of the 50-minute hour, which seemed infinite, and was in fact able to speak more freely when she controlled the duration herself by her lateness. She wished to remain "a woman of mystery," lest I discover that "there's really no one there."

Issues of time control are of course not limited to the narcissistic syndrome, but here one typically finds those patients who relish the last hour of the day because "when I leave there's nobody else to take up your thoughts;" those who either glance at their watch throughout the hour or fall into a transference sleep; those who start at the sound of the door-bell and either leap up prematurely in mid-sentence or fall silent for the last few minutes, and those who ostensibly never miss, need, or want more time.

These quantitative problems are closely tied to the qualitative nature of experienced time, which varies tremendously and is connected with issues of control and spontaneity. A patient with a profound work inhibition said:

When I try to structure long periods of work it just doesn't go...planning to do something robs the experience of its reality...a little voice saying—read from five to seven—ruins things...the only way is to go to the book-case when I feel like it and take out a book...and it's true not only for things that involve anxiety but for things that are pleasurable....

And time begins to take on a peculiar dimension...it's related to feelings of being mechanical or not being alive...it's hard to put my finger on, but time begins to be associated with a pressure on my forehead...as peculiar as that may sound...I don't know how to explain it...I'm simultaneously the participant and the observer and when that split occurs and you're watching yourself behave, then time is peculiar...not that it stands still or goes faster, but it weighs heavy...a tendency to be concerned with actual time...looking at clocks all the time...it's as if one is in jail counting time rather than living in time...I keep having this image of throwing a basketball up to the hoop...[?] I keep seeing it...[?] I see an unfettered ball floating through air...follow the ball wherever it's going...it's going where it wants to go...Even if it's something I like to do, when I get an order to do it, or give one to myself, I'm in jail....When I do something spontaneously without planning, then the time is lived time...time in which I'm alive....When I do something on orders from myself or someone else, even if it's something I like to do, then time is served time.

Several months later, when this problem had been partially resolved, he said:

When I first came to analysis, I had the idea that I should never cry, never be upset, always associate perfectly, have meaningful hours, etc....it took a long time to understand...I was disappointed in the first year of analysis....

Everything that went before should be erased from the record so that I couldn't remember it and you couldn't remember it....There's a pervasive theme of starting over again with a clean slate because any mistakes and vulnerability are just too difficult to admit or incorporate. I should start over again fresh...almost in the sense of being reborn....

If I read the papers or watch TV one morning and don't do

much work, then the day is spoiled and I can't do any more and I have to go to sleep and start again the next day...There isn't really any continuity, everything is discrete and there are artificial demarcations like going to bed and getting up in the morning and that officially starts a new life...If I do something and it's difficult, not perfect, then the day is ruined and I might as well go to sleep and awake reborn. ...Maybe tomorrow I can be perfect....

This excerpt marks, incidentally, an early point in the analysis of a fantasy of 'exceptionality' (Freud, 1916), which seems central to the narcissistic states and which takes protean forms such as reincarnation fantasies, Godhead fantasies, 'Peter Pan' fantasies, hermaphroditic fantasies, monster and vampire fantasies, sadomasochistic fantasies, etc. While these fantasies provide the content of many of the formal deviations noted above, they are beyond the scope of this paper and I hope to discuss them at another time. I will note in passing that these fantasies generally violate the limitations of time-space-causality and that, while in their pathological manifestations they are compensatory for the lost state of well-being, in their developmental aspect they are an essential precondition for the formation of an 'identity' or self-symbolizing system, one of the crucial defects of the narcissistic state. Having digressed thus far, I offer an example of such a fantasy in relation to time and immortality:

I feel a yearning to do away with myself, to join the Big Family...a crib scene, warm sand with a light on it and the rest in darkness and two stars...the eyes... the breasts...I can't stand the separateness of things....

The things which characterize something make it separate and different from others and who would want to be just one thing? If you recognize the separateness of the other then you recognize the separateness of yourself too....

My mother is dying and it's intolerable to permit it to happen...to think of someone going through that alone....

I can't stand the cruelty of separateness...it makes me angry—I would like to break the walls...an apocalyptic fantasy, when you see you can't take the stars and hold them, and you throw a rock at the sky and it breaks and everything falls....

I hear you saying—there are plenty of rocks in the street and you should try it sometime...Well, that's reasonable and so on, but I have this fantasy of living inside a glass bubble, one of those plastic souvenirs that you shake...I cannot abide living in a world this powerless! If the stars have any reality, millions of light years away...that's ridiculous, ludicrous, to throw a rock...

I guess there's a lot of anger and hatred towards you. I have been doing better, working better, feeling better, and of course you're responsible for that—but so what!

That's time...I can calculate it on a sheet of paper, quantitatively and qualitatively different....But it's like doing a time trial in some race—if you accept the race it's significant to do one half second better—BUT I DON'T ACCEPT THE RACE!...

I'm really a child and don't care about that....I'd just like to make the moon come and go as I please....There must be some other way of thinking about things instead of thinking that everything is animated and has feeling and wanting to close with it and not be alone.

While this patient rarely complained of specific time difficulties, he was in effect trying to make time stand still or regress by not sleeping, not answering his mail or telephone, discarding nothing, persistently repairing worn-out objects, preserving his world in photographs and taking no decisive action or commitment. This life-style had long pre-dated his mother's terminal illness, which only served to reactivate an earlier trauma.

Other patients keenly experience a peculiarity in their relation to the time continuum:

Whatever I was trying to do in the present was only a trial run that I would have to go back and recheck in the future...I couldn't do anything spontaneously in the present....Whenever I read something it was only a pre-trial, with the thought that I'd have to go back in the future and master the material...and now I don't feel like that....

I used to have such leftover business from things that hadn't been completed that my head was always full of things in the past I hadn't finished...and part of that feeling of not being alive was related to living partially in the past, partially in the future, and very little in the present....

That's most dear of the things I've gotten here...I may have recurrent depressions or anxiety but I'll do all of that essentially in the present from now on...I'm coping now with today's things, because yesterday's are taken care of.

This patient denied the reality of the imperfect present and, consequently, the continuity of his imperfect self, in the hope that tomorrow he might be reborn, perfect. This is, of course, a variant of the 'family romance' (Freud, 1909). Other patients cling obsessively to temporal bench-marks as 'a way of linking things up' in the absence of experiential self-continuity.

As a kid I used to try to visualize the way the weeks passed and think what would be at the end of a certain period of time....Now I think—in October I will be six months pregnant and need maternity clothes...or when Bill goes away I'll diet those two weeks and be ten pounds less....it's a way to understand time...a way of linking things up....

Now if I become pregnant we'll have the baby when I'm 29 and Bill 35, and 20 years from now I'll be 49 and Bill 55 and my mother is 52 and she'll be 72....

...to try to understand what happens when time passes or what happens when people grow up or grow older or die....I'm trying to understand life but I'm trying to do it in a very concrete way...what it all means...because it's too mysterious to understand in other ways.

The previous patient, in the mirroring transference, was emphasizing the difference between himself and his father. This patient, in the idealizing transference, is emphasizing the similarity between herself and her mother. As Freud (1909) has suggested, the similarity is necessary for the preservation of the species, and the difference necessary for its progress. In this broadest sense then, the 'self' may be seen as an artistic creation like a family romance fantasy or a transitional object, since it must be similar enough to the parent to belong to the same world and preserve the species identity, yet different enough to create one's own world and preserve the individual identity. Narcissistic patients share the human dilemma in their search to strike an ever-changing balance between these needs.

REFERENCES

Ajuriaguerra, J. de, Diatkine, R. & Badaracco, G. (1956). Psychanalyse et neurobiology. In La Psychanalyse d'Aujourd'hui, ed. S. Nacht. Paris: Presses Universitaires de France, pp. 437-498.

Bach, S. (1971). Notes on some imaginary companions. *Psychoanalytic Study of the Child* 26:159-171.

Bach, S. (1975). Narcissism, continuity and the uncanny. *International Journal of Psychoanalysis* 56:77-86.

Bach, S. & Schwartz, L. (1972). A dream of the Marquis de Sade—Psychoanalytic reflections on narcissistic trauma, decompensation, and the reconstitution of a delusional self. *Journal of the American Psychoanalytic Association* 20:451-475.

Bak, R. (1939). Regression of ego-orientation and libido in schizophrenia. *International Journal of Psychoanalysis* 20:64-71.

Bibring, E. (1953). The mechanism of depression. In *Affective Disorders: Psychoanalytic Contribution to their Study*, ed. P. Greenacre. New York: International Universities Press, pp. 13-48.

Bion, W. R. (1959). Attacks on linking. *International Journal of Psychoanalysis* 40:308-315.

Brazelton, T. B., Koslowski, B. & Main, M. (1974). The origins of reci-procity in the early mother-infant interaction. In *The Effect of the Infant on Its Caregiver*, eds. M. Lewis & L. Rosenblum. New York: Wiley, 49-77.

Deikman, A. J. (1966). De-automatization and the mystic experience. *Psychiatry* 29:324-338.

Dixon, J. C. (1957). Development of self recognition. *Journal of Genetic Psychology* 91:251-256.

Dodds, E. R. (1951). *The Greeks and the Irrational.* Berkeley: University of California Press.

Eliade, M. (1954). *The Myth of the Eternal Return: Cosmos and History,* trans. W. Trask. New York: Harper & Row, 1959.

Escalona, S. K. (1968). *The Roots of Individuality.* Chicago: Aldine.

Escalona, S. K., & Corman, H. H. (1971). The impact of mother's presence upon behavior: The first year. *Human Development* 14:2-15.

Escalona, S. K., & Corman, H. H. (1973). Basic modes of social interaction: Their emergence during the first two years. *Merril-Palmer Quarterly* 19:205-232.

Escalona, S. K., & Corman, H. H. (1974). Early life experience and the development of competence. *International Review of Psychoanalysis* 1:151-168.

Ferenczi, S. (1913). Stages in the development of the sense of reality. In *Sex in Psychoanalysis.* New York: Brunner, 1950, pp. 213-239.

Ferenczi, S. (1923). The dream of the "clever baby." In *Further Contributions to the Theory and Technique of Psychoanalysis.* London: Hogarth Press, 1960, pp. 349-350.

Fischer, R. (1969). Out on a (phantom) limb: Variations on the theme: Stability of body image and the golden section. *Perspectives in Biology and Medicine* 12:259-273.

Fischer, R. (1971). A cartography of the ecstatic and meditative states. *Science* 174:897-904.

Fraser, J. T. (1975). *Of Time, Passion and Knowledge: Reflections on the Strategy of Existence.* New York: Braziller.

Freud, S. (1909). Family romances. *Standard Edition* 9:235-242.

Freud, S. (1913). Totem and taboo: Some points of agreement between the mental lives of savages and neurotics. *Standard Edition* 13:vii-162.

Freud, S. (1916). Some character-types met with in psycho-analytic work. *Standard Edition* 14:309-333.

Freud, S. (1930). Civilization and its discontents. *Standard Edition* 21:64-145.

Freud, S. (1933). New introductory lectures on psycho-analysis. *Standard Edition* 22:1-182.

Gedo, J. E., & Goldberg, A. (1973). *Models of the Mind: A Psychoanalytic Theory.* Chicago: University of Chicago Press.

Grossman, W. I. (1967). Reflections on the relationships of introspection and psychoanalysis. *International Journal of Psychoanalysis* 48:16-31.

Grossman, W. I., & Simon, B. (1969). Anthropomorphism: Motive, meaning and causality in psychoanalytic theory. *Psychoanalytic Study of the Child* 24:78-113.

Hartmann, H. (1952). The mutual influences in the development of ego and id. In *Essays on Ego Psychology.* New York: International Universities Press, 1964, pp. 155-182.

Hartmann, H. (1939). *Ego Psychology and the Problem of Adaptation.* New York: International Universities Press, 1958.

Hermann, I. (1929). Das Ich und das Denken. *Imago* 15:325-348.

Homer (1968). *The Odyssey of Homer*, trans. R. Lattimore. New York: Harper Torchbooks.

Horowitz, M. J. (1972). Modes of representation of thought. *Journal of the American Psychoanalytic Association* 20:793-819.

Jacobson, E. (1957). On normal and pathological moods: Their nature and function. *Psychoanalytic Study of the Child* 12:73-113.

Jacobson, E. (1964). *The Self and the Object World.* New York: International Universities Press.

Kernberg, O. F. (1975). *Borderline Conditions and Pathological Narcissism.* New York: Aronson.

Klein, G. S. (1970). *Perception, Motives and Personality.* New York: Knopf.

Kohut, H. (1971). *The Analysis of the Self.* New York: International Universities Press.

Kohut, H. (1972). Thoughts on narcissism and narcissistic rage. *Psychoanalytic Study of the Child* 27:360-400.

Lacan, J. (1949). Le stade du miroir comme formateur de la fonction du Je, telle qu'elle nous est révélée dans l'expérience psychanalytique. In *Ecrits.* Paris: Le Seuil, 1966, pp. 93-101.

Laplanche, J., & Pontalis, J.-B. (1968). *The Language of Psycho-Analysis.* London: Hogarth Press, 1973.

Lewin, B. D. (1965). Reflections on affect. In *Drives, Affects, Behavior,* ed. M. Schur, vol. 2. New York: International Universities Press, pp. 23-37.

Lewin, B. D. (1968). *The Image and the Past.* New York: International Universities Press.

Luce, G. G. (1973). *Body Time: Physiological Rhythms and social stress.* New York: Bantam Books.

Mahler, M. (1965). On the significance of the normal separation-individuation phase: With reference to research in symbiotic child psychosis. In *Drives, Affects, Behavior,* ed. M. Schur, vol. 2. New York: International Universities Press, pp. 161-169.

Mahler, M. (1968). *On Human Symbiosis and the Vicissitudes of Individuation.* New York: International Universities Press.

Piaget, J. 1936 *The Origins of Intelligence in Children* (2nd ed). New York: International Universities Press, 1952.

Piaget, J. (1954). *The Construction of Reality in the Child.* New York: Basic Books.

Piaget, J. & Inhelder, B. (1948). *The Child's Conception of Space,* trans. F. J. Langdon & J L. Lunzer. New York: Norton, 1967.

Piaget, J. & Inhelder, B. (1966). *The Psychology of the Child.* New York: Basic Books, 1969.

Rapaport, D., ed. (1951). *Organization and Pathology of Thought.* New York: Columbia University Press.

Rapaport, D. (1957). The theory of ego autonomy: A generalization. In *The Collected Papers of David Rapaport,* ed. M. M. Gill. New York: Basic Books, 1967, pp. 722-744.

Reich, A. (1960). Pathologic forms of self-esteem regulation. *Psychoanalytic Study of the Child* 15:215-232.

Russo, J., & Simon, B. (1968). Homeric psychology and the oral epic tradition. *Journal of the History of Ideas* 29:483-498.

Sandler, J., & Joffe, W. G. (1965). Notes on childhood depression. *International Journal of Psychoanalysis* 46:88-96.

Sartre, J. P. (1960). *Les Séquestrés d'Altona*. Paris: Gallimard.

Schachtel, E. (1959). *Metamorphosis: On the Development of Affect, Perception, Attention, and Memory*. New York: Basic Books.

Schafer, R. (1968). *Aspects of Internalization*. New York: International Universities Press.

Simon, B. (1972). Models of mind and mental illness in ancient Greece: II. The Platonic model. *Journal of the History of the Behavioral Sciences* 8:389-404.

Simon, B. (1973a). Models of mind and mental illness in ancient Greece: II. *The Platonic model. Journal of the History of Behavioral Sciences* 9:3-17.

Simon, B. (1973b). Plato and Freud—The mind in conflict and the mind in dialogue. *Psychoanalytic Quarterly* 42:91-122.

Simon, B., & Weiner, H. (1966). Models of mind and mental illness in ancient Greece: I. The Homeric model of mind. *Journal of the History of Behavioral Sciences* 2:303-314.

Snell, B. (1953). *The Discovery of the Mind: The Greek Origins of European Thought*. New York: Harper Torchbook, 1960.

Spitz, R. A. (1957). *No and Yes: On the Genesis of Human Communication*. New York: International Universities Press.

Spitz, R. A. (1963). Life and the dialogue. In *Counterpoint: Libidinal Object and Subject*, ed. H. S. Gaskill. New York: International Universities Press, pp. 154-176.

Spitz, R. A. (1965). *The First Year of Life*. New York: International Universities Press.

Stein, M. H. (1965). States of consciousness in the analytic situation, including a note on the traumatic dream. In *Drives, Affects, Behavior*, ed. M. Schur, vol. 2. New York: International Universities Press, pp. 60-86.

Winnicott, D. W. (1958). The capacity to be alone. *International Journal of Psychoanalysis* 41:585-95.

Winnicott, D. W. (1960). Ego distortion in terms of true and false self In *The Maturational Processes and the Facilitating Environment.* London: Hogarth Press, 1965, pp. 140-152.

Winnicott, D. W. (1965). *The Maturational Processes and the Facilitating Environment.* New York: International Universities Press.

ON SADOMASOCHISM

CHAPTER 6

A Dream of the Marquis De Sade:
Psychoanalytic Reflections on Narcissistic Trauma, Decompensation, and the Reconstitution of a Delusional Self[1]

Sheldon Bach, Ph.D. & Lester Schwartz, M.D.

In the night of 16 February 1779, on the second anniversary of his incarceration at Vincennes, the Marquis de Sade had a dream which so moved him that he hastened to recount it to his wife the next day in a letter from prison:

> … My only comfort here is Petrarch. I read him with delight, with a passion like none other. But I do it the way Madame de Sévigné did with her daughter's letters: I read it slowly for fear of having read it. How beautifully written the book is!…Laura turns my head; I am like a child; I read about her all day and dream about her all night. Listen to a dream I had of her yesterday, while all the world was taking its pleasure.
>
> It was about midnight. I had just fallen asleep with the Life

---

[1] We wish to thank Drs. Ruth Eissler, William Grossman, Donald Kaplan, Lydia Landau and Martin Wangh, who read an earlier version of this paper and offered valuable criticism and suggestions.

of Petrarch in my hand. Suddenly she appeared to me...I saw her! The horror of the tomb had not impaired the brilliance of her charms, and her eyes had the same fire as when Petrarch sang of them. She was draped in black crepe with her lovely blond hair flowing carelessly above it. It was as if love, to preserve her beauty, had tried to soften the funereal form in which she appeared to me. "Why do you groan on earth?" she said to me. "Come and join me. No more ills, no more sorrows, no more troubles in the vast expanse that I inhabit. Have the courage to follow me there." At these words I flung myself at her feet calling: "O my Mother!" And my voice was choked with sobbing. She held out her hand and I covered it with my tears; she too shed tears. "When I dwelt in the world which you loathe," she said, "I used to enjoy beholding the future; I counted my descendants until I reached you, but I did not see you so unhappy." Then, engulfed in my tenderness and despair, I threw my arms about her neck to hold her back or to follow her and water her with my tears, but the ghost had disappeared. All that remained was my grief.

> *O voi che travagliate, ecco il cammino,*
> *Venite a me se'l passo altri no serra.*
> Petrarch, Sonnet LIX
> (Lely, 1965, pp. 309-310)

How are we to explain such a dream, the only one we have on record from a man who has been called a "wild beast" and "the most abominable scoundrel ever to inhabit the face of the earth," a man who has given his name to the worst perversions and who, by his own admission, has written "the most impure tale that has ever been told since our world began" (Sade, 1966, p. 253)? Let us begin by putting it in context.

Petrarch's Laura, Laure de Noves, was the wife of Hugues de Sade and consequently an ancestor of the Marquis. The *Life of Petrarch* which provides the day residue for the dream was written by the Marquis' uncle, the Abbé de Sade, a Petrarch scholar and bon vivant with whom the young Marquis lived between the ages of five and 10. There is yet another Laura, the Lady Laure de Lauris, whom the Marquis passionately loved and with whom he had an ill-fated liaison that was abruptly broken off by her only a few weeks before his actual marriage to the woman his father had chosen for him. Sixteen years later, on the anniversary of his second year in the prison of Vincennes and with an indefinite term still ahead of him, he falls asleep with his uncle's book in hand, and his mind returns to Laura.

He precedes the dream by remarking on his passion for Petrarch: he reads the book slowly *for fear of having read it.* By this he means that he is afraid of finishing it, afraid of losing Laura, just as Madame de Sévigné hesitates to part from her child. If we turn to the earlier pages of the letter from which this dream is extracted, we find him berating his wife for betraying him and expressing his anguish at not knowing how long he is to be confined. The dominant theme is clearly one of anxiety about separation and helplessness; he accuses his wife unjustly, and his thought reaches such a paroxysm of paranoia that he finds significance in every letter and number as a "signal" that might indicate the time of his release. It is in this context of enormous anxiety about loss and his own complete helplessness that "like a child…while all the world was taking its pleasure," he dreams.

Suddenly she appeared to me … I saw her!

The Marquis had been complaining in this letter about his intolerable isolation; he is allowed neither visitors nor association with other prisoners, and the attendant who feeds him spends only seven minutes a day in the cell. Separated from his wife, rejected by Laure de Lauris, Sade, on the second anniversary of his imprisonment and of his mother's death, dreams of a woman who will never leave him: the faithful Laura.

The horror of the tomb had not impaired the brilliance of her charms, and her eyes had the same fire as when Petrarch sang of them. She was draped in black crepe with her lovely blond hair floating carelessly above it. It was as if love, to preserve her beauty, had tried to soften the funereal form in which she appeared to me.

She is immortal, she retains her fire and brilliance after death and incarceration in the tomb; she is the idealized mother with whom he would merge.

> "Why do you groan on earth?" she said to me. "Come and join me. No more ills, no more sorrows, no more troubles in the vast expanse that I inhabit. Have the courage to follow me there."

Out of a distant time and grave, the omnipotent Laura appears and offers the prisoner his freedom; he need only follow her in an act of suicidal merging. In this same month of February, two years before, Sade had written: "My plight is terrible…but one way out is left…My mother calls out to me from the depths of her tomb: I seem to see her open her bosom once more to clasp me to it—the only refuge I have left. It is a comfort to me that I shall follow so closely…" (Lely, 1966, pp. 34-35) and again: "I am overwhelmed with despair…My blood is too hot to bear such terrible restrictions…If I am not released in four days, I shall crack my skull against these walls" (Lely, 1965, p. 269).

> At these words I flung myself at her feet calling: "O my Mother!" And my voice was choked with sobbing. She held out her hand and I covered it with my tears; she too shed tears. "When I dwelt in the world which you loathe," she said, "I used to enjoy beholding the future; I counted my descendants until I reached you, but I did not see you so unhappy."

He joins with the idealized dead mother in a mutual exchange of tears, and together they bemoan the loss of his promised happiness.

> Then, engulfed in my tenderness and despair, I threw my arms about her neck to hold her back or to follow her and water her with my tears, but the ghost had disappeared. All that remained was my grief.
> *O ye who travail, here is the way,*
> *Come to me if there is no other.*

The attempt to merge through a fluid exchange does not succeed. Once again, he is thrown back to that very despair which the dream was summoned to deny. He awakens in anguish seeking his lost hopes and expectations, and, driven back to fantasies of grandiosity, he assumes the "delusional identity" of the Marquis de Sade.

History and Family Romance

The Marquis de Sade was born on the 2nd of June 1740 in the house of the Prince de Condé, head of the younger branch of the ruling Bourbon family, to which his mother was closely related by marriage. His father, the Comte de Sade, Marshal of the Camp of the Royal Armies, was from one of the most important families of Provence. He was apparently a rather grim, pompous, and meticulous person who, at the time of Sade's birth, was out of the country on one of his frequent diplomatic missions.

His mother, the Comtesse de Sade, was lady-in-waiting to the Princesse de Condé and, at the death of the Prince and Princess about a year after the birth of the Marquis, she became involved in the rearing of their young son, Louis-Joseph de Bourbon, Prince de Condé. Although little enough is known of Sade's early childhood, there is a reference in *Aline et Valcour* which all of his biographers take to be autobiographical:

> I was related on my mother's side to the most powerful nobility in the kingdom; on my father's side, to the most distinguished families of Languedoc. I was born in Paris, in the lap of luxury, and from the moment I could think I believed that Fortune and Nature had conspired to heap their gifts upon me. I believed this because people were stupid enough to tell me so, and this absurd conviction made me haughty, domineering, and ill-tempered. I felt that the whole world should yield to my whims and that I merely needed to want something in order to have it. I need tell you only one incident from my childhood to

convince you how dangerous were the illusions that were fostered in me by such utter folly.

Born and raised in the palace of the Prince, whom my mother had the honor to serve and who was about my own age, I was encouraged to be with him as much as possible in order that our childhood friendship should be useful to me in later life. But my vanity was such that, knowing nothing of these schemes, I became angry one day because he would not yield to me while we were playing, and even angrier because he seemed to feel that his rank entitled him to act this way. I revenged myself by falling on him and striking him again and again, and it was only through force and violence that I could finally be separated from my adversary.

It was at about this time that my father was employed in diplomatic negotiations, and my mother joined him there. I was sent to my grandmother in Languedoc, and her blind affection for me only served to encourage all the faults that I have just confessed. (Lely, 1965, p. 37)

It seems clear that the young Prince referred to in this account was Louis de Bourbon. Interestingly enough, Sade's mother had intended to name him Louis, but because neither parent was present at the christening he was erroneously named Francois by the two servants who attended him there. Sade never accepted this error and on many occasions throughout his life continued to refer to himself as Louis, the given name of the Bourbon kings. In the light of this and other material, we believe that in some way Sade was unable to accept or to integrate the narcissistic insult of recognizing himself to be less than his playmate, Louis de Bourbon, Prince de Condé. The scene described sounds like an attack of murderous rage in which he attempts to rid himself of the other boy, his rival both for power and for the attention of his mother. It can also be read as a screen memory for some traumatic disillusionment both with himself and with his parents. Whether he was sent away from court because of this and similar incidents or whether he was dismissed because his parents went abroad, the implication of these events might well have convinced him that he was being punished and exiled for his pretentious claims.

However, rather than having the effect of reconciling the young Marquis to the inevitable renunciations imposed by reality, the incident seems only to have heightened his grandiose claims upon the world. After a year with his doting grandmother in Languedoc, he spends the years from five to 10 with his uncle, the Abbé de Sade, a libertine whose holy orders did not prevent him from pursuing both his studies in Petrarch and his amorous dalliance, for the last of which he was on at least one occasion apprehended by the police. By the age of fourteen the young Marquis has left school, begun his military training, and entered the army. We glimpse him in his adolescence and young adulthood as a military officer, impetuous and courageous but profligate and dissolute, the bane of his father's existence. Despairing of his constant debts, his exasperated father attempts to marry him off into the wealthy Montreuil family.

At this point the Marquis appears to be engaged to two young ladies at the same time: his father's choice, Mademoiselle de Montreuil, and his own beloved, Laure de Lauris. Both fathers have declared themselves opposed to this latter match, and when it is finally broken off, for reasons still unclear, de Sade writes to Laure in a frenzy of rage and desperation:

> Perjurer! ungrateful wretch! pray tell what has happened to those sentiments of lifelong devotion? Did you take my departure for flight? Did you believe that I could exist and flee from you?...Fie, monster, born to make my life miserable; stay there in Paris forever! May it one day become, through the deceitfulness and knavery of the scoundrel who will replace me in your heart, as odious to you as your own double-dealings have made it in my eyes!...But what am I saying? Oh, my dear, my divine friend! the sole support of my heart, the only love of my life, where, my beloved, is my despair leading me?...If I lose you I lose my existence, my life; I die, and by the cruelest of

deaths...My mind wanders, my love, I am no longer myself; let the tears which becloud my eyes, flow...I cannot survive such misfortunes.—What are you doing?...What has become of you?...What am I in your eyes? An object of horror? of love?...Tell me, how do you view me?... Beware of inconstancy; I do not deserve it. I confess to you that I shall be furious and there is no horror I shall not commit. The little business of the c...[clap?] ought to make you be sparing of me. I confess that I shall not conceal it from my rival, nor will that be the only secret I shall confide to him. There are no lengths—this I swear to you—to which I shall not go, no horrors to which I shall not stoop...But I blush to think of employing these means to keep you...Adieu, my beloved child, I adore you and love you a thousand times more than life itself. Come, now, say what you will, but I swear that we shall never be aught but one for the other. (Sade, 1965, pp. 121-124)

Two weeks after this passionate letter, Sade marries Mademoiselle de Montreuil. Thus begins that disastrous marriage during the course of which Sade seduces his sister-in-law, publicly flaunts his perversions, and so outrages his wife's family that a *lettre de cachet* is obtained which keeps him imprisoned almost continuously for 20 years. Nevertheless, despite the utter disruption of his life in the years that follow, despite a sentence of death passed upon him *in absentia,* despite grinding poverty, exile, and years of solitary imprisonment, 20 years later we still find Sade writing to his wife from prison: "Imperious, choleric, impetuous, extreme in everything, of a disorderly wealth of imagination on human conduct such as life never saw the equal of, there you have me in a couple of words; one thing more, you must either kill me or take me as I am, for I shall not change" (Lely, 1962, p. 256).

This grandiosity, this perverse willfulness, this monumental refusal to conform in the face of overwhelming force, all take on a certain awesomeness and grandeur which may have misled some of Sade's proponents into joining the Marquis in his self-exaltation rather than trying to understand him.

Delusional Identity

There seems little doubt, in reviewing Sade's biography, his letters, and his work, that at times he suffered from a psychotic disorder. His object relations we shall discuss at length; his reality testing and reality sense are too often faulty; there is evidence from his letters of a formal thought disorder and of psychotic decompensations into suicidally depressive and paranoid states, with experiences of significance and ideas of reference. But what is most interesting about de Sade is not his psychiatric diagnosis, nor yet the repeated provocative behavior which led to a life of incarceration, but rather those qualities which allowed him to survive the long years of imprisonment, to maintain his unique sense of identity, and to produce his eccentric and extraordinary work. Chief among these qualities are certain grandiose and megalomaniacal trends, with such a remarkable emphasis on issues of power and self-assertion that we were inevitably led to further consideration of narcissistic phenomena.

In our reading of de Sade we were impressed by what seemed to be a persistent and vastly hypertrophied grandiose self-image crucial to his view of himself, and clearly defensive and compensatory in nature. We were also struck by de Sade's exquisite idealizations of which the dream of Laura is but one example. In this series of idealized women we have mentioned only Laure de Noves and Laure de Lauris, but there were others as well. For the student of de Sade, there remains the puzzling contrast between the extraordinarily keen sensibilities of his poetic idealizations and the crude and scatological extravagance of his self-assertive fantasies.

In a recent series of publications, Kohut (1966, 1968) has formulated a developmental sequence of narcissism that seems helpful to us for an understanding of these questions. Out of an original primal narcissism, Kohut postulates the emergence of two major structures. One, the grandiose self, is a necessary stage in the development of a stable self-image. This stage is characterized by certain grandiose fantasies, with drive accompaniments of a predominantly exhibitionistic nature displaying the perfection of the self, and it requires a mirroring object for its successful development.

The other development of narcissistic libido is the formation of an idealized parent imago, which combines elements of object relations together with an investment of these objects with the perfection of the self.

Basically, our thesis is that the identity of the Marquis de Sade, as we know it from his writings, represents a compensatory hypercathected grandiose self—a delusional identity—constantly being constructed and reconstructed in an attempt to restitute that grandiose self-representation which had been disrupted in childhood. This delusional identity is related to one kind of imaginary companion, a distorted reappearance of that grandiose image of the self which existed prior to the traumatic disillusionment (Bach, 1971). We see this delusional identity as a continuation of the nuclear grandiose core hypothesized in our reconstruction of his early identification with Louis de Bourbon.

As we know, the integrity of the self in the earliest years is dependent on the support, mirroring, and participation of the mother. Kohut (1968), writing of childhood disappointments in idealized objects and the idealized self, tells of patients finding "substitutes for the idealized parent imago and its functions by creating erotized replacements and through frantic hypercathexis of the grandiose self" (p. 95). In analysis, under circumstances in which the idealized transference is disturbed, the patient "may turn to archaic precursors of the idealized parent imago or may abandon it altogether and regress further to reactively mobilized archaic stages of the grandiose self" or of the "auto-erotic body self" (p. 94).

In the object-libidinal sphere, the process of regression involves a retreat to earlier positions of development either as a defense against or as an attempt to solve conflicts about objects in the present. We would expect a similar process in the narcissistic sphere: an attempt either defensively to recapture or to begin to construct stages in which the self unquestionably possesses that power and perfection which is currently being threatened. In psychotic individuals, this process protects against a total fragmentation of the self, against a loss of significance and self-coherence, represented by fantasies of being dropped, crushed, dismembered, and destroyed, or of being wraith-like, nonhuman, nonexistent, or already dead. Although fantasies obviously combine both object-libidinal and narcissistic elements in an often inseparable amalgam, in states of extreme pathology involving a basic narcissistic fault, it is this latter aspect which is frequently the most salient and which may pre-empt the fantasy function. It is this aspect of de Sade's fantasies that will especially concern us here[2].

The writings of the Marquis de Sade play a peculiarly central role in his attempts to maintain his restitutive identity. So far as we know, these writings begin in prison, and although the Marquis engaged in perverse sadomasochistic acts prior to his imprisonment, it is only in his books that he permitted himself those excesses of torture, mutilation, and murder which have become associated with his name. From hints in his letters it would appear that these fantasies were linked to masturbation—especially anal masturbation—a point to which we shall return later.

In certain ways the writings and the development of the delusional identity may be seen as aspects of the same process, marked at first by that peculiar playfulness often associated with transitional phenomena, perverse acting-out, and certain types of art (Winnicott, 1953; Khan, 1965), but slipping more and more into the deadly seriousness of a psychotic struggle for survival. The public as a whole has tended to accept the delusional identity as a reality. Thus, Sade's books have been confined to the *enfer* of libraries, his name has been used to terrorize children, and the man himself was persecuted by the public authorities

---

[2] In his monograph, Kohut (1971) traces the narcissistic regression in the psychoses "through the following way stations: (a) the disintegration of higher forms of narcissism; (b) the regression to archaic narcissistic positions; (c) the breakdown of the archaic narcissistic positions (including the loss of the *narcissistically cathected* archaic objects), thus the fragmentation of self and archaic self-objects; and (d) the secondary (restitutive) resurrection of the archaic self and of the archaic narcissistic objects in a manifestly psychotic form" (p. 6).

throughout his life in a manner unwarranted by his actual deeds.

To the reader unfamiliar with de Sade, a brief excerpt should suffice to explain these reactions. We shall quote from his acknowledged masterpiece, in which the delusional identity finds perhaps its clearest expression. But first, a word of introduction to the book.

In 1785, during the course of a 10-year imprisonment in the Bastille, the Marquis de Sade wrote an extraordinary and terrifying manuscript, *The 120 Days of Sodom*. Four years later, during the storming of the Bastille, the manuscript was lost and thought to be destroyed.

Sade considered this work his magnum opus, and its loss led him to "shed tears of blood." Certain critics believe that many of his later writings were, in a sense, largely attempts to reconstitute the missing manuscript of *The 120 Days* (Lely, 1965). We shall later see that the theme of loss and restitution plays a major role in the work itself, as well as in Sade's life.

Although Sade was never to know it, the manuscript was in fact recovered, preserved by a French family for three generations, sold to a German connoisseur, first published in 1904 by the German psychiatrist Iwan Bloch, and later published in a definitive edition in 1931 by the great Sade scholar Maurice Heine.

The book should be of interest if only from a historical viewpoint, for it is an attempt—a century before Krafft-Ebing and Freud—to classify the sexual aberrations and to illuminate personality through the study of sexual behavior, and it gives us the opportunity to learn something about sadomasochism from its most notorious and articulate exponent. It is undoubtedly a major work of pornography and one that has influenced many great writers, but it is also more than this. Written during years of incarceration when Sade felt himself persecuted and abused, it is a cry of outrage and an act of desperation by a man who turned his life into a rage against extinction.

For there is evidence that Sade had begun to decompensate during the course of his many years of imprisonment. And although *The 120 Days* is presented as an adventure in which the libertines are willfully engaged, it might be more accurate to view it as the description of a catastrophe that befell Sade and that he was powerless to prevent. The book may thus be seen as a record of the acute stage of his psychosis, an attempt at delusional restitution and, in some ways, a therapeutic endeavor.

The book employs a story-telling device familiar from the *Thousand and One Nights* and the *Decameron*. Toward the end of the reign of Louis XIV, four libertines, the Duc de Blangis, his brother the Bishop, the Supreme Court President Curval, and a financier named Durcet prepare for an orgy by isolating themselves in the desolate and impregnable Chateau de Silling. These four villains, incorrigibly monstrous and perverse, have obtained their great wealth and power through unbridled viciousness, corruption, thievery, and murder. They bring with them to the Chateau 42 "objects of lust" who are in their complete power: their beautiful young wives who are also their daughters, together with a seraglio of sixteen young boys and girls kidnapped from their parents; eight sodomistic "fuckers," selected by reason of their monstrous dimensions; four sexagenarian duennas, eaten and ravaged by chancres; six kitchen maids and servants and, finally, four narrator-procuresses "grown gray in the service," Duclos, Champville, Martaine, and the frightful Desgranges.

Between a certain November 1st and the following February 28th, the narrator-procuresses, taking turns by month, tell the story of their lives, incorporating 150 tales of perversions which the Duc and his guests often re-enact on the spot. In the course of countless orgies, a crescendo of horrors that in fact lasts beyond the appointed date, 30 victims die in frightful torment. Only 12 return to Paris with the Duc and his three accomplices.

The book is divided into four sections of which the first 150 perversions or "passions" are simple, the next 150 complex, the next 150 criminal, and the final 150 murderous. Although the manuscript is completed only in outline, Sade had worked out the placement of these 600 passions and made notes for himself on their very carefully arranged progression. On examination, the passions of Book I can be seen to consist essentially of pregenital polymorphous perversions with a primary coprophagic and masochistic emphasis. This theme is continued in Book II with the use of multiple subjects of all kinds. Book III begins with homosexual and bestial sodomy, both punishable by death in Sade's day, and proceeds to more and more explicit tortures of the victims. In Book IV pleasure is essentially obtained through murder, after having subjected the victims to the most excruciating tortures.

As we read the storytellers' narratives, we are struck by the theme of the disappearance of objects and various attempts to deny the loss, to manipulate it in fantasy, and to make restitution. As Duclos proceeds with the first month's tale, we learn that she was born in a monastery of an unknown father, we hear of her childhood sexual adventures with the monks and, on the second day of the narrative, we are told of her mother's mysterious disappearance. In a denial typical of Sade and his heroines, Duclos disclaims any feelings of grief and maintains along with her sister that

> ... As for Mother, I don't care what's happened to her, as a matter of fact, even if it's the worst I'm perfectly delighted, and all I hope is that the whore is far enough away so I'll never see her again for the rest of my life. (Sade, 1966, p. 287)

When the Duc asks if there was reason for hating her mother, Duclos is unable to account for her antipathy and can only suppose it was inspired by Nature, to which the Duc replies:

> It is madness to suppose one owes something to one's mother. And upon what, then, would gratitude be based? Is one to be thankful that she discharged when someone once fucked her?...Does that mother of ours give us happiness in giving us life?...Hardly. She casts us into a world beset with dangers, and once in it, 'tis for us to manage as best we can. (ibid, p. 293)

The Duc then goes on to describe with relish the keen delight he experienced when he murdered his own mother. Following this, in a return of the denied, one of the young captive girls is found to be sobbing at the thought of her own mother's death and is thereupon brutally silenced by the Duc.

Continuing with her life story, Duclos relates how she and her sister then enrolled in a brothel, where they shortly witnessed the following scene:

> ...one morning someone came and asked for a girl named Rosalie, one of the most lovely blondes it were possible to behold...Immediately she entered, he had her sit down on a very high stool used especially for this ceremony. As soon as she was settled, he removed all her combs and hairpins and down all the way to the floor floated in a cloud the superb golden hair that adorned Rosalie's head. He drew a comb from his pocket, combed her hair, took handfuls of it, tangled it, kissed it, everything that he did was accompanied by remarks praising the beauty of that hair in which he took such a keen and exclusive interest. At last, from out of his trousers he pulled a smart little prick, already quite stiff, and he promptly enveloped it in his Dulcinea's hair; once well wrapped, he began to fondle his dart and discharged...He extricated his defunct engine, I saw that my companion's hair was matted with glistening fuck; she cleaned it, put it up again, and our lovers separated. (ibid, p. 297)

Although one might interpret this as a typical fetishistic fantasy or as a displaced homosexual idealization of the phallus, in the context of the book we are inclined to view this and similar fantasies as a regressive and restitutive attempt to maintain the existence of an archaic idealized object. The resemblance to the Laura dream is striking: the elevated beauty, the brilliance and nimbus of the hair, the watering with tears or sperm, and the ultimate separation; but now there is a mocking comparison of Rosalie with Dulcinea. Again the denied returns in a disguised and degraded form: sperm is substituted for tears and an attempt is made to reunite in a kind of *unio mystica* through a fluid exchange which in other fantasies involves urine, saliva, and all bodily liquids. But the fluid is finally spent; drives cannot be made to do the work of narcissistic and object cathexes. The conflict between the need for an object and the denial of its importance is not resolved.

Indeed, throughout the first book we find a predominantly masochistic theme that implies an attempt to maintain or re-create the object at the expense of the self. As the passions proceed, however, the idealized object tends to fade more and more and to be replaced by an emphasis on the aggrandized self. Ultimately the objects become completely dehumanized, and the self can be authenticated only through the extravagance of the destruction it wreaks. Here is an example from Book II of the Laura-Rosalie fantasy, one step further along the continuum to sadism: "He has himself frigged by his lackey while the girl, naked, balances upon a narrow pedestal; all the while he is being frigged, she may neither budge nor lose her equilibrium" (p. 587). Once again the girl is on a pedestal, but now her position has become more problematic. Although her enforced immobility may suggest the denial of a primal scene or even necrophilic fantasies, we feel that the essential function here is to serve as a mirror for an aggrandized self that becomes threatened whenever the object asserts its own separateness or individuality, however slight.

In the earlier passions the girl must not move or she will forfeit her pay; in the later passions it is her life that is at forfeit:

> He makes her sit down in an armchair balanced on springs; her weight releases a number of springs connected to iron rings which bind her tightly to the chair. Certain levers and gears advance twenty daggers until their points graze her skin; the man frigs himself, the while explaining that the least movement of the chair will cause her to be stabbed. He sprays his fuck upon her, in so doing touching the chair very delicately with his foot. (ibid, p. 609)

Here the object is pinioned and cannot move; its only attribute is to be an extension of the aggrandized self. If it moves, it dies. Already, the objects have taken on the stillness and silence of death. Ultimately, they will be discarded and replaced by others.

And in fact, the last book is entirely devoted to murderous pas-

sions. For purposes of illustration, we have chosen a slaughter perpe-
trated by the Duc himself upon Augustine, a beautiful 15-year-old
girl abducted by our heroes from a convent in Montpellier:

Escorted by Desgranges and Duclos, the Duc and Curval make a
journey to the cellars with Augustine in the course of that night;
her ass has been preserved in excellent condition, 'tis now lashed
to tatters, then the two brothers alternately embugger her, but
guard their seed, and then the Duc gives her fifty-eight wounds in
the buttocks, pours boiling oil into each gash. He drives a hot iron
into her cunt, another into her ass, and fucks her wounded
charms, his prick sheathed in a sealskin condom which worsens
the already lamentable state of her privities. That accomplished,
the flesh is peeled away from the bones of her arms and legs,
which bones are sawed in several different places, then her nerves
are laid bare in four adjacent places, the nerve ends are tied to a
short stick which, like a tourniquet, is twisted, thus drawing forth
the aforesaid nerves, which are very delicate parts of the human
anatomy and which, when mistreated, cause the patient to suffer
much. Augustine's agonies are unheard-of.

   She is given some respite and allowed to recruit her
strength, then Messieurs resume work, but this time, as the
nerves are pulled into sight, they are scraped with the blade of
a knife. The friends complete that operation and now move
elsewhere; a hole is bored in her throat, her tongue is drawn
back, down, and passed through it, 'tis a comical effect, they
broil her remaining breast, then, clutching a scalpel, the Duc
thrusts his hand into her cunt and cuts through the partition
dividing the anus from the vagina; he throws aside the scalpel,
reintroduces his hand, and rummaging about in her entrails,
forces her to shit through her cunt, another amusing stunt; then,
availing himself of the same entrance, he reaches up and tears
open her stomach. Next, they concentrate upon her visage: cut
away her ears, burn her nasal passages, blind her eyes with
molten sealing wax, girdle her cranium, hang her by the hair,

attach heavy stones to her feet, and allow her to drop: the top of the skull remains dangling.

She was still breathing when she fell, and the Duc encunted her in this sorry state; he discharged and came away only the more enraged. They split her belly, opened her, and applied fire to her entrails; scalpel in hand, the President burrows in her chest and harasses her heart, puncturing it in several places. 'Twas only then her soul fled her body; at the age of fifteen years and eight months thus perished one of the most heavenly creatures ever formed by Nature's skillful hand. Etc. Her eulogy. (ibid, pp. 658-659)

If we now compare this abominable fantasy with the dream of Laura, that idealized vision of womankind deriving from the troubadour poets, we are again struck by certain similarities. It can hardly escape our attention that here too we are dealing with an idealization and a subsequent disappearance or fall, nor can we fail to notice that few lovers in history have taken a more direct approach to the heart of their beloved.

Both dream and passion take place in the dark of night and make reference to a primal scene: in the dream the idealized mother appears to comfort him, in the passion it is the self that re-enacts a sadistic primal scene. In the dream Sade groans in sorrow, in the passion it is Augustine who is made to groan; in the dream Laura's eyes are on fire, her hair flows carelessly, in the passion Augustine's eyes are blinded with molten wax, her hair torn off. In the dream Laura *did not know* he was so unhappy, in the passion Augustine's sufferings are witnessed and yet unheard of; in the dream Sade speaks of his passion for Laura, in the fantasy Augustine must endure the passion. In the dream Sade throws his arms about Laura's neck to hold her back; in the passion he tortures while exquisitely prolonging Augustine's existence. In the dream Sade is *like a child* who is being destroyed, in the passion it is the child Augustine who is in fact destroyed. In the dream Sade is a helpless witness to his own destruction; in the fantasy, the destroyed self is projected into a split-off fragment, while the aggrandized megalomaniacal self *becomes* the destroyer. Passivity is turned into activity, the pain of self-destruction into the pleasure of destroying, but the price paid is the sacrifice of the idealized object and the idealized good self.

Devouring and destructive fantasies become explicitly equated in the final "Hell Passion" in which 15 young girls called "material" are branded, labeled, and propelled through a gaping gullet-like window whence they fall into the bowels of a cellar where they are tortured, dismembered, and slowly reduced to anonymous bits and pieces.

In the end, the fear of the self fragmenting and falling apart has become manifest; the narcissistic "cement" provided by the idealized mirroring self-object is no longer there to hold the fragments together. He assumes a compensatory delusional identification with the Bad Mother and Destroying Nature; he must "destroy the universe and dismember the cosmos;" he becomes death in order to avoid death. Faced with this fantasy of world destruction, the reader recoils in horror and disgust. Slowly we understand that his object in writing is to devastate us in order to master his own fear of annihilation.

Anal Economy and Metamorphosis

Commentators on *The 120 Days* have viewed with consternation and disgust the presence of coprophagia in more than half of the 600 passions (Lely, 1965). For us, however, it forms an integral part of the work when regarded as a manifestation of narcissistic phenomena.

Clinically, the grandiose self is usually found to be built around an anal core. It is only at this stage that there is sufficient self-object differentiation and cognitive development for the structure of the grandiose self to be relatively stable. Thus the struggle around anal functioning is often the first testing ground for the powers of the grandiose self, and it is through this modality that the self proclaims its entitlement to do anything it wants, with anything it wants, in any way that it wants, and particularly in ways that are forbidden. It is here that negativism itself can become the object of idealization.

Prior to this, however, we believe that a paradigm for the experience of the grandiose self is to be found in the idealization of the bowel products. For this is the first concrete evidence of the power and perfection of the self, the first tangible gift of love, and one that is usually received with wonder and admiration.

But it is also the focus of the first great disillusionment in the self's perfection, for the child must come to terms with the fact that his creation and gift is eventually treated as though it were worthless and even offensive. In a pathological regression, as the failing grandiose self is forced into more and more primitive denials of the curtailment of its powers, it eventually retreats to a denial that this initial disillusionment ever occurred.

For Sade, anal exhibitionism is the predominant mode of claiming attention for the aggrandized delusional self. Buttocks, anus, and feces are proclaimed as exemplars of beauty and perfection. Bowel products and their equivalents are to be treasured, savored, and adored. In effect, *The 120 Days* itself is like a bowel movement or an anal baby, an unsurpassed masterpiece whose brilliance, uniqueness, and importance must not fail to impress us. Thus, the first half of the denial in fantasy is: *My feces remain idealized:*

> She once sent me to the home of an elderly Knight of Malta who opened a kind of wardrobe filled with cubbyholes, each of which housed a porcelain chamber pot containing a turd; the old rake had made arrangements with a sister of his, abbess of one of the most considerable convents in Paris; that obliging girl, upon his request, every morning sent him a crate of fresh shit produced by her prettiest little pension-naires. He filed away each perfor-mance according to a classifying system, and when I arrived he bade me take down such and such a number, and it proved to be the most venerable. I presented the pot to him.
>
> "Oh yes," said he, "that belongs to a girl of sixteen, lovely as the day. Frig me while I eat her gift." (ibid, p. 414)

The second half of the denial in fantasy runs: Not only do my feces remain idealized, but *your ideals are in fact nothing but feces:*

He has some pious women recruited for his pleasure, beats them with a crucifix and rosaries, and then has each of them pose as a statue of the Virgin upon an altar, but pose in a cramped position from which they are not to budge. They must remain thus throughout an exceedingly long mass; when at last the Elevation occurs, each woman is to shit upon the Host. (ibid, p. 589)

In this state where ideals are degraded and the bowel contents themselves become idealized, they can be used as a kind of restitutional cement to patch all flaws in the grandiose self. Thus the denial of disillusionment is effectuated through a magical anal economy that equates all body parts and admits of no loss, differentiation, or diminution of the self. Human physiology is degraded into a jigsaw puzzle of small parts that are equated with food and feces and become interchangeable. The body products: blood, sweat, tears, saliva, urine, feces; the body contents: nerves, marrow, bones, viscera, brains; the mental content: souls, morals, values, principles, ideals; all become metamorphosed by the fantasy into the standardized parts of an insane anal technology. It is through the coprophagia that all objects become what they eat, reduced to an elementary common denominator which can be manipulated for the purpose of self-aggrandizement. People become reified, objectified and replaceable; corpse and excrement become one. But let us hear what de Sade himself has to say about this magical reduction:

And what after all is murder: a small rearrangement of matter, some changes in its disposition, some molecules that are disassembled and plunged back into the cauldron of nature whence they emerge some time later assuming another form on earth; and where is the harm in all that?

Thus, like the alchemist who transmutes base metals into gold, Sade's powers of fantasy have transformed the narcissistic trauma into a grandiose affirmation of the self and its omnipotence.

Discussion

We know that the Marquis de Sade, before his imprisonment, had engaged in perverse sadomasochistic activities and that, despite warnings,
he had persisted in them with sufficient indiscretion so that the legal
records of his prosecution still remain. Once in prison, his outlets were
apparently restricted to masturbation, to his insistently proliferating
fantasies, and to his writings, which begin at this time. For de Sade, his
art continues his acting out, for it serves the double function of provok-
ing punishment on the one hand and of being a vital element in his
self-affirmation on the other. Through these writings he continues to
demonstrate his power to his imaginary readers who are both his mirroring audience and his victims, and whose reactions of horror, disgust,
and outrage make manifest to him in the most vivid way possible the
effects of his self-assertion. Projected into the future is the fantasy that
his thoughts will have a profound effect on the values of all mankind,
thus ensuring his immortality.

This function of affirmation is also served by fantasies of infinite
and ultimate revenge. Of course, revenge fantasies appear in de Sade's
adult life directed toward those whom he blames for his persecution
and imprisonment. But behind this, one seems to discern the fantasy
that the person who shattered the grandiose self-image must be endlessly destroyed in his turn. Thus, Sade often identifies with the
aggressor who ravishes, despoils, and murders a beautiful and innocent
child, a representative of the perfect childhood self. Sadistic fantasies
here seem to function as attempts to prevent the final dissolution of
the delusional self, to prevent a yielding or submission that is equated
with death.

Masochistic fantasies, on the other hand, are evoked as the idealized
parental imago fades, and represent more and more desperate attempts
to experience *its* presence, to submit to *its* power. In *The 120 Days*, it is
noteworthy that the perversions change from masochism to sadism
and ultimately to murder as the idealized images disappear. Basically,
we understand the masochistic fantasies as restitutional attempts to

reanimate and cling to idealized imagos which have been denied and destroyed as their promised omnipotence failed. This is followed by a return to more archaic fantasies of the delusional self whose existence is validated and affirmed through sadism and murder.

Both of these primitive maneuvers require above all a *vividness* in the effect sought or produced by the self. It is the priority given to this vividness which stamps these fantasies with their strange and bizarre quality, and it is this emphasis on brilliance, intensity, and sensation—in contrast to pallor, stillness, and silence—that suggests a denial of the fantasy of death.

For we imagine that the grandiose self originates in sensations of feeling intensely alive, and that it remains close enough to the body experience so that traumatic disruptions are literally equated with physical damage—as though one were being torn apart, shredded, mutilated, and destroyed, or pinioned, stifled, silenced, and annihilated. This may be the source of a lifelong sense of terror and outrage, an equivalent to what we sometimes see in people who have suffered early and severe physical damage: the exceptions (Freud, 1916). Here the compensatory use of invulnerable self-images protects the self from the constant threat of its own destruction. But why are these images incorporated into sexual fantasies?

Eissler (1958), in discussing the question of the emotional conviction of one's existence, proposes that "orgasm is the strongest affirmation possible to man...endowed with the power to confirm, create, and affirm conviction" (p. 242). Nydes, in "The Magical Experience of the Masturbation Fantasy" (1950), maintains that "As the climax of the masturbation fantasy, the orgasm is a triumph of *realization,* which for an instant gives imminent life and power to the thoughts that surge on its crest. The tactile illusion in particular fortifies the hallucinatory quality of the experience" (p. 306).

We have seen that the threatened aggrandized self makes sexual use of objects in order to affirm its power and existence, but we see this insistence on triumphant affirmation as a denial of a deeper anxiety. For it is startling to note with what passivity the victims in *The 120 Days* submit to their gruesome fate: they neither scheme, struggle, nor

attempt to escape, although in fact they greatly outnumber their torturers. They seem to welcome their death, if only as a liberation from
the torment of their life.

We believe that these victims represent a split-off part of Sade's
ego, personified and externalized in the form of a beating fantasy: I
observe that a child is suffering, I observe that a child is dying. But
here the wish goes beyond the classical regressive distortion of a wish
to be loved by the parent; it is the endopsychic perception of Sade's
own wish to die. Torturer and victim represent both sides of an
intrapsychic conflict. Omnipotent sexual fantasies are, in the long
run, simply a frantic means of sustaining the delusional self in the
face of a longing to submit to the reconstituted idealized self-object, a
personification of the yearning for death. Now we begin to understand why the victims submit so meekly, why the torturers prolong
their agonies indefinitely, why the whole mad charade must continue
until exhaustion, only to begin anew. The real issue is not only that
the delusional self must keep trying to affirm itself, but that there is
an insoluble conflict between its affirmation or survival and the
longed-for quiescence of death.

Rereading de Sade, one at times has the impression of being with a
small child in the midst of an endless temper tantrum, raging against
God, against the world, against institutions, against beloved objects
and ideals, against life itself—but all this seems only a pale reflection
of his rage against himself. In the presence of such colossal fury, we
are once again reminded of the autobiographical reference in *Aline
and Valcour* where the young Sade falls upon the Prince, his childhood companion, with such violence and murderous intent that they
can only be separated by force.

Can we read this as a screen memory in which Fortune and Nature—his parents—have led him to believe that the whole world
should yield to his whim and that he need merely want something in
order to have it? And then—one day—shockingly and traumatically
disillusioned, he turns with a violent fury upon the young Prince—his
ideal self—in a narcissistic rage and with intent to commit murder upon his own grandiose image. Afterward, so the story goes, his parents

voyage abroad and he is sent to live with his grandmother. Those who promised so much have proven devastatingly disappointing; he has lost his idealized objects as well. Now he must reconstruct a restitutive false self—a self to which everything is permitted since it has suffered so grievous an injury (Freud, 1916), a self to which rage becomes a kind of affirmation because its function is to perpetually reassure him that long ago there had not been an internal act of murder which left behind a lifeless corpse. It is this narcissistic fantasy that "a child is being murdered"—my childhood grandiose self is being destroyed—endlessly carried out and just as endlessly denied, that finds expression in the murderous sadistic fantasies of *The 120 Days*.

But it is also expressed in the dream of Laura. In "The Theme of the Three Caskets," Freud (1913) has pointed to the typical reversals that mask the figure of death: the beautiful woman who stands for the terrible Goddess, the apparent choice that represents a stark necessity, but here Death itself has become a narcissistically idealized corpse. Laura is a magical omnipotent figure, a restitutive and "delusionally" idealized *self*-image whose brilliance is not impaired even by death and who summons him to a blissful merger in the tomb. Much as he longs to, he cannot surrender because it would mean acknowledging that very image of the dead self against which he has struggled throughout his life. Yet, in another sense, his perpetual entombment may represent just such an acknowledgment. In certain cases we find that the idealization of death eventually wins out, and we then see a kind of spectacular suicide, a triumphantly aggrandized death. Indeed, in some cultural contexts, this idealized suicide has become institutionalized as a way of providing a final narcissistic triumph over unendurable humiliation.

Summary

In this paper we examine a dream of the Marquis de Sade and a series of perverse fantasies from one of his major works, viewing them both as attempts to cope with narcissistic decompensation. We suggest that the public image of the Marquis de Sade is a manifestation of a "delusional grandiose self," constructed in a restitutive attempt to recathect a traumatically disrupted childhood narcissistic self-object.

On the basis of a biographical fragment, we offer some speculations about the nature of this traumatic disruption and the restitutional attempts that follow. We relate these ideas to current concepts of narcissistic pathology and find them particularly congruent with the formulations advanced by Kohut.

We illustrate the unique emphasis that Sade places on anal fantasies and coprophagia, and we comment on the special relationship of the anal stage both to processes of idealization and disillusionment and to the formation of the narcissistic self-object.

In the context of Sade's psychosis, his narcissistic pathology, and the struggle to master his narcissistic rage, we view the masochistic fantasies as attempts to restitute delusionally idealized self-objects, and the sadistic fantasies as efforts to animate a delusional grandiose self. We see the sexualization of these fantasies as an attempt to deny experiences of self-fragmentation, bodily disruption, and "death of the self." We present a series of fantasies about murder and death, and we explore their relationship to narcissistic trauma, restitution and triumph.

REFERENCES

Bach, S. (1971). Notes on some imaginary companions. *Psychoanalytic Study of the Child* 26:159-171.

Eissler, K. R. (1958). Notes on problems of technique in the psychoanalytic treatment of adolescents—With some remarks on perversions. *Psychoanalytic Study of the Child* 13:223-254.

Freud, S. (1913). The theme of the three caskets. *Standard Edition* 12:289-302.

Freud, S. (1916). Some character-types met with in psycho-analytic work. *Standard Edition* 14: 309-333.

Khan, M. M. R. (1965). The function of intimacy and acting out in perversion. In *Sexual Behavior and the Law,* ed. R. Slovenko. Springfield, IL: Charles C Thomas, p. 397-412.

Kohut, H. (1966). Forms and transformations of narcissism. *Journal of the American Psychoanalytic Association* 14:243-272.

Kohut, H. (1968). The psychoanalytic treatment of narcissistic personality disorders—Outline of a systematic approach. *Psychoanalytic Study of the Child* 23:86-113.

Kohut, H. (1971). *The Analysis of the Self.* New York: International Universities Press.

Lely, G. (1962). *The Marquis de Sade: A Biography*, trans. Alec Brown. New York: Grove Press.

Lely, G. (1965). *Vie du marquis de Sade*. Paris: Pauvert.

Lely, G. (1966). *The Marquis de Sade: Selected Letters*, sel. by G. Lely, trans. W. J Strachan, ed. M. Crosland. New York: October House.

Nydes, J. (1950). The magical experience of the masturbation fantasy. *American Journal of Psychotherapy* 4:303-310.

Sade, D.-A.-F. (1931-1935). *Les 120 Journées de Sodome, où l'Ecole du libertinage par le marquis de Sade.* Edition critique tablie sur le manuscrit original autographe par Maurice Heine. Paris: S. et C.

Sade, D.-A.-F. (1965). *The Marquis de Sade: The complete Justine, Philosophy in the Bedroom and other Writings,* compiled & translated by R. Seaver & A. Wainhouse. New York: Grove Press.

Sade, D.-A.-F. (1966). *The Marquis de Sade: The 120 Days of Sodom and other writings,* compiled & translated by A. Wainhouse & R. Seaver. New York: Grove Press.

Winnicott, D. W. (1953). Transitional objects and transitional phenomena-A study of the first not-me possession. *International Journal of Psychoanalysis* 34:89-97.

CHAPTER 7

On Sadomasochistic Object Relations

We need, in love, to practice only this:
letting each other go. For holding on
comes easily; we do not need to learn it...

Rilke: Requiem

In one of the more philosophical passages of the Marquis de Sade's *The 120 Days of Sodom,* the Duke reflects with sadness and resignation that people are generally so difficult to comprehend. "Yes," replies his friend, "most people are indeed an enigma. And perhaps that is why it is *easier* every time to fuck a man than to try to understand him."

This aphorism of the Divine Marquis seems especially appropriate for a discussion of perversions, for it speaks to the regressive nature of perversion and thus to the sadomasochist in each of us. No doubt it is easier to exploit a person than to relate to him, for relationships require a dialogue, whereas usage can be simple and unilateral, requiring only force, intimidation, or cunning. In this sense psychoanalysis may be viewed as the opposite of a perversion, because in principle it embraces the difficult task of understanding a person rather than using him, although it, too, can easily enough become a perversion itself.

I would like to talk about one of the more ubiquitous perversions of everyday life in which the individual rather than using a fetish or fantasy as a prosthesis to replace a missing part of his ego, uses instead a mode of relating that one of my patient's called a "technical" relationship, one that falls under the more general heading of narcissistic object relations.

165

Of course sadomasochistic relations may or may not include actual perversions, but they always include sadomasochistic fantasies that may be conscious or deeply unconscious. They cover a continuum of nosologies from the neurotic through the psychotic, but I believe they are developmentally related to the sexual perversions because, like them, they arise as a defense against and an attempt to repair some traumatic loss that has not been adequately mourned. This loss usually occurs in childhood or adolescence and may take the form of loss of a parent, loss of the parent's love through neglect or abusive treatment that the child denies, or a feeling of loss of the self through childhood illness, traumatic disillusionment, or overwhelming castration anxiety. In this view, sadomasochistic relations may be seen as a kind of denied or pathological mourning, a repetitive attempt to disclaim the loss or to repair it in fantasy, but an attempt that does not lead to resolution because in some dissociated part of the psyche that loss remains disavowed.

The issue is complex because we are dealing with the interdependence of drive and object relations, for if, as Waelder (1930, pp. 72-73) notes, "the act of love...comes closest to being a complete and equable solution of the ego's contradictory tasks..." then the failure of that act of love, as in a perverse relation, may be understood as a failure of multiple tasks in many lines of development. Here, I can do no more than touch upon some of these lines, each of which must be given due weight to achieve both a theoretically plausible and clinically successful outcome.

From a certain perspective, one might say that a person has a perversion *instead* of having a relationship. To the extent that a relationship is pathologically defective and lacks the capacity for whole object love, we may say that a perversion or a character perversion exists. But just as perverse drive gratification may be a flight from intimate object relations, so perverse object relations may defend against anxieties about drives.

Regarding the severity of sadomasochistic pathology, a distinction might be made between those cases where the preoedipal and oedipal struggle with the parents has been over instinct prohibition and those cases where the struggle has been over recognition of the self. Cases where the parents condemn the behavior but recognize the child as a separate entity tend to fall into the range of neurotic perversions, and often enough the instinctual condemnation illuminates rather than eliminates the ego—"Your instincts are terrible but there *is* a you there." On the other hand, cases of parental nonrecognition, emotional absence, or a lack of mutual pleasure between parent and child force the child to flee to the sadomasochistic drives in an effort to deny the loss and to buttress a failing sense of self. Let me start with an example of this latter type:

> A young man whose chief complaints have been chronic depersonalization and an unbroken series of sadomasochistic relationships with women reported with some astonishment that he was learning to cuddle and fondle his friend's children, something that he didn't know how to do before the analysis. He was astonished that they liked it so much and realized that he had never been cuddled himself and that his own parents were remote and distant. He remembered how afraid he was as a child to ask for anything and convinced that he must do everything for himself.
>
> I noted that he still has ways of doing things for himself when he needs fondling, like masturbating or getting high on drugs.
>
> He said he can't believe that anyone would want to love him, which is why in sex he ties women up and forces them to love him and makes them come even when they don't want to....
>
> There was a long silence, and then he observed in a tone of awe that a strange image had come into his mind of someone lying there screaming...being beaten up...a memory of crowds coming to watch someone broken on the wheel...someone being beaten to death with a stick...
>
> I said that's just like cuddling and fondling, but with a minus sign in front of it.

He answered after a while that the most personal relationship he ever had was when his father came after him with a
whip to beat him. "I really had his exclusive attention then, like
I never did at any other time.... It's just like in my fantasies
when I force women to have sex with me and to like it too...I
suppose you can get to like it if it's the only kind of fondling
you've ever known."

In this way we arrived at the beating fantasy, the essential element
of the masochistic perversion that Freud (1919) described seventy
years ago. In that formulation, conflicts around oedipal wishes lead to
an anal regression and the punishing and resexualized wish that we
have seen: I want my father to beat me as a way of loving me. It is
worth noting this patient's report that although his mother and father
took good care of him, neither one seemed to derive any real *pleasure*
from being with him, nor he from them.

A few months later this young man met someone on the street
and became confused about whether it was me or someone
who resembled me. He said that he could never recognize anybody, couldn't remember names and that he didn't understand
what motivated people. He plaintively added: "I really don't
know anything about people as human beings I just have a
kind of technical relationship to them I don't know what you
can do to help me...(?) Suppose I expressed sadness and you
comforted me and I took that comfort...then how would I get
up and leave? I can picture myself begging at the door—please
can I stay—I can't go! At home there was nobody with the patience to listen....Nobody sat with me as a kid....And when I
grew up in adolescence and someone listened to me sympathetically, I fell in love!... if somebody listened sympathetically,
that's all it took. I tried to merge with them, to surrender all
autonomy, and then it evolved into a contest—I'm controlling
you, you're controlling me....(How did that happen?) I would
spend long nights with some girl and at some point it came to

controlling them, tying them up...then I could play out the fantasy that she would always be where I wanted her to be and always accessible for what I wanted...and the less I knew about her the better, because if I knew who she really was it would make that fantasy impossible...if she lived in the real world she couldn't always be mine....And that must be why I didn't recognize you on the street!... you're supposed to be here in your office waiting for me always and not running around West End Avenue..."

At this point we were able to do some work on how he ties me up in the transference by maintaining a "technical" rather than a personal relationship, keeping himself distant, tantalizing me with half-truths, forcing me to wait on his pleasure, and frustrating my therapeutic efforts. Over the next few years we saw this theme in its transformations as an expression of oedipal rivalry and aggression, as a defense against homosexual impulses and the wish to be beaten as a defense against castration anxiety and a means of enhancing his potency, as a way of firming up ego boundaries and reviving a failing sense of self and as a participation in the primal scene. No one of these perspectives or interpretations magically undid the problem, which was molded into his character and ego pathology, and I continually had to remind myself that in such cases we are attempting no less than to help someone separate, maintain object constancy, and achieve whole object love.

It is worth noting the vicissitudes of this patient's attempts to love. Starting from situation in which he experiences both parents as unrelated and dead through some combination of his projected rage and their own failure, he provokes his father into beating him not only as a defense against this rage and a punishment for oedipal wishes, but also to keep his father and himself *in love,* to revivify their relationship. In adolescence he falls in love with anyone who listens sympathetically, tries to surrender to them, and "and at some point it came to...tying them up....Then I could play out the fantasy that she would always be where I wanted her to be and always accessible for what I wanted...." The attempt to love has somehow miscarried and become instead an attempt to control, and although the patient is aware that this is only a fantasy, he prefers it to reality.

Because it may not be entirely clear how the attempt to love becomes transformed into a sadistic fantasy that glues both participants together, perhaps we can look at the beating fantasy from what appears to be the other side:

A young woman with a disturbed maternal relationship who had also been beaten by her father seemed to be forever in search of some kind of symbiotic experience. As we worked on this she explained:

"It's like when I ask to be blindfolded in sex and tied up...if I'm blindfolded I can imagine that he's tuned in right along with me whereas in reality you can see how he's *not* with you more than he's with you...the fantasy is he will take care of you, will feed you, wash your hair, dress you,...you can just *be,* it's a fantasy of being perceived in one's essential being...the enigma and the indirectness leave room for the fantasy of being understood....And the other thing about that fantasy is that it can never be satisfied...you have to keep it in that charged space between people that's never fulfilled...[How do you mean?] I don't feel perceived in the act of consummation the way I do beforehand...before *it's the apex of power,* it's all charged...they can consummate with any other woman... but not with me....I retain my uniqueness because they're still interested, and there must be something special in me to keep them from going where they can be gratified..."

With this patient the teasing and castrating behavior was designed to retain a sense of power that the consummation would destroy because it would demolish her body-phallus fantasy, make *her* feel castrated and empty and make her in reality dependent upon an imperfect object. More concretely, she was trying to recreate a situation in which all her father's attention was focused on her, but to prevent a consummation that would feel like the longed-for but humiliating lash of his whip. "If I'm blindfolded I can imagine that he's tuned in right along with me whereas in reality you can see how he's *not* with you more than he's with you...."

It is certainly striking how both these patients *insist* on their desire not to learn anything real about their partners or the analyst because their fantasies of being "tuned in," or merged with an idealized other become endangered by rage and devaluation if that other person is realistically perceived. But one of them also complains of his *incapacity* to know anything about his partner or anyone else. My clinical impression is that this latter complaint is also to the point and that some of these people cover their deficit in understanding others with a variety of defenses, just as someone who cannot admit he is partially deaf may pretend to understand, may read lips, claim that nothing is worth hearing, or become hypervigilant and paranoid. Thus, their deficit in understanding others may be patched over by their "technical" mode of relating, in much the same way as the pervert uses his fetish to patch over a deficit in the body ego. This mode of relating is both an adaptive way to deal with their interpersonal deficit and a defense against the rage and devaluation that would destroy the object entirely.

We should note the instability of the narcissistic position, since at one moment the patient is sunk in masochistic surrender to the idealized lover whom she *knows* to be a figment of her imagination, whereas at the next moment she is sadistically manipulating the same lover, willingly exchanging the pleasures of sexual consummation for the pleasure of sexualized power. These oscillations between masochism and sadism and between passivity and activity are typical of such cases, and one may also find masochistic content being expressed within a sadistic structure or vice versa. But for the moment I want to emphasize the alternation between reality and its denial in fantasy.

For, however, we may choose to conceptualize this phenomenon in which both the reality and its disavowal remain in conscious awareness, it seems true that in his *experience,* the sadomasochist feels himself to be living in two worlds: the fantasy world where he plays the *game of the idealized omnipotent self and object,* and the real world, which seems too dangerous to exist in. In the fantasied world of the idealized merger, the laws of space, time, and logic, which promote differentiation, are suspended: separation, death, and mourning do not exist.

With my own series of cases, discussion of this "two world" phenomenon almost always seemed to elicit material about the parents and some strange aspects of *their* relationship to reality. Let me give an example:

> A man who was in a state of tormented jealousy and paranoia that he knew to be unjustified said: "I know in the real world that my girlfriend has a right to do what she wants to do, but that doesn't matter...there's a different world in which I live, where my feelings really are, and in that world she has no rights..." He then remembered a time at school when he was caught breaking the rules and his mother had said: "I'll go tell the teacher what a good boy you are and he'll let you off." He had screamed at her: "Mom, join the real world, they caught me and now I have to pay!" His mother had, in fact, never joined the real world, but he himself had become a voyager between the two worlds of reality and omnipotent fantasy in order to stay in touch with her.

In 1940 Freud had remarked with some wonder at the pervert's ability to both affirm and deny the existence of the maternal phallus and had conceptualized this behavior as reflecting a split in the ego. Traditionally, of course, the fetishistic perversion and even the character perversion has been explained as due to the traumatic sight of the maternal genitalia (Arlow, 1971), but I do not believe it has been adequately explained why this sight may be traumatic for some and not for others. From my perspective, one may surmise that in some cases the *whole* mother and not only her genitals has been traumatic or, to put it more concretely, that some of those children who find the sight traumatic have discovered not only a fantasied gap in the genital area but also an actual gap in relatedness, and that the child's entire psyche has been mobilized to deny and to patch over this gap. In certain cases one can regard this fantasy of a frightening genital nothingness as the ultimate body metaphor for a series of developmental losses culminating in the fear that there is *no one there* to love or be loved by and no possibility of finding some libidinal connection behind the screen of technical relatedness. These parents are the sort of people about whom one might say: "There's no *there* there." Let me give some examples:

A woman with sadomasochistic fantasies, commenting on her mother's presence said: "You speak to her on the telephone and she's not there...other people say uh-huh or mm...mmm...or you just know that they're there, but with her you wonder has she left the telephone....Is she gone? Where has she gone?"

This same question—where has she gone?—became the leitmotif that was repeatedly acted out in the treatment of a man who said about his mother—"She was always absent in my presence." He recounted how his mother had sent him to a doctor as a youngster because he slept too much, but he slept to avoid the emptiness and the pain of her absence...he remembers the doctor asking him questions, but it was a useless experience because it was his mother who should have awakened him by asking him what was the matter or talking to him or being alive or present in his presence....When he was a kid he used to miss her and ask over and over again where she was...where has she gone? He would read *Playboy* magazine to stimulate himself and keep him awake....

He remembered that he sucked his thumb for a long time; the thumb provided a good feeling of connection that he didn't have with his mother—at least he knew where his thumb was! It was like an addiction, and he gave it up only when he turned to masturbation and that was like an addiction, and then he turned to women, and now with his current woman he is in a state of constant jealousy and driven to ask her where she is going and what she is doing and interrogate her over every detail even though it hurts them both, and when he sees that she is as miserable as he is, then he can stop because it means that she loves him....

We may note again how the attempt to love miscarries, is replaced by fetishistic substitutes, becomes embodied in a merger fantasy that is thwarted and finally turns to sadomasochism in a tormented attempt to discharge the rage and regain contact through the induction of a mutually addictive sexualized misery: '"If I can make you feel as bad as I feel, then I know that you love me and we can retrieve our lost togetherness!" The utter loneliness, misery, and despair of the sadist reaches its apogee in the mad acts of the Marquis de Sade or King Frederick Wilhelm beating his subjects while shouting—"You must love me!"—but both sadist and masochist form a couple united in a common enterprise, each seeking in their own way to complete themselves through the realization of a perfect union.

In this case it seems clear that the sadism is in the service of recapturing the lost object, aggressively punishing it for straying, and maintaining a sexual excitement that will keep both self and object idealized, libidinized, and alive, so that his mother will never again be lost or dead to him and he will never again suffer excruciating pain. In playing this sadomasochistic game, however, he avoids mourning the loss of his mother or renouncing her, which would be necessary in order for the frozen developmental process to resume.

You may wonder why I say that the patient avoids mourning the loss of his mother when I reported that from an early age he was already bemoaning her absence and frantically seeking substitute satisfactions to help him feel alive. In part, of course, this is a retrospective account and he became increasingly aware of the significance of his mother's absence only as analysis progressed. More important, he had split off a part of his psyche so that he could remain close to his mother in her own omnipotent fantasy world, whereas another part of him was strongly connected to reality. Thus, like the pervert who behaves as if he both affirmed and denied the existence of the maternal phallus, he behaved as if he both affirmed and denied the existence of a loving and idealized mother, and so long as this dissociation persisted, his mourning could never be complete. Finally, the very defenses that enabled him to survive this cumulative trauma kept him fixated at an anal-sadistic-rapprochement level: he denied his loss by constantly seeking and finding substitute gratifications, he identified with the lost object and became a loser himself, and, most important, he renounced the oedipal struggle by partially identifying with his mother and taking the father for his love-object.

Thus his masochism kept him attached to the *idealized mother of pain,* the mother who was never really there and whose absence was so excruciating, but whom he reactively idealized and was omnipotently attached to in his masochistic fantasies. His sadism, on the other hand, was a denial of his need for her, a manic assertion that he could be omnipotently powerful by himself but that, in the end, was a primitive identification with the aggressive, omnipotent, and androgynous mother of pain.

Most of the time such children appear to be caught in a double bind, because although their sense of being effective is *discouraged* so that they feel no power and no way of having any real impact upon the parent, their sense of omnipotence and guilt is *encouraged* so that they feel responsible for the parent's failure, depression, and rage. One then witnesses a pathetic situation in which the child or adult, even while being physically or mentally abused, feels that he has brought the situation upon himself but is powerless to effect any change.

It is sometimes as early as infancy that the fateful choice to live in pain rather than to lose the object may already have begun, a choice that the sadomasochist repeats at each developmental stage. There may be a history of early maternal insensitivity or deprivation resulting in head banging, hair pulling, skin problems, or eating and sleeping disorders, which can be seen as precursors of masochistic adaptations to the unpleasurable maternal dyad (Novick & Novick,

1987). In addition, the environment may have conspired with some object loss through the mother's depression, the loss of a caretaker, the birth of a sibling, or a childhood illness, all of which may intensify the sadomasochistic struggle. The conflict achieves heightened impetus in rapprochement, when the basic paradigm of clinging or going-in-search (Hermann, 1976) and shadowing or darting-away (Mahler, 1972) becomes embroiled in the sadomasochistic refusal to resolve the conflict of separation.

This failure to phase-adequately resolve separation has important consequences for subsequent difficulties in handling the heightened sexual fantasies and excitement of the oedipal period and problems around integrating a sexual identity. For sadomasochism in the service of repairing narcissistic vulnerability is also fueled by the impermissability of healthy sexual expression, as could be clearly seen in one of my male patients whose mother had wanted a little girl and had taught him that his phallus and his phallic strivings were unacceptable. He retained these strivings through a combination of drugs, masturbation, and perverse relationships, in which the perversions could be viewed as an idealized or denigrated prescription for what was necessary to complete his sexual identity and sense of self. It may be that one of the reasons we see fewer classical perversions these days is not only that social opportunities have expanded, but also that so many of these people now use drugs to help camouflage and patch over the defect in their ego functioning and reality sense.

This defect in reality sense or split in the ego, which is bridged by the fetish or ritual in the classical perversions, is bridged by the mode of relating in sadomasochistic relationships. And just as each fetish or perverse ritual must be unique for the bridge to hold or the patch to fit and function in the perverse act, so one finds a related intolerance for flexible behavior in sadomasochistic relationships. We may presume that this is a reflection of narcissistic intolerance for self-other differentiation as well as an anal omnipotence that declares: "I want what I want when I want it!" But the demand that everything feel just right is reparative as well, because in the childhood of these patients hardly anything felt right for them at all, that is, just as the patient was once a narcissistic extension of the parent, he now makes the partner or the analyst into a narcissistic extension of himself.

We may recall here Stoller's (1988) formulation that "at the center of every erotic fantasy is a childhood trauma which is contained by the fantasy" and that presumably guarantees its uniqueness. I believe this to be true also for sadomasochistic relations which are, after all, a way of loving, and that it is the combination of early separation problems with the unique traumata from specific developmental phases that characterizes these relationships. One might say that these patients have to some degree failed to adequately integrate the mother of nurturance and the mother of frustration, or the mother of pleasure and the mother of pain.

Ordinarily, if this integration has been achieved, then under the impetus of the incest taboo and castration threat the child goes in search of a replacement object to love. Going-in-search involves narcissistic affirmation in all phases, but also an acknowledgment of the reality of object failure and loss and the resulting anger that leads to a painful separation. This painful disengagement and symbolic internalization characterizes separation and differentiation, whether in rapprochement, in the oedipal phase, in adolescence, or in *mourning*, which is also a process in which the lost object is separated from by painful detachment and internalized.

It is precisely these painful detachments that the sadomasochist is unable to tolerate because his anger is experienced as an unbearably destructive separation from the object. Thus the masochist says: "Do anything you want to me but don't leave me," and the "anything you want" feels pleasurable because it means that his partner is still with him. The pain of suffering defends against the greater pain of loss.

The sadist turns this around and in a sort of temper tantrum plays at destroying the object in order to achieve pleasure, but it is only a false game because in the complicity of the perversions, the object is seldom destroyed or even harmed, while the pleasure of gratification through discharge only temporarily overcomes the pain of separation. Even in those rare instances where the object is destroyed, the identification with the lost object is often so extreme that suicidal thoughts and reunion-in-death fantasies predominate, as Schwartz and I have shown in our study of the Marquis de Sade (Bach & Schwartz, 1972). So if the masochist says: "Do anything you want to me but don't leave me," the sadist proclaims: "I can do anything I want to you and you'll still always be there!"

Thus the narcissistic sadist denies his object needs by overvaluing the importance of his drive discharge, whereas the narcissistic masochist denies his drive needs by overemphasizing the importance of his object attachments. Since the sadist and masochist are often the same person at different times or in different topographical states, sadomasochism may be viewed as a pathological oscillation between overvaluation of the drives and overvaluation of the object. In both masochism and sadism, however, holding on to the object typically wins out over letting go because at the stage of incomplete separation where the sadomasochist is fixated, letting go means losing not only the object but also losing a part of oneself.

It is in order to avoid this loss that the sadomasochist flees from the real world of dependency to the world of his fantasies where he can play the false game of the idealized self and object. I call it a false game because, as we have seen, it takes place in that split-off world of perversion that is acknowledged as both real and unreal at the same time (Freud, 1940; Steingart, 1983). But whereas the child's game is in the service of discriminating reality, uses the transitional object as a help in letting go and is on the developmental line toward independence and creativity, the sadomasochist's game is in the service of confounding reality, uses the fetish as a help in holding on, and is on the regressive line toward merger and stereotypy. The child's game involves *playing*, from which he may quickly make the transition to reality, but the pervert's game involves *play-acting*, never allowing the object to be real

It is also a false game because it requires the suppression of real emotionality, especially anger, and the substitution instead of a "technical relationship," that is, a withdrawal of cathexes so that one is dealing with part-objects or self-objects in a world of one's own creation. In this world of dehumanized part-objects that is typified by pornographic literature, a regressive anal economy prevails: all objects are interchangeable and one can scarcely be distinguished from the other; the most horrifying sadistic and masochistic fantasies have no real consequence, and *nothing is ever permanently lost* (Bach & Schwartz, 1972).

Unfortunately, in our real psychic economy, if nothing is ever permanently lost then nothing can ever be truly gained. For the price the sadomasochist pays by denying castration, loss, and death is to remain forever frozen into a lifeless stereotype that he is doomed to repeat. Where no loss, mourning, or renunciation is possible, then no progression is possible from one set of ambivalent life conflicts to another.

This fantasy of part-objects manipulated without loss unfolds in a world that the sadomasochist has split off or dissociated, in an altered state of consciousness characterized by extreme sexual excitement, sharply diminished reflective self-awareness, and a diminished sense that his acts are his own and under voluntary control. While in this altered state he feels as if hypnotized or in an *erotic haze,* and under its spell events take on a hyper-real and hallucinatory quality that make them seem larger and more compelling than reality itself. What I call the *erotic haze* serves to deny that reality is not in accord with fantasy, just as my patient had herself blindfolded in order not to notice that her lover was really *not* in tune with her. Variations on this denial range from closing one's eyes in sex or on the analytic couch to a characterological preference for the vague, the amorphous, and the ambiguous (Arlow, 1971; Lewin, 1948).

But in this state one also finds hyper-realistic imagery, images that in their hallucinatory clarity seem to deny that the object was lost and to proclaim instead: "No! It's not that she's gone! On the contrary, I see her more clearly and brilliantly than ever!" This is particularly striking in the works of Sade where the memory of his dead mother is transformed into that of a ravaged whoremonger whose image, in a moment of passion, becomes once again more glorious, bright, and beautiful than it was in life, a veritable resurrection of the dead imago. One recalls here the many visually concretized denials of loss in fantasy, from the luminescence of dead souls and the incandescence of the wake to the brightness of fetishistic perceptions and the screen memory (Greenacre, 1968).

While the sense of voluntary action and reflective self-awareness *decreases* during the sadomasochistic act, the sense of aliveness *increases*, so that the patient feels he is being lived by his instincts or his id. The fascination of this regressive state is known to many, but it is especially attractive to people who feel chronically alienated, anxious, or depressed. In some cases this sadomasochistic sexualization defends against a profound libidinal deadness in the patient traceable to a defective libidinization in the early mother-child matrix[1]. In other cases we can see how the idealization of the drives is used as a defense against the intimacy of object relations and the fear of loss, because to the sadomasochist, the danger of losing his objects momentarily outweighs the fear of his drives.

Sooner or later, however, he begins to fear the loss of boundaries and becomes anxious and guilty about his omnipotent sexual and destructive fantasies. Many patients do not have the capacity to move easily from this fantasy world to the real world and to feel relaxed in both spaces: they cannot, as it were, get them together. It is important for the treatment to help such patients integrate these dissociated states of consciousness. But although it is essential that this split-off area be brought into the transference, analyzing it is no small task since it is precisely at this point of diminished reality testing and reflective self-awareness that the therapeutic alliance tends to break down.

In the area of the split these patients appear concrete, tend to view the world in stark either-or fluctuation, seem unable to comprehend ambivalence, and may have difficulty in appreciating that a single reality can be understood in different ways by different people. Since this appreciation of multiple perspectives is a basic prerequisite for transference interpretation, these patients have often been regarded

---

[1] See, for example, *Perfume* by Patrick Suskind (1991) and Chapters 4 and 8, this volume.

as unanalyzable, oppositional or, in another sense, "perverse." The problems these patients have in differentiating and separating from their objects is reflected endopsychically in their inability to differentiate and separate from their own point of view or to take perspective on their own thought processes and thus to develop reflective self-awareness. In some ways it might not be misleading to compare sadomasochistic alternations and ambivalence to that of a person with pathological mourning, someone who frantically oscillates between believing that the love object is dead,and believing that it is still alive, but who does so in such a way that true mourning never becomes possible. Thus, instead of mourning, we find a split in the ego, and instead of separation through painful detachment and symbolic internalizations, we find repeated attempts at reunion with the mother of pain through the false game of the idealized self and object.

For although, as Freud (1919) noted, sadomasochistic object relations are inextricably linked to beating fantasies, in many cases interpretation of the beating fantasies alone may not produce therapeutic success. In these cases there are difficulties on the way to whole object love, and I see the goal of analysis as *opening pathways to object love.* Let me try to sketch some implications for therapy that will be elaborated in later chapters.

Just as the child cannot usually develop object love without having experienced some kind of satisfying union with the mother, the narcissistic patient cannot develop object love without having experienced some deep trust in the analytic process as it is exemplified through the analyst (Ellman, 1991). I am suggesting that, in addition to the beating fantasy, a more regressive fantasy of union with the omnipotent self and object must be analyzed and worked through before an enduring change can take place. The working through of this fantasy requires dealing with that split-off area of omnipotent objects that is defended by pseudo-emotionality and a frozen aggression that prevents separation and mourning from taking place. Once separation and mourning have been facilitated, the patient is enabled to again take up the developmental line of dependence-independence that had been blocked and replaced by sadomasochistic oscillations.

Another way of putting this is that these patients get better as they learn to be in a transference relationship that is not sadomasochistic. This is more complex than it may seem, however, because in the transference they do everything possible to subtly provoke either sadistic or masochistic reactions that are difficult for the analyst to discern, to understand, and to control. One sometimes sees in consultation cases where the sadomasochistic transference has been interpreted seemingly to no avail, or in which it has been jointly acted out in ongoing squabbles about who is going to control whom until both parties to the analysis have reached a state of mutual exasperation and exhaustion. Sometimes confrontive interpretations simply repeat the beating fantasy in another form, so that the patient is secretly gratified while being beaten with interpretations. This is but one situation in which the treatment itself can become a kind of perversion. To a certain extent, of course, incidents like this must be re-created before they can be understood, but the hope is that they will not be repeated indefinitely in the transference as they are in life.

In certain cases the analyst may not have fully appreciated that the patient' mental organization is in some respects still at a primitive level and that you cannot explicate the transference, which is a metaphor, to a patient whose mind cannot embrace the cognitive flexibility of metaphors. What this means in practice is that such a patient will confuse or confabulate what should be transferential and symbolic issues into *real* issues of love or death, and will struggle with you as if you were *in fact* trying to rape or kill him.

If certain of these patients are persistently confronted with the analyst's reality before a reliable autonomy has developed, then two perversions of treatment may ensue. In the first, the patient becomes acquiescent and agrees, but does not develop a genuine sense of self, and a prolonged pseudo-analysis results. In the second, the patient disagrees and eventually either leaves or conforms, but he becomes internally isolated, suspicious, and schizoid. He learns, in short, to keep his thoughts to himself and renews his conviction that there is no one in the world he can really trust and nothing to believe in.

Because the person with narcissistic pathology and sadomasochistic tendencies has never learned to trust his objects, he can never feel truly at home in the world. One of my patients constantly compared his life experience to that of a character in Hemingway who says: "When you're born they put you into the game and they tell you the rules and the first time they catch you off base they kill you." In the world of the sadomasochist there is no margin for error, no compassion, and no forgiveness. It is consequently very difficult to help these patients learn to love, to separate, and to mourn.

It seems that the sadomasochist interposes an impersonal or technical relationship between his desire and his object. This alienates him both from himself and from the object of his desire (Khan, 1979) in the interest of denying his dependence upon objects that have failed him in the past. This denial takes the form of manic or grandiose assertions of exceptionality, perfection, and omnipotence, *the game of the idealized self and object,* which includes denial of separation and sexual identity, denial of loss and castration, and denial of helplessness and depression. The masochist's longed-for surrender to an idealized other, or the sadist's merger with his grandiose omnipotent self is the ultimate way of avoiding the ambivalence conflict between dependence and independence. One might say that in searching to avoid a real dependence upon an actual fallible object, the sadomasochist substitutes a fantasied dependence upon an idealized infallible object. In this way, much like those political terrorists exiled from their homeland, the sadomasochist spends his days in fantasies of recapturing a lost Paradise that never in fact existed, while at the same time refusing to compromise by living in the real world that might actually be possible.

REFERENCES

Arlow, J. (1971). Character perversion. *In Currents in Psychoanalysis,* ed. I. Marcus. New York: International Universities Press, pp. 317-336.

Bach, S., & Schwartz, L. (1972). A dream of the Marquis de Sade: Psychoanalytic reflections on narcissistic trauma, decompensation, and the reconstitution of a delusional self. *Journal of the American Psychoanalytic Association* 20:451-475.

Ellman, S. (1991). *Freud's Technique Papers: A Contemporary Perspective*. Northvale, NJ: Aronson.

Freud, S. (1919). A child is being beaten: A contribution to the study of sexual perversions. *Standard Edition* 17:179-204.

Freud, S. (1940). Splitting of the ego in the process of defense. *Standard Edition* 23:275-278.

Greenacre, P. (1968). Perversions: General considerations regarding their genetic and dynamic background. *Psychoanalytic Study of the Child* 23: 47-62.

Hermann, I. (1976). Clinging—going-in-search: A contrasting pair of instincts and their relation to sadism and masochism. *Psychoanalytic Quarterly* 45:5-36.

Khan, M. M. (1979). *Alienation in Perversions*. New York: International Universities Press.

Lewin, B. D. (1948). The nature of reality, the meaning of nothing, with an addendum on concentration. *Psychoanalytic Quarterly* 17:524-526.

Mahler, M. S. Rapprochement subphase of the separation-individuation process. *Psychoanalytic Quarterly* 41:487-506.

Novick, K. K., & Novick, J. (1987). The essence of masochism. *Psychoanalytic Study of the Child* 42:353-384.

Steingart, I. (1983). *Pathological Play in Borderline and Narcissistic Personalities*. New York: S. P. Scientific Books.

Stoller, R. (1988). Panel on sadomasochism in the perversions. American Psychological Association, December.

Suskind, P. (1991). *Perfume: The Story of a Murderer*. New York: Knopf.

Waelder, R. (1930). The principle of multiple function: Observations on overdetermination. In *Psychoanalysis: Observation, Theory, Application*, ed. S. Guttman. New York: International Universities Press, 1976, pp. 68-83.

CHAPTER 8

Sadomasochism in Clinical Practice and Everyday Life

ranz Kafka once observed that the primary fact of childhood is the slow, persistent, and forceful induction of the child into the great lie, by which he meant the hypocrisy of civilization. Freud, of course, had made a related observation when he suggested that civilization engenders discontents because the civilizing process relies on the repression of instincts or needs which will thereafter always be seeking expression and satisfaction.

But Freud suggested a third alternative to either totally rejecting the great lie of civilization or sporadically rebelling against it. He felt that the ego could, by deforming itself, avoid a direct confrontation between its own needs and the demands of civilization. "In this way," he concluded, "the inconsistencies, eccentricities and follies of men would appear in a similar light to their sexual perversions, through the acceptance of which they spare themselves repressions" (Freud, 1924, pp. 152-153).

Now the socialization of the child begins from the day of its birth, and we know that each phase of development builds upon previous phases in a transformative way. But in our own culture one of the key periods of forceful socialization of the child is the anal phase when toilet training and willful struggles with the parents normally intrude on the child in a major way; when he is constantly beset with such prohibitions as "Don't hit! Don't break! Don't run away!" that give this period its name, "the terrible twos." Nowadays we generally view this period in a larger developmental context so that I have come to refer to it, only half-jokingly, as the anal-depressive-rapprochement-gender-identity phase, because all of these developments are going on simultaneously. It is often at this time that one is able to see most clearly whether the relationship between parents and child will become one based primarily on mutuality or one based primarily on some variety of overly forceful, unilateral socialization.

If the child is socialized predominantly through object related love of the parents and the prohibitions are reasonably negotiated, then mutuality will tend to predominate. But if he is socialized pre-dominantly through terror and fear of abandonment, whether overt or covert, then the suppressed urges and needs will generally emerge from undercover, often in the secretive and object *un*related ways that we call perversions, either sexual or of everyday life. I believe this is true whether the child complies masochistically or rebels defiantly, for the compliance always cloaks hidden rebellion just as the rebellion always cloaks a hidden desire for surrender. Worst of all, the child who is socialized by fear and force often has no inkling of what a mutual relationship might feel like or even how one comes to exist, and he will become an adult who will likewise have a defective understanding of mutuality and love. Let me begin by presenting two ordinary clinical examples, the first of which seemed neither particularly noteworthy nor perverse to the patient when he came for analysis.

This man, a dermatologist, while speaking of his adolescence and college days, once mentioned that he had played on the football teams in both high school and college and was kept on varsity because, although not a very good player, he was outstanding at blocking and tackling. Curiously, he loved to practice tackling and would do so for hours on end, often returning to the clubhouse bloody and bruised but strangely exhilarated. The coaches admired him for his dedication, but he himself didn't quite understand why the blocking and tackling thrilled him so.

I noted he had recently mentioned that his mother and father were physically quite distant and that they would never kiss, hug, or even touch one another, and that usually neither one of them touched him. I suggested that he had spent his adolescent years violently banging into tackling dummies and other men's bodies out of some desperate longing to be touched, and particularly to be touched by his mother. He began to sob, as if some trigger point had actually been touched, and recounted a chronological history of incidents ranging from sexual gropings of a little girl when he was 3 years old to repeated impromptu wrestling with a friend in high school, which had gotten him accused of homosexuality. It became clear that even his choice of dermatology as a profession was to some extent conditioned by his intense need for skin contact with another human being.

This patient was also something of a Don Juan, and although his actual sexual practices were unremarkable, his desperate need for touch and sexual contact many times a day had in fact led to a major distortion of loving. Although he wanted to be a caring person and needed to feel that he was giving pleasure to his partners, his insatiable need for sexualized touching inevitably led him to seductions, infidelities, and painfully ruptured relationships.

My second example is from a gay male patient, a banker whose sexual orientation was not in question but who had come because of difficulties with work and relationships. While he also felt that what he most wanted was to have a loving and enduring relationship, he constantly found himself in leather bars with one-night pickups indulging in sadomasochistic acts like licking their boots or being fist fucked, which afterwards disgusted him and made him feel loathsome. He viewed himself as a geisha girl, seducing strong men by his compliant availability, but then leaving them first because of his fear of being abandoned. Indeed, he himself had twice been emotionally abandoned by a mother who throughout his childhood was distant and physically unresponsive and who later in life left the family for a lesbian relationship.

Now I want to emphasize that although the dermatologist's sexual practice was usually missionary position copulation, while the gay banker's was usually masturbation, fellatio, or anal intercourse with actual or fantasied humiliation and domination, it seemed to me that certain of their dynamics were very similar and that the essence of their perversions lay, not in their sexual orientation nor even their sexual practices, but in the nature of their object relationships. For although *perversion* has historically meant sexual behavior that is pathological because it deviates in object choice or aim from the ostensible norm of heterosexual genital intercourse, I am using it here in the larger sense of an ego defect that interferes with the adequate resolution of object choice.

Both these accomplished men were sensitive, intelligent, and moral human beings who were struggling with all their might to make loving and meaningful human relationships and were tortured by their inability to do so. Both their analyses proceeded along similar lines and eventually enabled them to love in a way that felt more satisfactory to them. But I am getting ahead of my story.

How did it happen that I saw related dynamics and a similar evolution in these two men, one of whom was gay and practiced anal licking and fist fucking while the other was straight and practiced missionary sex? Despite the apparent differences, the similarity that seemed crucial to me was that they were both sadomasochistically fixated and that this fixation was contributing more than anything else to their difficulties in forming loving relationships. Of course, I should differentiate these two cases, which I view as perverse yet organized attempts at establishing object relationships, from a lower level of fragmented, indiscriminate perverse activities like subway flashing, which are basically efforts to establish self-cohesion and are chaotic attempts at canceling object relationships.

Freud considered the beating fantasy to be the essence of sadomasochism, and I related to you how I began to uncover the dermatologist's beating fantasy by connecting it with his need to be touched by his mother. This need to be touched had been transformed into a need for brutal and violent contact with other men's bodies and connected to an unconscious fantasy of being beaten by his father. By contrast, the gay banker's beating fantasy was being consciously reenacted in leather bars when he got men to abuse him, but it was also being unconsciously reenacted in certain repeated failures in his business life. Both these men had their object relationships and their love lives structured by their beating fantasies. How had this come about?

First, let me make it clear that I believe sadomasochism, like most other psychological phenomena, is both complex and multiply determined. I have elsewhere (Bach, 1995) discussed other important factors, including endogenous temperamental factors such as aggression in the infant that might make it difficult or impossible for any caretaker to respond in a good-enough way, thus compromising the regulation of a dyad, which then becomes the matrix for sadomasochism. I have also found sadomasochistic pathology to arise when the mother is endangered, sick, or unhappy and the child dedicates his life to curing or rescuing her, a frequent motif in members of our own profession. Sadomasochistic pathology often follows a variety of childhood traumas that lead to an intensification of annihilation or castration anxiety. It also frequently results from a prolonged childhood illness like polio or rheumatic fever where the child becomes isolated from his cohort, afraid for his life, and creates a pain-seeking and omnipotent fantasy world in compensation. Thus every vicissitude of life and any developmental phase may contribute to the formation of sadomasochism. The thread that binds them all together is that relationships with primary objects become oriented predominantly toward pain rather than toward pleasure, and that what feels longed-for, reassuring, and familiar is some variety of painful rather than pleasurable interaction. You may notice that I treat addiction to the giving or receiving of pain, that is, sadism or masochism, as two reversible sides of the same coin. In my last book (1995), I made the distinction between two narcissistic types, the overinflated, grandiose, and aggressive sadist who is defending against his weakness and vulnerability, and the deflated, helpless and dependent masochist, who is defending against his latent grandiosity and aggression. Thus, in my experience, every sadist is a latent masochist and every masochist a potential sadist, depending on the time and the context.

But let me return to my two cases and explore one particular aspect of how this addiction to pain rather than pleasure arises. The beating fantasy in both these cases took the form of "A man is beating someone," and in a previous analysis the gay banker's fantasy had been interpreted as relating to oedipal competition with his father, who was indeed a powerful and frightening figure. Now although the beating fantasy is one of Freud's great clinical discoveries, it seems likely that part of his clinical material came from the analysis of his own daughter and perhaps this in some way affected his ability to fully understand its consequences. At the oedipal level where he was working with Anna, he could formulate that the wish to be beaten by the father is "not only the punishment for the forbidden genital relation, but also the regressive substitute for that relation" (Freud, 1919, p. 189). He could then go on to conclude that "people who harbor phantasies of this kind develop a special sensitiveness and irritability towards anyone whom they can include in the class of fathers. They are easily offended by a person of this kind, and in that way (to their own sorrow and cost) bring about the realization of the imagined situation of being beaten by their father" (Freud, 1919, p. 195), a brilliant clinical formulation as true today as it was in 1919.

What he overlooked, perhaps because of both historical and countertransferential difficulties, was the fantasy's preoedipal function in maintaining the dependent tie to the father or mother or analyst, a function which I have read as: "Do anything you want to me, beat me if you wish with whips or interpretations, but don't ever leave me." Here the fantasy works to retain the tie to the mother of pain and to avoid the establishment of newer and more appropriate object relations. And indeed, it seems possible that Anna Freud's beating fantasies, despite years of analysis, may have finally disappeared only after she had separated from her father-analyst and found a life of her own in her relationship with Dorothy Burlingham (Young-Bruehl, 1988).

So, among many other aspects of sadomasochism, the one that I am going to emphasize here is its origins in the early environmental tie to the caretaker. The mothers of both these patients manifested a narcissistic style of relating which, in my experience, is often found in parents of children who later develop either distorted love relationships or frankly sexual perversions. Because of the parents' self-preoccupations, they can at best attend to their children only sporadically, a condition known as intermittent decathexis (Furman and Furman, 1984), which undermines the child's sense of self and object constancy. Even worse, the basic fabric of the ego is impaired because the parents' difficulties with cognitive and emotional self-regulation are passed on to the child in the form of disorganized, contradictory, and incompatible procedural knowledge. This procedural knowledge, which consists of abilities and rules that we learn without being aware of them, are, like the grammar of our first language, a nonconscious grammar of skills, goals, procedures, and regulatory interactions with others that make us feel like we belong in this world and know what we're doing there, just as we speak our first language without thinking about it. Because these children have internalized disordered regulatory processes and contradictory procedural skills from their environment, they never feel at home in the world and always feel deviant, no matter how successful they may appear objectively. Perversions of all sorts are one kind of sexualized attempt to compensate for these hidden feelings of deviance and defectiveness.

Although these parents I am discussing often appear normal to the casual observer, they all live in a world of their own to which the child feels he has little or no access. Children learn to access their parents' cognitive and emotional states from the very beginning, and we have experimental and developmental evidence of how profoundly an infant is affected when, for example, the mother either avoids or aggressively pursues eye contact, or when she neutralizes her own facial expression as an experimental condition. If you can imagine this neutral, impassive-faced experimental condition as a permanent way of relating, then you can imagine what it is like to have as your primary object a Sphinxlike caretaker whose mental and emotional experience remains a mystery to you. Obviously, the caretaker does not always have to be impassive; it works equally badly if she is emotionally labile, alexithymic, or in denial of her feelings. The point is that her own true feelings and thoughts remain mysterious because they cannot be consistently correlated with either the child's own emotional states or with events in the real world. So the child cannot construe the caretaker's mind and the caretaker remains a mystery, neither knowing the child nor being known by him. The child becomes confused and disoriented; he feels that the world makes no sense and he cannot feel at home in it.

The parent's inconsistency and changeability are experienced by the child as a series of repeated betrayals—a cumulative trauma that undermines the solidity of the self and object representations. In the child's mind, questions of which mother is real intermingle with questions of which self is real. The child fights against deep attachment to someone so emotionally unpredictable and he feels constantly enraged. Typically, the rage cannot be expressed and the child ends by shaming and blaming himself for not being able to reach the mother whom he has idealized to protect her from his aggression.

Furthermore, this type of caretaker is also anhedonic; that is, she derives little or no pleasure from the parent—child relationship and ultimately provides no pleasure to the child. In all of my cases this lack of mutual pleasure in the dyad or even an outright sharing of suffering with the mother of pain, beginning in infancy and continuing through each developmental stage, has been a prominent factor in the development of sadomasochism. Characteristically, this mutual lack of pleasure also pervades the transference in the early years of analysis, making the management of the countertransference exquisitely difficult.

Typically, the child of such a caretaker is consciously or unconsciously enraged at her, but cannot display it because she is all that he has. Such caretakers do not allow their children any freedom, and the child clings to them because he has not been encouraged to develop his own agency. These sadomasochistic dyads are a closely coupled system without autonomy for either caretaker or child, who have indeed both become each other's slaves. A normal dyad is loosely coupled, so that while each partner can experience togetherness, he can also experience moments of aloneness, autonomy, and effectance.

Since the child cannot express his hatred *to* the caretaker and is also not obtaining any pleasure *from* her, the rage tends to get sexualized and displaced elsewhere in a perverted demand for love that reminds one of King Frederick William of Bavaria who used to beat his subjects while shouting: "I will *make* you love me!"

This close coupling of the sadomasochistic dyad not only precludes autonomy but it effectively excludes the oedipal third, whether father or mother, so that an illusory dyadic closeness is maintained at the expense of an entry into the real, triadic, oedipal world. In some way these children are both tied to their caretakers and yet always trying to escape from them. As adults, they develop similar love-hate relationships with others in which they seem bound to the relationship through pain. My patient the gay banker, whose beating fantasies were enacted in leather bars, was able to find a loving relationship with a man only after psychologically separating from his mother by working through the early ties that had left him addicted to painful interactions. Before that, after every visit to his mother he would find himself having anonymous masochistic sex, a compensatory repetition that became clear only in the analysis. As a child he had desperately wanted his impassive mother and his egotistical father to respond to him in some intimate way that would confirm their relationships and reaffirm his existence. This need led him to increasingly provocative behaviors in order to evoke any kind of response, and the symbolic beatings that he provoked from his father were later reenacted as real beatings in leather bars.

In this very brief account, I have touched on certain aspects of perversion while necessarily omitting many others. I have modified the definition of perversion from the usual "deviation in object choice or aim from heterosexual genital intercourse," which I find problematic in many ways, to the larger sense of a "deviation that interferes with the normal resolution of object choice" or "an incapacity to relate to an object as a whole person rather than as a self-object or thing," a definition I find more relevant for psychoanalysis.

I have made some rather obvious connections, the most obvious being that if the caretaker cannot consistently relate to the child as a whole person in a mutual relationship, then the child may have problems later in life with loving relations. These problems will often emerge as sadomasochistic character pathology with beating fantasies and regulatory difficulties that sometimes lead to deviant sexual behaviors and sometimes to drug abuse, eating disorders, and somatic pathology.

From one perspective all of these syndromes can be viewed as disorders of self-regulation and mutual regulation, resulting from the dysregulations between parent and child that I described and which Ferenczi (1933) first characterized as "confusion of tongues." But the degree of disruption may vary widely from a totally chaotic and fragmented self organization to a relatively cohesive one. Patients who feel quite fragmented may make desperate attempts at establishing self-cohesion and self-regulation through any and all modalities, such as filling and emptying the body of food, altering states of consciousness with drugs, creating somatic sensations in different parts of the body, or employing sexuality in a frantic attempt to revitalize the self and retain self-cohesion, as do certain sadistic sexual criminals. With all these patients there is either an acute or cumulative environmental trauma, and they recount this trauma through enactments in the transference rather than by symbolic verbal means. In the early part of treatment they tend to react poorly to symbolic interpretations, often experiencing them as a repetition of the original environmental trauma. Nevertheless, it is important to eventually interpret internal conflicts in order to enable the patient's sense of agency and allow him to feel responsible for his life.

In the treatment itself, my clinical emphasis is usually on the sadomasochistic pathology in the relationship rather than on its symptomatic manifestation as a disorder of sexuality, of drug abuse or of psyche-soma. So that another way of thinking about perversion is as a disorder of sexual regulation and especially of pleasure-pain regulation in the dyad. And although neither of my patients, the gay banker or the dermatologist, suffered from the more primitive chaotic disorganizations, they both had enormous problems with self-regulation. For example, they both had an incapacity to be alone and were perpetually on the prowl for homosexual or heterosexual contacts in order to make a connection, to feel alive, and to allay their anxieties. In so doing they were both ultimately seeking to replay the original dyadic relationship with their caregivers, but this time to get it correctly regulated. Despite countless attempts on both their parts to work this out in real life with a variety of partners, it was only in the psychoanalytic transference relationship that this became a genuine possibility.

In the transference, of course, we eventually expect to see some permutation of the sadomasochistic relations that originally brought the patient into treatment. Our hope is that before they become explosive, we will have built up enough analytic trust to enable the patient to talk about them rather than to abandon the analysis or embroil it in perpetual enactments. The treatment of sadomasochism is one of our most difficult tasks and ultimately, as Freud noted, we must call up the ghosts in order to put them to rest. And while it is indeed tragic if the treatment ends in yet another sadomasochistic impasse, of which the patient might already have had more than his share, I imagine that anyone who has practiced long enough has at least one ending of this sort on his conscience. A redeeming thought is that we continue to talk and theorize about our clinical practice, as I did for so many years with Dr. Lester Schwartz after we wrote our paper together on the Marquis de Sade (Bach & Schwartz, 1972). I believe that to view the therapeutic situation as a human dilemma in which we are mutually engaged and to accept responsibility for our ignorance and our mistakes, is to take one step away from the perversions in the ongoing struggle toward stable and loving commitments.

REFERENCES

Bach, S. (1995). *The Language of Perversion and the Language of Love.* Northvale, NJ: Aronson.

Bach, S., & Schwartz, L. (1972). A dream of the Marquis de Sade: Psychoanalytic reflections on narcissistic trauma, decompensation, and the reconstitution of a delusional self. *Journal of the American Psychoanalytic Association* 20:451-475.

Ferenczi, S. (1933), Confusion of tongues between adults and children. In *Final Contributions to the Problems and Methods of Psycho-Analysis*. London: Hogarth Press, 1955, pp. 156-167.

Freud, S. (1919). A child is being beaten: A contribution to the study of sexual perversions. *Standard Edition* 17:179-204.

Freud, S. (1924). The loss of reality in neurosis and psychosis. *Standard Edition* 19:181-188.

Furman, R. A., & Furman, E. (1984), Intermittent decathexis—A type of parental dysfunction. *International Journal of Psycho-Analysis* 65:423-433.

Young-Bruehl, E. (1988). *Anna Freud: A Biography*. New York: Summit Books.

HOLISTIC CLINICAL MANAGEMENT

CHAPTER 9

Problems of Narcissistic Love

T here was a time, just a few decades ago, when the leading expert on the treatment of narcissism kept a crown and scepter beneath his chair that he would present to his grandiose narcissistic patient at an appropriate moment. Most of us have abandoned this form of deliberate shock therapy because we have come to understand that the counter-transference that produced it is in fact one of the most difficult aspects of the treatment and that, as Freud (1914) noted, our envy for the blissful libidinal position of narcissists, beautiful people, great cats, and children may account to some extent for our difficulty in empathizing with them.

This increasing understanding of narcissism has also widened our diagnostic net beyond the type of narcissist who presents with haughty grandiosity, a sense of entitlement, and shallow and devalued relationships, which I shall call the *overinflated* narcissistic type. Now we may also include in this category those patients who show the "other side of the coin" (Bach, 1977; Broucek, 1982; Gabbard, 1989) and present with complementary feelings of inferiority and hypersensitivity, boredom and uncertainty, and chronic idealizations followed by disillusionments, which I shall call the *deflated* narcissistic type. One tends to think that the overinflated narcissistic type has too much pathological narcissism, whereas the deflated narcissistic type has too little healthy narcissism, but we shall later see that this formulation is somewhat

oversimplified and that both types share a common defect of representational constancy.

Those overinflated patients who present with grandiosity and entitlement tend to form a mirroring transference (Kohut, 1971), in which
the patient insists that the therapist should *reflect* or mirror the patient's grandiose wishes; whereas those who present with depletion and
inferiority tend to form an idealizing transference, in which the patient
insists that the therapist should *embody* his grandiose wishes. While
many narcissistic patients alternate between feelings of grandiosity and
inferiority, the literature has tended to emphasize the grandiose or
overinflated patient, sometimes reserving other diagnoses such as regressed oral hysteric, infantile personality, or masochistic character for
the type who presents with depletion and inferiority. For long time the
treatment of the narcissistic disorders was embroiled in a lively debate
between proponents of conflict and of deficit, but the passage of time
suggests that framing the issues in these terms is not entirely clarifying,
if only because it now seems apparent that developmental deficits lead
to unresolvable conflicts and that unresolvable conflicts engender developmental failures (Auerbach, 1993; Eagle, 1984).

Although overinflated and deflated narcissists are ideal types reflecting only presenting aspects of the personality, I include both in the
diagnosis of narcissism because I feel that the one is often simply the
overt or the covert face of the other (Akhtar & Thomson, 1982). Indeed, an important part of the therapeutic task consists in uncovering
the sense of depletion and inferiority in the overinflated-type narcissist
and in uncovering the grandiosity and entitlement in the deflated-type
narcissist. I also include on this continuum certain patients with narcissistic character disorders who present with symptoms of
perversion, addiction, eating disorders, or psychosomatic complaints,
because I believe these are structurally related and therefore show a
similar evolution in the transference and treatment. I might mention
here my impression that these patients frequently show a history of
unusual sensitivities as young children, so that they might require unusually nurturant or devoted parenting to successfully manage their
unusual temperaments (Ellman, 1992; Suomi, 1991).

In all these conditions there appears to be a difficulty with evocative constancy, that is, a weakened capacity to evoke or hold on to the object representation when the object is absent, or to hold on to the self representation when the object is not there to sustain it. The overinflated narcissist is someone whose sense of his *objects* is fading and who compensates by overinflating himself and insisting he is so powerful that he doesn't need objects, whereas the deflated narcissist is someone whose sense of *himself* is fading and who compensates by overinflating an object and then clinging to this idealized figure for stability.

All these patients have related difficulties either with the immediate experience of themselves as the center of thought, feelings, and action (subjective awareness) or with the awareness of themselves as an object among other objects, a self among other selves (objective self-awareness). At first view, the overinflated narcissist has difficulty being aware of himself as an object in a world of other people, whereas the deflated narcissist has difficulty in the immediate experience of himself as a center of thought, feelings, and action. But both types have persistent difficulties moving back and forth between these two perspectives on the self and integrating them into their representational world (Bach, 1980, 1985).

The normal or neurotic is able to experience both himself and his objects as cohesive and alive because in normal development the self and object representations grow and mature simultaneously, and self-love develops concurrently with object love. But in narcissistic development the overinflated narcissist can experience himself as cohesive and alive only at the expense of devitalizing his objects, whereas the deflated narcissist can keep his objects cohesive and alive only at the expense of devitalizing and fragmenting himself. Because self- and object constancy are the foundation of symbolism, these representational deficits have corresponding symbolic and cognitive deficits such as difficulties in dealing with multiple points of view, in tolerating ambiguity, and so forth. But before exploring how this develops, let me first situate this syndrome on the diagnostic continuum.

The narcissistic personality type can be distinguished from the borderline personality by his better functioning in the real world and by his more cohesive and integrated self- and object representations, leading to a greater degree of fused or modulated aggression. While in the borderline pattern the aggression leaks out and can explode at any moment, in the narcissistic patient whose representational world and sense of self is more stable, the aggression is often linked to particular experiences of narcissistic injury and may yield to interpretation or repair of that injury.

The narcissistic personality disorder can be distinguished from neurotic disorders of the hysterical and obsessive kind by the development of a predominantly narcissistic transference, that is, a transference in which boundaries between self and object are permeable to a greater or lesser degree and can be seen to dissolve within the analytic transference situation, but rarely outside it. There are innumerable practical clues to this situation; for example, the narcissistic patient may often not bother to explain the context of what he is saying because he assumes you are either one with him or not worth informing at all, whereas the neurotic patient will generally tell you what you need to know in order to understand him. Thus the narcissistic patient may speak for days about someone before you discover whether this is a friend, a lover, or some former acquaintance; he may allude to people without actually naming them or allude to events without actually describing them so that after a while you begin to feel as if you too were living in a narcissistic haze and are somewhat disoriented as to time, place, and person. These are merely manifestations of the fact that the narcissistic patient's inner world is focused primarily upon himself or a self-object and that his whole-object relationships are weak and less differentiated.

I believe that many of the narcissistic disorders share a developmental origin in what I have called the anal/depressive/rapprochement/ bisexual phase. This is the pregenital phase that includes Freud's anal stage, Klein's movement from paranoia to reparation and object-love[1],

---

[1] I have, of course, advanced Klein's timetable while retaining her conceptualization, in the belief that this realignment is more in keeping with our current understanding of child development.

Mahler's rapprochement sub-phase, and the bisexual flux characteristic of this period. This is the period when the toddler is first gaining objective self-awareness, the ability to view himself from someone else's perspective, and when he is particularly vulnerable to experiences of humiliation and shame. Shame is the affect that regulates exhibitionism and self-esteem, and in helping to demarcate the boundaries of our difference and separation from others it becomes intimately linked with self and object representations. But even though the interactions at this time are particularly conducive to shame experiences and narcissistic pathology, subsequent developmental restructurings may alter or modify the outcome or may initiate pathology at a later time.

Frequently, however, one finds that events in this period have started a sequence of developmental failures, conflicts and regressions that give rise to the typical problems associated with the continuum of the narcissistic disorders. Some of these problems are:

A: *Disturbances of self-constancy and of self-regulation*

1. There is a subtle disturbance in the sense of bodily continuity so that the patient may experience his body as strange or different, shading into hypochondriacal preoccupations.

2. There is a subtle disturbance of the sense of mental and emotional continuity so that the patient may fear his thoughts and feelings as potentially unstable or subject to sudden and inexplicable shifts, that is, a mild person may momentarily experience himself as Frankenstein.

3. There is a disturbance of self-continuity across alternate states of consciousness, so that the patient's sense of himself may become fragile in states of fatigue, of high arousal, of intoxication, or in dream or dream-like states. There are similar disturbances of the sense of self at moments of transition such as from waking to sleeping, on arriving or departing, traveling, moving, and so forth. All these disturbances of bodily and emotional continuity may be clinically hidden behind some simple statement such as: "I don't feel like myself today." These transitional disturbances shade into:

B: *Disturbances of separateness*

These patients show anxiety at separation or an inability to separate or a difficulty in being alone, which in the deflated narcissistic type is often a symptom or presenting complaint and in the overinflated narcissistic type is generally handled by denial or counter-phobic and manic mechanisms.

C: *Disturbances of object constancy and object relatedness*

One finds a certain interchangeability of objects, shallowness of object relations, or sadomasochistic object relations that tend to be manifestly sadistic in the overinflated type and manifestly masochistic in the deflated type, with the other side of the coin always present in the latent content.

D: *Disturbances of reality testing and of mourning*

The overinflated narcissistic type frequently displays a denial of his limitations, his finiteness, or his vulnerability; he has grandiose fantasies of brilliance, power, and entitlement, and he shows a persistent refusal to admit or to mourn the loss of his own omnipotence. The deflated narcissistic type presents with the obverse feelings of inadequacy, extreme vulnerability, and depression and, while bemoaning the loss of his own omnipotence, he seems to be desperately seeking an omnipotent object to unite with, to idealize, and to appropriate its power.

E: *Disturbances of sexual identity*

Although sexual disturbances are most obvious in narcissistic patients with eating disorders or sexual perversions where they may be consciously acted out, at a less conscious level most narcissistic patients have a persistent desire to be or to become both sexes and they display sexual confusion and androgynous fantasies. This sexual confusion is related to disturbances of separateness and of self constancy, and to an omnipotent denial of limitations.

Diagnostically, one may divide the narcissistic continuum into higher and lower levels according to functioning, but this becomes confusing because of the often enormous discrepancies between the pathology of the inner life and the frequently excellent outward adaptation in this character type. If one were to make a division, I would prefer to make it in terms of those patients who are more or less able to accept symbolic rather than actual gratifications, a point of major importance as we turn to considerations of treatment, especially of the milder addictions and eating disorders.

Narcissistic personalities with addictions and eating disorders are the clearest examples of the disturbances of self-regulation enumerated earlier. The narcissistic addict, bulimic, or anorectic *is attempting by substance abuse to regulate his emotions in order to achieve a state of well being.* In successful psychoanalysis the patient becomes addicted to a human relationship instead of to a substance. This addictive relationship helps the patient manage his anxieties, depressions, and feelings of emptiness in a better way than with earlier objects and develops his ability to regulate himself and eventually to wean himself from the relationship. This therapeutic object relationship (Grunes, 1984) offers the patient a chance to interact with a separate but constant object and to analyze his difficulties in handling both separateness and object constancy.

Although substance abusers and eating disorders offer the most dramatic examples, all the narcissistic disorders may be thought of as showing addictive tendencies. Thus the overinflated narcissist is addicted to a mirroring figure or "yes-man," while the deflated narcissist is addicted to an idealized other who infuses him with life, while both types show "withdrawal symptoms" when the self-object is removed. Such patients may become dependent upon or addicted to the treatment before they have developed real trust in the situation, putting them in conflict between their addictive needs and their potential vulnerability. The natural evolution of the therapy along standard analytic lines, by accepting the patient's projections and without any role playing by the therapist, results in the provision of precisely that sort of therapeutic object relationship that each particular patient needs. But analytic trust may have to be slowly established and then reestablished after each shift in the transference situation (Ellman, 1992).

It is important to note that while the higher level narcissistic patient is able to use the therapeutic object relationship to help himself compensate for deficiencies of self- and object constancy and of self-regulation, patients at the lower level of the continuum may find it difficult to accept a relationship that provides only *symbolic* rather than actual gratifications. Because the development of evocative constancy underlies symbol formation (Auerbach, 1993), such patients have not yet reached that stage where symbolic words replace enactments or acting out. An important treatment goal is to bring this about through a holding environment that provides a constant yet separate object, as well as through understanding, clarification, appropriate therapeutic responses, and, eventually, interpretation.

Although one may quite legitimately view the narcissistic disorders as deep characterological defenses against both libidinal and aggressive conflicts, I find that this conceptualization often leads to ignoring the basic disturbances of self- and object representations and evocative constancy and sometimes encourages premature attempts to break through the narcissistic defenses. Such premature confrontations often lead to narcissistic rage reactions in the overinflated patients and to a pseudo-acquiescence in the deflated patients, but not to structural growth. Effective interpretation of libidinal and aggressive conflicts becomes possible only as self and object representations become more differentiated, constant, and cohesive. This point is clinically marked when the patient begins to experience that *the same reality can be viewed in different ways by different people and that his point of view and the therapist's point of view can both have reality and legitimacy.* This is another way of talking about the attainment of mutual trust in the analytic situation (Ellman, 1991), a trust that these patients lack and that must be affirmed and reaffirmed at different stages of the analysis. Before that time, interpretations of libidinal and aggressive conflict are often counterproductive and, indeed, may spring more from the therapist's countertransference than from the patient's needs.

Many clinicians agree that the countertransference is the major stumbling block in treating narcissistic patients, either because we cannot tolerate the consistent disregard shown for our human rights and our very existence by the overinflated, entitled narcissist, or because we cannot tolerate the idealizations projected onto us by the insecure and deflated narcissistic patient. It may help to remember that behind the former's entitlement lie profound feelings of inadequacy, and behind the latter's experienced inadequacy lie deeper feelings of grandiose entitlement. As the treatment progresses and the defenses are analyzed, these complementary sides should emerge, and ultimately the presenting distinctions between the two types should dissolve as a more complete human being emerges. Of course, no real-life analysis proceeds in so schematic a fashion since in analyzing the narcissistic structures and defenses we are simultaneously uncovering the libidinal and aggressive conflicts and dealing with them as we do in any ordinary analysis.

But as the dissociation decreases so that the patient feels *himself* to be more of a whole and trustworthy person, the patient also begins to experience the *therapist* as more of a whole and trustworthy object. Sometimes the therapist also begins to see the patient in a more complete way and, most interestingly the therapist may feel that he himself has grown from the experience as his own countertransference splits have been dealt with and overcome.

One of the earliest signs of this growing trust may appear in the countertransference with the overinflated patient, when the therapist begins to feel that he is no longer walking on eggshells, and that he can from time to time say exactly what he thinks without totally disrupting the treatment. Similarly, it is a sign of progress when the deflated patient can disagree and maintain his own position without fear, shame, or overcompensation. The emergence of a real dialogue between two separate people signals a new phase in the treatment, but this important goal may require considerable patience, understanding, and technical dexterity to achieve.

Trained as we all have been in a therapeutic model that assumes we are talking to another separate, distinct, and individuated person, it is often quite difficult to imagine the extent to which people suffering from narcissistic problems may live in a world of fusion, merger, and omnipotent fantasies. So it may come as an unwelcome surprise to both parties to abruptly discover that the person with whom we have been working for some time really does not share certain of our basic assumptions about how the world operates.

A few months ago I was consulted by a very competent therapist who had been treating a patient for more than two years with quite positive results. A problem arose when for the first time the therapist needed to change an appointment and offered the patient some alternate hours. Much to the therapist's surprise the patient, who was normally deflated and acquiescent, became outraged at the thought that the therapist could change hours whenever she wanted to, whereas the patient was obliged to conform to the therapist's availability when changing hours. The patient stated with absolute sincerity that she did not see how she could continue in treatment with someone who was so untrustworthy as to change an hour, although in fact the patient herself had frequently changed hours for business reasons, whereas the therapist had never done so before.

The therapist was stunned, as I have been in similar situations, at this unsuspected revelation of the extent of her patient's narcissistic vulnerability. No appeals to reason, no interpretations of the projection or of the transference, no parallels with any childhood feelings or previous situations were of any avail, and, with the treatment hanging in the balance, the therapist had come for consultation. With an increased understanding of what was at issue, she was fortunately able to turn the situation around, but we took the occasion to explore in just how many different areas the therapist's own assumptions about the world were not necessarily shared by the patient. We concluded that for a very long time she would have to make continual allowance for the fact that, in some way, she and her patient were living in different worlds (Bach, 1985) that overlapped to only a limited degree. Each time that their worlds or perspectives clashed, analytic trust would be disrupted and would need to be slowly reestablished. This patient had felt throughout her life that if she made the slightest mistake her parents might discard her like a used Kleenex, and she was treating the therapist in much the same way. But it took a long time before this interpretation could be made.

The kind of incident I describe is, of course, commonplace to anyone who has worked with narcissistic patients, and one that frequently makes the therapist feel he must tread very gingerly. For no matter how many times we experience it, it is always a shock to our own narcissism to realize that another person who seems so like us on the outside may, on the inside, think or feel so differently from us.

It is at this point of the absolutely inevitable transference-countertransference crises that treatment techniques may differ. Instead of advising my supervisee to hand her patient a golden crown or to confront the irrationality of her behavior, I noted it was a positive step that this deflated and compliant patient's grandiosity had finally emerged, be it in ever so distorted a form, and I advocated treating her sense of betrayal by the therapist as a valuable and legitimate feeling.

I must emphasize that all attempts at analyzing the transference in a symbolic way had utterly failed and probably should not have been attempted, because the patient was clearly not yet able to understand that the same reality can be viewed in different ways by different people and that her point of view and the therapist's point of view might both be legitimate. I take it as an axiom that unless we first come to experience the patient's point of view as legitimate, not only as a transference reaction but also as an experiential reality for us, then the patient will hardly ever come to experience that our point of view can also be legitimate. We are looking as it were, to enter the patient's world or psychic reality or to find the kernel of experiential truth in whatever his position may be.

If the patient is coerced, however subtle the method, into accepting our point of view without truly believing it, then his narcissism has not matured but has only been circumvented, and it is very likely to emerge again in distorted and unexpected ways. This situation is related to the unfortunate circumstance we used to encounter in training situations where candidates were assigned to an analyst, which sometimes led the candidate to conclude that his training analysis was "for the Institute" and that he would need a second analysis "for himself." I believe it is of crucial importance for every person to have an analysis that belongs to himself and not to his analyst, no matter how noble and well-intentioned that analyst might be.

But I have mentioned elsewhere the dilemma involved in having to make this unfortunate choice. In principle the treatment should belong to both participants and be a mutually cooperative endeavor or, if not, that fact should be the subject of interpretation or of self-reflection on the part of the analyst. But for mutuality to exist we must have two participants who feel themselves to be autonomous people, capable of saying "yes" and "no" to each other while maintaining respect for each other's point of view. But it is precisely this capacity to form a mature object relationship, a working alliance, or a transference neurosis that is lacking in narcissistic patients to a greater or lesser degree, depending on the extent of disruption to their self-awareness and evocative constancy. A mature relationship and a true transference neurosis require both a self and other who are whole, vital, and unfragmented.

Clearly, the young woman who felt betrayed and ready to leave treatment because her therapist asked her to change an hour had not yet reached this stage of relatedness. And my point is that until she does, we are better advised to take our therapeutic stance within her world rather than attempt prematurely to confront and force her into ours. Although patients of the deflated narcissistic type may acquiesce to our confrontations and interpretations under the sway of the idealizing transference or the threat of losing us, they may only be repeating in the transference that surrender to an ambivalently idealized figure that traumatized them in the first place.

Likewise the overinflated narcissistic type, when prematurely confronted, may become enraged or even leave treatment, as this young woman considered doing. She, however, had been in treatment for some years and was on the verge of transition from insecurity to grandiosity in certain areas, a progressive movement for her. In this case her libidinal attachment to the therapist was sufficient to stand the strain of her ruptured narcissism, but if the same event had occurred two years earlier she might have left treatment without being able to understand why.

One may imagine that we are dealing here with an economic issue, constantly attempting to assess whether the weight of the patient's attachment will bear the strain of our interventions. And, indeed, this is nothing more than we ordinarily do in maintaining friendships and marriages, although to put it so bluntly might make it sound crass. But perhaps rather than only calculate whether, for example, our spouse's affections will tolerate yet another night away from home, what we also concurrently do is to put ourselves in the other's place and try to empathize with how our spouse might feel about it. And it seems we should always do this with our patients, for to treat them mechanically can only result in their reacting to us in a similar mechanical fashion.

All too many of our narcissistic patients have been brought up in mechanical ways. They have been socialized and trained to behave like human beings, but many feel inside as if they were only performing a ritual, going through the motions and, deep down, they know there is something wrong, something not real, something missing.

While many of these patterns may indeed suffer from castration anxiety or penis envy, what they are also complaining of missing is an essential human quality, an inability to be in the world and to feel autonomous, self-sufficient, sexual, and alive. Ultimately, their complaints of inferiority, boredom, meaninglessness, and hypochondriasis refer to this feeling of emptiness that the deflated narcissist may express openly and that the overinflated narcissist defends against with counterphobic activity and manic denial. Although the grandiose narcissist seems to feel entitled to everything, whereas his deflated counterpart appears to feel entitled to nothing, deep down neither of them feels that he has a right to a life of his own. Indeed, many of our narcissistic patients do not feel a right to their own life, and certainly those with addictive problems like bulimics and anorectics do not feel a right even to their own bodies.

It may now become clearer why I place so much emphasis on the narcissistic patient emotionally owning his treatment, because for someone who may not feel a right even to his own life or his own body, it will be a constant problem to feel that he has a right to his own treatment.

As you may anticipate, the issue goes far deeper than finding a benevolent therapist who will permit the patient to have a voice in his
treatment. By the time we see such patients, intricate defensive operations have evolved so that they are no longer capable or even desirous
of collaborating in their treatment. Instead, the deflated narcissist
wants *you* to control him so that he becomes your slave and is em-
powered by you, and the grandiose narcissist wants to control *you* so
that you become his slave and are unable to help him. This plunges us
squarely into problems of sadomasochism.

It should not be surprising to discover that sadomasochism is so
ubiquitous in the narcissistic disorders since I have already suggested
that a frequent fixation point is in the anal/depressive/rapprochement/
bisexual phase. We are all familiar with both the clinging and the sadistic
aspects of anality and rapprochement and the alternating omnipotence
and helplessness characteristic of this age.

It is at this time that the toddler is beginning to integrate his sense
of wholeness and aliveness *(subjective awareness)* with his parents'
and his own developing perspective on him-self as one person among
many others *(objective self-awareness)*. It is also at this time that he is
struggling to integrate the extremes of overinflated and deflated self-
representations and object representations. Externally, one sees this in
the clinging and sadistic behavior that has made this period known as
the "terrible twos." When this struggle to develop evocative constancy
and to modulate and regulate the self- and object representations
does not go well, then the representational stage is already set for the
child to slip easily into the mode of sadomasochism.

Indeed, we might see this stage as a decisive preoedipal influence
on the future love life of the child. We have noted that the normal or
neurotic can experience both himself and his objects as cohesive and
alive because in normal development the self and object representations develop simultaneously and self-love develops concurrently
with object love. In the narcissistic disorders, however, this process
seems to have gone awry.

The overinflated narcissist denigrates his objects yet needs them
to love him, while the deflated narcissist idealizes his objects, who

repeatedly disillusion him. These distortions of the love life arise because of self love and object love have not developed interdependently, and this lack of reciprocity gives them a pathological distortion.

Let me take as an example the case of a mother who lacked self-esteem and masochistically allowed herself to be denigrated by her husband. She then endowed her baby son with her lost phallic-narcissistic powers and he grew up to be an overinflated narcissist, denigrating the very mother who admired him. In this case one might say that the growth of the child's object love for his mother had not kept pace with the growth of his self-love leading to a pathological imbalance in favor of a distorted self-love.

Another example is the case of a very self-centered mother whose narcissism, for complicated reasons, did not extend to her daughter. Unrecognized and unsupported by her mother, this little girl turned to idealizing her father in order to stay alive. In later life she becomes a deflated narcissistic type, feeling inferior and insecure, always looking to worship a powerful man who would protect her. In this case one might say that the growth of the little girl's self-love had not kept pace with the growth of her object love, with a pathological imbalance favoring a distorted object love.

When this struggle to modulate self- and object representations and to develop evocative constancy does not go well, the child is constantly faced with insoluble either-or dilemmas. He cannot arrive at a point that will allow him multiple perspectives on the events in his world, nor a vision that will even slightly legitimize both his view and the view of others. Thus each interaction becomes a battle over the preservation of his very existence, a struggle to the death, a sadomasochistic encounter.

We find that the sadomasochistic attitude runs like a red thread through all the narcissistic disorders: not only the sexual perversions but also the addictions, the eating disorders, and the psychosomatic disorders, as well as the more common character disorders. Alternations between sadism and masochism are ubiquitous and they parallel and reflect fluctuations in self-inflation and self-depletion, in objective and subjective self-awareness and in self-regulation.

I would not want to leave you with the impression that sadomasochism is uniquely an issue of self-representations and self-regulation, for we know that it also involves fascinating problems of pleasure in pain, sexualization of aggression, anal fixations, and issues of autonomy. Normal relationships are loosely coupled systems that leave room for each partner's autonomy, but narcissistic and sadomasochistic relationships are tightly coupled systems which leave little space for individual autonomy. Such relationships are totally entwined, controlling and controlled which is one reason they are often of unusual intensity but also tend to burn out rather rapidly.

Although most patients with narcissistic and borderline transferences will show sadomasochistic fantasies, only some will show actual sexual perversions. While all these patients have undifferentiated self- and object representations, the development of an actual perversion seems to require some particular elision of the relationship to reality.

I have suggested that many sadomasochistic relationships are connected to some early loss that has not been mourned, so that sadomasochistic fluctuations may be viewed as a kind of pathological mourning, a frantic oscillation between admitting that the object is lost or dead and asserting that it is still alive and available. But this, too, can be seen as a problem of object constancy, although there are always elements of defense and compromise formation as well. Our concern is how to deal with the sadomasochist transference and countertransference that will inevitably arise when we work with these patients.

I feel that our attitude in beginning the treatment may be crucial in this respect, and I have mentioned how important it is for the patient to experience the treatment as a collaborative endeavor rather than as the analyst's exclusive province. While a true collaboration may be something that the patient has never before experienced in either his work, his relationships, or his previous therapies, we should nevertheless endeavor to achieve this throughout the vicissitudes of a transference that may run the gamut from mildly to profoundly sadomasochistic. And in order to achieve this goal with patients whose symptoms are grandiosity, idealization, disparagement, and denial, we can do no better than to learn to deal with our own parallel feelings, which will constantly be aroused in our ongoing struggles with the inevitable narcissistic countertransference.

REFERENCES

Akhtar, S., & Thomson, J. A. (1982). Overview: Narcissistic personality disorder. *American Journal of Psychiatry* 139:12-20.

Auerbach, J. S. (1993). The origins of narcissism and narcissistic personality disorder: a theoretical and empirical reformulation. In *Empirical Studies of Psychoanalytic Theories: vol. 4. Psychoanalytic Perspectives on Psychopathology*, ed. J. M. Masling & R. F. Bornstein. Washington, DC: American Psychological Association, pp. 43-110.

Bach, S. (1974). Notes on some imaginary companions. *Psychoanalytic Study of the Child* 26:159-171.

Bach, S. (1977). On the narcissistic state of consciousness. *International Journal of Psycho-Analysis* 58:209-233.

Bach, S. (1980). Self-love and object-love: Some problems of self and object constancy, Differentiation, and integration. In *Rapprochement: The Critical Subphase of Separation-Individuation*, ed. R. Lax, S. Bach, & J. A. Burland. New York: Aronson, pp. 171-197.

Bach, S. (1985). *Narcissistic States and the Therapeutic Process.* New York: Aronson.

Broucek, F. (1991). *Shame and the Self.* New York: Guilford.

Eagle, M. N. (1984). *Recent Developments in Psychoanalysis: A Critical Evaluation.* New York: McGraw-Hill.

Ellman, S. (1991). *Freud's Technique Papers: A Contemporary Perspective.* Northvale, NJ: Aronson.

Ellman, S. (1992). Psychoanalytic theory, dream formation, and REM sleep. In *Interface of Psychoanalysis and Psychology*, eds. J. Barron, M. N. Eagle, & D. Wolitzky. Washington, DC: American Psychological Association.

Freud, S. (1914). On narcissism: An introduction. *Standard Edition* 14:73-102.

Gabbard, G. O. (1989). Two subtypes of narcissistic personality disorder. *Bulletin of the Menninger Clinic* 53:527-532.

Grunes, M. (1984). The therapeutic object relationship. *Psychoanalytic Review* 71:123-143.

Kohut, H. (1971). *The Analysis of the Self.* New York: International Universities Press.

Suomi, S. J. (1991). Early stress and adult emotional reactivity in rhesus monkeys. In *The Childhood Environment and Adult Disease (Ciba Foundation Symposium 156),* ed. D. Barker. Chichester, England: John Wiley & Sons, Ltd, pp. 171-188.

CHAPTER 10

On Treating the Difficult Patient

P erhaps the primary problem in engaging the difficult patient is to build and retain what Ellman (1991) has called analytic trust. These difficult patients have generally lost their faith not only in their caregivers, spouses and other objects, but also in the world itself as a place of expectable and manageable contingencies. Imagine what it would be like to inhabit a world where you never feel certain that your loved ones will be there when you come home, and not even certain that your home will still be there. Imagine what it is like to turn on your kitchen stove or your car ignition, always half-expecting them to explode. Imagine what it is like to feel that the air you breathe is toxic or that the air supply is running out. These patients have lost their trust not only in people but also in the environment as a reliable place that will hold them safely. So one task we have is to restore this faith, and to rebuild it again and again as it inevitably gets lost in the vicissitudes of the transference.

We do this by making the analytic consulting room a safe and reliable place and by being absolutely truthful with the patient about everything that occurs in this place and that happens between us. Whenever the situation becomes momentarily unreliable, sometime because we have failed as we inevitably must over the course of years, we recognize this and analyze our own reactions as well as the patient's, for there is no way that a patient who mistrusts everything will trust us at all if we insist on leaving ourselves out of the equation. There is a way of being absolutely straight with the patient without indulging in confessions, apologia, or gross parameters, and this way is different and must be worked out with each individual patient.

I say "worked out" with the patient because, even if the patient is unable to engage in mutual collaboration, as most of these patients at first are not, *we* are always collaborating with them by going along with their vision of reality even when they reject ours. In the transference regression these patients do not really experience themselves as completely separate, and so they cannot believe or coexist with separate psychic realities. The idea that the same reality can be viewed in different ways by different people, and that the patient's *and* the analyst's views can both have truth and legitimacy, is often beyond their emotional comprehension. Thus a true collaboration between two independent people may be impossible, and we must defer to the patient's vision of reality until he becomes able to tolerate our presence and psychic reality in the room with him.

By this means we enter the patient's phenomenal world and begin to build analytic trust, which at first may be more of a trust in the safety of the analytic setup than in us as an object. For in many cases we do not really exist as an object until we make a mistake, or until something happens to make us loom up as a threatening stranger. Such disruptions of the budding narcissistic transference and the therapeutic alliance may result from the patient's impulses or our own ineptness, expressed in a mutual enactment or a projective identification, but they demand immediate understanding and rectification.

Each episode of attempted alliance, disruption of the alliance, and repair raises the mutual trust to a higher level—we have gone through something together and survived it. Each episode of mismatch, disruption, and repair is also an ongoing process of regulation of the dyadic system. I am emphasizing the simultaneous emergence and interplay of mutual trust and mutual regulation in the analytic dyad. What do I mean by mutual regulation?

In the days when psychologists still experimented with conditioning rats, a well-known cartoon showed one rat in a cage telling another: "I've got this guy trained by now—every time I press the lever, he gives me a pellet of food!" The psychologist, of course, felt that he was conditioning or regulating the rat, but indeed they had arrived at a jointly satisfactory state of mutual regulation. They could trust each other to be constant, reliable, mutually satisfying objects. Now this sort of mutual regulation is continually occurring, often without awareness, in the successful mother-infant dyad and also in the successful patient-analyst dyad. The analytic dyad is unusual in the analyst's insistence that dysregulations should ultimately be verbalized and analyzed, not just remedied or glossed over. But since so many of our difficult patients are products of poorly regulated mother-infant dyads or badly regulated family systems, it is not always easy to know how to handle any immediate situation.

Let me be doubly concrete and imagine a situation where a new patient complains of being too hot or too cold in the consulting room and asks that the temperature be regulated. Do we simply comply as social convention demands, do we question and investigate further, or, having checked that the temperature is normal, do we make an interpretation about possible emotional reactions and physiological changes? I suspect there is no cookbook answer to this kind of question, and that the complexities of mutual regulation in the treatment process can be addressed only through the complexities of mutual discussion in the supervision process in which the two parties have learned to trust each other and to speak openly. In this sense, good supervision is similar to good therapy.

But I hope that by now I have made it clear why I feel that analytic trust is based on and grows with successful mutual regulation. The patient arrives to find you always there and mostly on time; his own irregularities of arrival and of thought and emotion are met with temperance and understanding; the couch is always there, the temperature is usually comfortable, and nothing physical ever explodes. Slowly, he begins to develop trust, first in the physical regularities of the analytic holding world, then in the process by which each mismatch is slowly understood and repaired, then in the reliability of the analyst as some kind of part object or self object and, ultimately, in the reliability of the analyst as a separate whole object.

Meanwhile, we are uncovering and analyzing those regulatory difficulties that most of these patients have even if they don't know it. I am talking about disturbances of breathing, of sleeping, of eating, of bodily functioning, and of orientation in the world, but I also include disturbances of emotional regulation that are inseparable from the physiological, for example, dysregulation of affect so that highs and lows are too extreme, too prolonged, or too rapidly cycled and unpredictable. Above all, I am referring to a kind of intermittent cathexis of the object (Furman & Furman, 1984) so that object constancy is almost always in question. Many of these patients have experienced this intermittent cathexis from their own caregivers, who attended to them only when they were needed as narcissistic objects. When grown up, they tend not only to repeat this intermittent cathexis with their own objects but also to experience themselves as only intermittently alive and coherent; their own self-constancy is always in question. Of course, regulatory problems like disturbances in orientation, emotional regulation or intermittent cathexis will emerge in the transference anyhow, with the patient either doing it to you or getting you to do it to him. But since these transference reactions are so often accompanied by intense rage and other blinding emotions, I think the analyst is at a great advantage if the subject has already been raised and discussed in a historical context.

Although the earliest nonverbal and verbal interactions can profoundly influence brain chemistry and synaptic growth, I believe that later verbal interactions and mutual regulation can also influence brain chemistry and alter behavior at least as much as psychotropic medications. Over the course of the first few years infants learn to respond at the symbolic level as well as at the sensorimotor levels of the mother-infant interaction. But even adults, and particularly difficult patients, continue to respond at the sensorimotor-physiological level, precisely because that is where the earliest mutual regulation went awry. These sensorimotor-physiological responses frequently manifest themselves in inappropriate or negative transference reactions or enactments, which are often as hard for the patient to understand as they are for us. I try in the first sessions with these patients to get an overview not only of the dynamic picture but also a history of the early dysregulation with which it is entwined. This frequently interests the patient sufficiently so that he may try to fill in the missing data or to verify it on his own initiative. I find that working with this from the very beginning is a big help in dealing with transference disruptions, in understanding and managing them, and in arriving at the better regulated interaction that is the foundation of basic trust.

Naturally, I go along with those patients who refuse to talk about anything but the immediate here and now, but I treat it as a kind of defensive distortion. Normally, past, present and future interconnect and continually retranscribe each other, so that touching a life at any point should connect us with the whole. But with difficult patients it is easier to move the case if one has a handle on both the past and the present.

Since there is little time for theoretical discussion, let me simply state my belief that controversies such as here and now versus then and there, deficit versus conflict, hermeneutics versus science, interpretation versus holding, and other similar shibboleths are often false dichotomies that promote political correctness and keep us from thinking and speaking about what we actually do. I recall that in the not too distant past the fear of employing parameters made a whole generation of analysts talk and act as if the political police were just around the corner. So in the multiplicity of positions about the analyst's stance with the patient, it still seems to me that the best place to be most of the time is as close to the patient's phenomenal world as possible.

Just to put a little flesh on these bones, here is a brief example from a recent consultation.

A competent and experienced analyst presents a young professional woman, attractive and successful, whom he has seen in therapy for three months and who is threatening to quit. The patient complains of her need to attach herself to some man, but when he gets too close she feels obliged to break it off. She divorced her husband after starting an affair with an older man who lived in another country. When this older man phoned her to break off the relationship, she developed frightening somatic symptoms; called the Emergency Medical Service, and threw herself into the arms of the responding ambulance driver who was obliged to hold her and caress her to calm her down. She then had a brief affair with this driver that helped carry her through the period of breakup with the older man. She is able to say that her mother was always nervous and agitated, that the beloved older man was, in her own words, "a fantasy father figure" and that her father used to rub her legs to put her to sleep, but none of this seems to help her or to engage her.

When the therapist takes a long weekend vacation, she goes to a psychic who gives her a piece of rock that makes her feel more calm and secure. Over the weekend she joins a group of Buddhists who meditate and chant. When the therapist tries to connect these enactments with his absence, she appears to find him vaguely amusing and seems unaffected. Shortly thereafter she complains that therapy is boring, is not helping, and makes plans to leave. The therapist repeatedly focuses on her need to attach herself to some man and to break it off when he gets too close, but when this interpretation does not seem to help, he comes for a consultation. Talking with the therapist in the way that I have here helps him find a way into the case. He now remembers that when the patient first went to kindergarten, her mother dropped her off in front of the schoolhouse and she became disoriented and never found her way to the classroom. He remembers that the patient always envied those little girls whose mothers shampooed their hair, because her mother never touched her like that. As the therapist begins to inquire into other areas of self- and mutual regulation, the patient becomes more responsive. As a young woman she felt that she lacked "discipline," and she moved to Germany in the hope that living in Germany might instill some discipline in her. Now he helps her understand that her "lack of discipline" is really an inability to self-regulate, connected to her mother's failures to help her regulate when she was a child. The patient stops talking about leaving and becomes more interested in her history. The treatment is under way.

I have been emphasizing mutual regulatory processes both because they are terribly important with the more disturbed patient and also because we normally don't hear much about them in Freudian theory, where the economic point of view has gone out of fashion. Nevertheless, many of these patients *know* there is something wrong with their regulatory processes but are unable to conceptualize it, and have given themselves explanations such as "I don't have any discipline," "My trouble is I love too much," "I'm disorganized and disoriented and it's genetic," and so on. They are often interested to discover that these lifelong issues may stem from a chronic dysregulation of the dyad or family system, and that self-regulation can be learned.

Approaching these issues from the economic or regulatory side is usually much easier for difficult patients, most of whom have problems with reflective self-awareness and symbolization. The patient who went to see a psychic while her analyst was away could not see any connection between these two events, and would probably have been frightened and fled if she had. But I do believe that talking with her about the stone the psychic gave her and her psychophysiological reactions to its solidity and permanence would have elicited her own feelings of tenuousness and impermanence, which underlie her belief that she lacked discipline. I would then anticipate associations about childhood attempts at self-healing by playing with solid objects or putting herself in situations, like the Buddhist chanting, which gave her a temporary sense of solidity and stability. If she became interested in this, one might track the changes in her feelings of insubstantiality and, only after a long time, begin to relate these to the analyst's physical or emotional absence.

Now even in this oversimplified case vignette, there are so many things going on simultaneously and so many possible theoretical levels and viewpoints that the clinician may well wonder how to sort it out or where to begin. Do we address the patient's complaint that she needs to attach herself to some man but then feels compelled to break it off? The therapist did try to make just such transference interpretations when she threatened to quit, but to no avail. Should we address her affair with the oedipal older man who calmed her and soothed her like her own father when he used to rub her legs to put her to sleep? She makes these connections herself, because she knows about the Oedipus complex, but they touch nothing in her. Should we deal with her anger at her mother, who abandoned her on her first day at school and presumably never shampooed her lovingly as she imagined other mothers did? Should we interpret her father's leg massages as substitutes for her mother's shampoos? While all these dynamic connections are valid enough, I am reasonably sure that initially they would get nowhere.

If we are only able to listen carefully enough, patients will usually prescribe exactly what is necessary for their healing to begin. In this case, in response to a long weekend break, the patient reacts by finding a hard, permanent, massageable object, and a state of consciousness in which she can feel alone yet surrounded by others. So we know that she is unusually sensitive to separations but is able to deal with them only in a concrete way. She requires a regulatory dyad that will stabilize and solidify both her self-regulation and her analytic trust, yet at the same time she is likely to struggle against those very parameters such as increased frequency and use of the couch that will help the dyad become regulatory. We handle this by remaining phenomenologically close to her concrete use of objects and things in the interests of self-regulation, while at the same time trying to relate them to her earlier history of dysregulation.

Thus, with these patients, we start from the concrete and move to the abstract, we start from the physical and move to the mental and emotional, just as we always start from whatever is self-centered and only gradually move to whatever is object-centered. We do this because their deficiencies of symbolization and self-awareness lead them to communicate impulsively by enactments that are sometimes unintelligible and often uninterpretable. They respond at this behavioral and sensorimotor level because their basic mistrust and ongoing

dysregulation have prevented them from developing the kind of separateness and transitional space, the impulse control, the symbolic
abilities, and the degree of self-reflection that would be prerequisite
for the use of classical analytic technique.

One might say that classical technique assumes a large degree of
shared reality between analyst and patient, an assumption that usually does not hold with the difficult patient. One way that children
learn about reality is by reading their mother's face and learning that
she has a mind and feelings that are sometimes the same as theirs and
sometimes different. Ideally, they learn that their own feelings and
their mother's feelings both have reality and legitimacy. But when
difficult patients say, "I never knew what my mother was thinking or
feeling," they are telling you that they still can't read how other people
think or feel and that they still can't believe that their own feelings are
real or legitimate.

Caregivers convey reality by legitimizing the child's emotions and
thoughts. If the mother's face conveys one meaning and her
metacommunication in a different modality conveys another meaning,
then the child may not become schizophrenic but he is likely to become a difficult patient. Problems of reality are tremendously
amplified in the psychoanalytic situation, not only because of the potential conflict between the psychic realities of patient and analyst but
also because of the many different levels of reality on which the
treatment exists. Do the patient and analyst really love each other or
really want to kill each other, or is it only metaphorical? At times it
certainly feels real enough to both participants. Ideally, the analyst
can move freely between levels of reality and encompass the metaphor, but the difficult patient, who could never read his mother's face
and be sure of reality, has big problems achieving this.

In the psychoanalytic situation this often emerges as an underlying sadomasochistic struggle over whose version of reality should be
accepted. Freud (1915) speaks of "women of elemental passionateness" who treat transference love as real love and "refuse to accept the
psychical in place of the material" (pp. 166-167). But one cannot interpret the transference, which is a metaphor, to a patient whose

mental organization is unable to accommodate the symbolism of metaphor. In practice this means that such patients will confuse or confabulate what should be transferential and symbolic issues with real issues of love or death, and will struggle with the analyst as if he were in fact refusing to love them or trying to rape or kill them. The patient I discussed had a very real fear of her own "elemental passionateness," which was one reason she was so hesitant to allow herself to become deeply involved in treatment.

These patients are unable to understand that the same reality can be viewed in different ways by different people and that their point of view and the analyst's point of view can both have reality and legitimacy. This is because of their great difficulty shifting between levels of meaning, symbolism, and reality, but it is precisely at these shifts or transitions between levels, contexts, and frameworks that most transference disruptions occur and also that the greatest potential for change emerges (Bach, 1994).

The patient, who, in response to a weekend break, goes to a psychic and gets a rock to calm her, would very likely have become angry and upset had the analyst continued to insist on the connection between these two events. I believe that to conceptualize this as denial is misleading. She would have experienced the analyst's insistent interpretations just as she experienced her mother's dropping her off outside the schoolhouse, as a dysregulation and a desertion. She would have become confused and disoriented and would have felt lost. This confusion, which is a mental disorientation at transitions between levels of symbolism and contextual frameworks, may often be expressed or paralleled by a physical disorientation at transitions between places and events.

In treatment we hold the patient in the analytic framework, and a good deal of our effort goes toward maintaining and adjusting that framework, which the patient is constantly probing in order to test the levels of reality and learn how much he can trust us. Through enactments and counterenactments, through projective identifications that are contained and metabolized, through constructions and interpretations and through the vicissitudes of the transference, a transitional space develops in which confusion, ambiguity, and separation can be tolerated and explored. This feels to the patient very much as if, instead of being dropped off outside the school, the analyst had instead taken her by the hand and accompanied her into the classroom.

Eventually, a psychoanalytic space develops that is able to contain two whole, autonomous individuals who are capable of loving and hating each other and of trying to deal with each other's psychic realities. By then the patient's language and verbal behavior will truly be linked to his sensorimotor and nonverbal behavior and the analyst's interpretations will be heard not as boundary violations or contradictory communications, but as potentially helpful contributions. But by then, of course, the treatment is almost over.

One may well ask, as indeed this book's editor[1], Dr. Carolyn Ellman, did ask me, "So what's Freudian about that?" Upon reflection, one of the things that seems Freudian to me is that I was trained as a Freudian analyst and still believe that the classical method is the paradigm we strive for with the ideal analytic patient. The modifications that Freudian analysts have evolved over the years originated with classical technique and have a historical continuity with it. They were introduced as it became clear that classical technique didn't always work well enough for patients with severe problems of trust, of self-regulation, of self-reflexivity, and of symbolization. The classical method, when strictly enforced with these patients, sometimes resulted in losing the patient completely or producing a stalemate or a pseudoanalysis, where the patient goes through the motions of an analysis out of compliance or desperation, but without belief.

Working from the technical stance I described, these difficult patients often may and sometimes may not become amenable to strict classical technique. But at least they always know that the transference feelings they experienced in the treatment felt real to them and were acknowledged by me, and that the unconscious fantasies that

---

[1] This chapter was originally published in the book *The Modern Freudians: Contemporary Psychoanalytic Technique.*

emerged were their fantasies and not mine. For people who already have difficulty moving between levels of reality, nothing can be more important than learning to trust their own feelings in the heat of the analytic situation. If they can also learn to accept *my* feelings, then they have come a very long way toward resolving the sadomasochistic struggle over whose version of reality can be trusted. And the primacy of this struggle, between awareness and defense, between self and other, and between love and hate is, after all, an essential part of what we understand as the Freudian vision of life and of psychoanalysts.

REFERENCES

Bach, S. (1994). *The Language of Perversion and the Language of Love.* Northvale, NJ: Aronson.

Ellman, C., Grand, S., Silvan, M., & Ellman, S., eds. (1998). *The Modern Freudians: Contemporary Psychoanalytic Technique.* Northvale, NJ: Jason Aronson.

Ellman, S. (1991). *Freud's Technique Papers: A Contemporary Perspective.* Northvale, NJ: Aronson.

Freud, S. (1915). Observations on transference love. *Standard Edition* 12:159-171.

Furman, R. A., & Furman, E. (1984), Intermittent decathexis—A type of parental dysfunction. *International Journal of Psycho-Analysis* 65:423-433.

Schore, A. N. (1994), *Affect Regulation and the Origin of the Self: The Neurobiology of Emotional Development.* Hillsdale, NJ: Lawrence Erlbaum Associates.

CHAPTER 11

The Sense of Aliveness and
Feelings of Being Real

A number of years ago I began work with a patient named Susan who helped me to think more about certain essential features of life, namely, the experience of aliveness and the feeling of being real. This young woman recalled that she had never been touched by her mother in any sensuous or life-affirming way, and that the mother would also recoil at any attempts on Susan's part to touch or hug her. But this was only one of a number of factors that combined to leave her with the feeling that she wasn't really alive or that she didn't feel real.

Although Susan was in her late twenties and had managed to graduate from an Ivy League college, she had never been able to organize herself sufficiently to hold any kind of a job or to do anything to support herself. She was at that time being supported by the man she lived with, a successful investment banker, and she spent her days tending to the house, watching daytime serials, having erotic daydreams and bogged down in repeatedly failed efforts to start some little business of her own that her boyfriend had offered to bankroll. Although she was obviously quite bright, her reporting about her business efforts was so vague and circumstantial that I couldn't get a clear idea of what was really going wrong. I could sense a profound shame about her inability to accomplish anything substantial in life, although this was often defended against by put-downs of other people or boasting about her own superior tastes. I never commented on this because she seemed too narcissistically vulnerable, but from time to time she would make a sarcastic remark suggesting that she knew only too well that her characterization of other people as "losers" applied most profoundly to herself.

One day about two months into the analysis, she was describing to me the difficulty she had in following directions while driving her car, and on inquiry she explained that she had the same difficulty reading a map. I have often seen such difficulties in adults, who as children, had never been able to orient themselves around their mothers, and this usually resolves as the analysis progresses and the patient begins to orient for the first time around the analyst (Bach, 1977, 2006). And in fact this happened in the course of Susan's analysis. But there was something subtly different in this description and, suddenly suspecting that she might be struggling with some neurological deficit, on the spur of the moment I wondered if she would see a neuropsychologist.

The extensive testing surprised us all. As the neuropsychologist said: "I never would have suspected from talking to her beforehand how poorly she would do on these tests. She has compensated to an astonishing degree for these major visual and psychomotor disabilities; someone with this degree of impairment usually acts as if they're partially blind and often needs a person to help them around and explain things to them."

So Susan was started on a course of sensory retraining and visual correction that involved wearing contact lenses, multiple intensive focusing and visual exercises and so forth, and was tried on medication for ADHD. The initial improvement was dramatic, but what was even more interesting was the change this produced in her self-image and her re-interpretation of her history. Facts now became clarified that had long been obscured in a cloud of shame. She was able to realize and to tell me that, throughout her life and even at her prestigious university, she had never been able to read more than one or two pages of a book, and had consistently fudged the rest, while concealing from others and then eventually from herself the extent of her disability. This applied not only to reading but in general to almost everything that she could not immediately grasp and that had to be explained to her. Thus, in effect, she was hindered from learning anything that she didn't already know, both because of structural difficulties with reading and word processing, and because a blanket of shame kept her from admitting her own ignorance.

These difficulties had existed from the very beginning of her schooling and, while her intelligence allowed her to find work-arounds so that her grades were more or less acceptable, she knew that she couldn't tell anyone about this, that she was different from her peers and she had a deep feeling that she was profoundly isolated, alone and lonely. She developed a kind of false identity of a sarcastic joker that she deployed with her peers and this allowed her to feel superior and misunderstood when they rejected her.

I decided to become actively engaged in referring her to doctors and coordinating the complicated assessment and treatment situation. I had made the decision to do this after it became crystal clear to me that she was totally unable to manage it by herself, just as she had been totally unable to manage the normal affairs of everyday life. She had in fact been in a previous analysis for about three years and a therapy before that, which had changed nothing at all despite many interpretations of her masochism and passive aggression. Although Susan recognized some truth in these observations, she felt that at the time they were useless to her. The analysis ended when her analyst gave her a deadline to go get a job, reproached her for not trying hard enough and then referred her to a social worker for supportive treatment. Considering all of this in context, I had decided to risk whatever transference problems might be created by my unusual activity; I did not want her to have yet another analysis where the protocol was respected but the patient died.

Susan was immensely grateful that I had taken her neurological disability seriously, which she herself had never been able to do, and this trust allowed her to tell me things that she had never before revealed to anyone. She had been raised in an upper middle-class family where both parents were unsuccessful professionals trying to keep up appearances. It turned out that her family was extremely dysfunctional; the mother had had numerous affairs that the children knew about and the father had lost most of the money they had inherited. The parents themselves didn't seem to know how to manage in life, and they were quite incapable of teaching Susan how to plan, how to organize, how to study or how to find out what might be meaningful to her in her own life. We saw a typical example one weekend when her parents came to visit with the intention of taking her out for a birthday dinner but, after an hour of wrangling, were unable to get the entire family out of the house to actually accomplish this task.

A few months into the analysis when Susan was supposed to be doing eye exercises to help with her severe visual disabilities, I accidentally discovered that she wasn't doing them at all because she was unable to sit by herself for longer than a few minutes. So I suggested that she bring them into the session, where she set them up on my bookcase and found that she was able to do the required fifteen minutes by herself while I watched and we occasionally talked.

As this was going on, I remember thinking about sitting with my own children as they did their homework. At this point, Susan began to talk about how as a child no one ever sat with her while she was doing her homework, nor helped her to brush her teeth or get to sleep or performed the other regulating and monitoring activities that parents usually do and that go without notice.

Although reliable data on her infancy was lacking, we learned that her mother had been quite depressed in her early years and that she was brought up in an atmosphere of benign neglect—ostensibly loved by both parents but completely unattended to. By the age of seven this situation was so clear to her that she recalls making a bet with a visiting girlfriend that she could write an obscenity on some large drawing paper and show it to her mother who was in deep conversation with her own friend and that she wouldn't even notice it! And in fact Mother looked at the drawing and said something like: "Yes, Yes, dear! Very beautiful…," thus, confirming Susan's cynicism and despair at ever being able to be recognized or to depend on any adult. Although this was an experiment worthy of Piaget, this precocious little girl was destined to become an adult incapable of functioning in the real world.

It took me a long time to understand many aspects of how this destiny was realized. There seemed to be multiple causes, for example, a neurological defect that was not remediated but instead intensified by parental neglect, though some might argue that the original defect itself might have been the product of early misattunement. I will not go into that here, but rather confine myself to the issue of how Susan's sense of aliveness and realness was affected by her psychic and somatic situation, and how the parametric insertion of my own reality into this equation might have affected the outcome.

But first, just to give you a phenomenal sense of how it felt to inhabit Susan's world, let me cite almost at random some things she used to say about her body and her mind:

One day, after a while in analysis, she said to her older brother: "You know, no one ever touched us or hugged us when we were growing up." He said: "That's true, so let's do it now." So they gave each other a big hug and held on for several minutes, just hugging each other.

One day after she realized that if you want to be touched you have to touch other people too, she began to give massages to her boyfriend. He said that no one had ever massaged him like that before; it was highly unusual. She said: "Yes!" She knew that must be true. She then went on to describe how she would touch each bone, tendon and integument as if exploring them for the first time. She said: "It's as if a Martian came down to earth and was trying to figure out all about human anatomy by touching people."

Once she said: "It takes hard work to make things real. I have to keep telling myself—try, try, try to really look at someone or something, try to really talk to someone and be authentic." While she was doing her eye exercises she remarked: "I need someone to watch me while I'm doing it. It makes it alive and meaningful...otherwise it's just a task and I lose interest and can't go on. It's very important to me that you're watching me and really looking..."

She had just previously been talking about an acquaintance she was attracted to, Roberto, who observes her all the time, watches her closely, is tuned in to her. "It makes me feel alive, like I really exist. When no one is watching me it feels like Berkley's tree that falls unobserved in the forest---did it ever really happen?"

Susan's eyes had never really caught my attention, but after a year or so I thought that I began to notice a glint in her eyes that I hadn't seen before. I wasn't certain of my observation and I wondered: Was it because her depression was lifting, was it because she was actually seeing better as a result of her eye exercises, was it the medication, was it that she had seen a glint in my eyes for the first time and was able to reflect it?

When I told her about this, she was interested but did not seem surprised and said: "It's because I'm seeing you clearly for the first time. Before you looked like some cardboard image, not real or three dimensional, and I think that it's maybe because now I'm focusing on you where you really are—before I was always focusing either in front of you or behind you and that made things looks peculiar, fluid, not solid, unreal..."

One day as she was coming in to the session she touched her finger to her thumb and said: "It's a miracle—the fingers seem to know where the thumb is without thinking about it! My body is coming alive!"

One day after about a year of analysis, she said to me: "You know, when I first came here I had to tell you everything that happened to me in all the details because otherwise it didn't feel real. Now I don't have to do that anymore." Although I was interested in how this worked, she said that she didn't want to talk about it anymore. I think that at the time it all still felt too fragile for her and she couldn't risk talking about it.

In the first year or two when she remembered to give me a check for the previous month, there was almost always some mistake in it: an incorrect date, a numbered sum that didn't match the written sum, etc. At first I didn't inspect the checks for fear of humiliating her, but when I had to return them because the bank wouldn't cash them, I realized that this was an even greater humiliation and began to go over them carefully. I also began to understand how difficult it was even for me to really believe in the extent of her deficit. She was, after all, an Ivy League graduate and even the neuropsychologist had been astonished at the discrepancy between her presentation and her test results. Such was the extent of the False Self she had created and lived with, deceiving even herself.

When she wrote checks in my presence she scribbled them hastily, but I soon learned that she was convinced that no matter how carefully she worked, it would never come out right, so it was less humiliating to appear to not even try. This had been a guiding principle since she was a child. It later came out that each month's bill would come to her as a great surprise, since she could never fully believe that one month would follow the next, that our work would actually continue and that I would really be there for each appointment with her.

So this defect in her sense of reality and of her own existence was inevitably coupled with doubts about the substantial existence of other people. I knew that her mother had scarcely touched her and had rejected her hugs, but I now learned that her boyfriend, Steven, also did not welcome touching or cuddling and would rarely have sex with her. Nevertheless, he insisted that they sleep in the same bed together and often repeated that he couldn't live without her. In his work as an investment banker he was travelling almost three quarters of the year, but he would phone her fairly often and tell her how much he missed her. Although they had been living together for a few years and she was being supported like a princess, she herself felt that their relationship was extremely strange and frustrating, but she couldn't leave because she felt unable to take care of herself financially and unable to have a life of her own. She was ambivalent about demanding marriage because she didn't feel entitled to it, because she felt she had nothing to offer, because she was afraid of upsetting the equilibrium, and because she was terrified at even the thought of having children.

Because Susan was rather pretty, smart and nervously outgoing, she had no difficulty in attracting men and she was sometimes propositioned when Steven was out of town. She felt very tempted because they barely ever had sex, but at the same time she felt guilty because she was being kept in high style and also because she truly loved Steven, or as deeply as she was capable of loving anyone.

After one brief flirtation with a man she said: "With Steven I feel like his shadow, but with this man I felt like there were two people in the room." At another time she said: "I started making out with this guy and for just a few minutes I had a glimpse of what normal people might feel like when they're having sex and why it might be fun." For her it was never really fun, but rather a task to be more or less successfully negotiated. At the beginning of analysis she was always somewhere outside of herself and observing herself, unable to maintain a state of subjectivity or to give herself wholeheartedly to anyone or anything.

She believed that her boyfriend loved her at the beginning and admired her and really expected her to do great things. Now that she's frozen and hasn't been able to move he has become terribly disappointed, disillusioned—he still loves her but has withdrawn and no longer wants sex—she no longer thrills him like she did. He actually told her one day—"I had great hopes for you and I got disillusioned again and again. I still love you and will support you but I'm just not turned on anymore..."

From as far back as she could remember, Susan had always felt that she didn't belong. We have seen why she felt that she didn't belong with her mother, and when she turned to her father she again found someone who loved her but so ineptly, with such confusion, anxiety and turmoil, that there was no belonging there either.

But since human beings are like pack animals, feeling that one does not belong to the pack contributes to feelings of not being real and not being alive. Patients who feel they are not alive or real and do not belong very often feel that they do not belong to the human race at all, that, literally, they are not human. Think of how people who live in the world of pornography and leather sometimes talk of themselves as being "on the prowl." Think of Gregor Samsa in Kafka's Metamorphosis, who awakens one day to find himself changed into a monstrous verminous bug. This is often how many of these patients feel, although the analyst may never realize this or have a very hard time believing it.

In the first year of treatment I met Susan in the waiting room taking off her ear buds and asked her what she was listening to. She told me with great excitement about an electronic music group of which she had been a devoted fan for many years. It turned out that they often performed in helmets, metal finger gloves and costumes that made them look like robots, and that one of their first albums was titled *Human After All* and their most recent one was called *Alive!*

When I enquired about this she said: "Sure! Think of Frankenstein, the Golem, Batman, the Tin Woodman, Blade Runner. It's archetypical!"

It belatedly dawned on me that this might be exactly how Susan felt, and one day when she was talking about how much better she was doing, I asked her about it. She said: "I'll try to describe to you what it felt like, although I'm not sure how clear I can be. It was like living in a shadow world, a half-world of darkness; everything was vague and obscure, unclear and half-alive. Not exactly like being like an animal—more like being half a person and half an animal, like those figures that are half woman and half fish, or half man and half horse. I would look out into the light and be dazzled by it; there was never even a thought that I could be out there and possibly become a whole person, a real human being and live in a human world the way I feel I do today!"

In a moment I will offer some thoughts about common countertransference issues with these patients and with psychosomatic issues in general. But first I want to continue with Susan's story.

Steven had gone on a long trip during which their communication had been very sporadic. Susan kind of fell apart when he didn't phone her for almost a week. She became unable to schedule or keep any appointments, to stick to any task or work consecutively for more than a few minutes, to keep her mind on any one thing, or to eliminate what she called the constant background "chatter," that is, the unspoken voices that she heard in her head reproaching her for not being more efficient, for being lazy, stupid, undisciplined, etc. As usual, she then began to fantasize about hooking up with some other guy, but she talked about it with me and eventually she didn't even try. Towards the end of the trip she and Steven spoke on the phone and she reminded him that it was their anniversary the day after he returned. He said—"Great, let's go out and have a special dinner together and celebrate!"

Before he returned she made several conflicting appointments for herself and in the process, effectively interfered with their dinner together. He got very upset and said: "I don't know who you are...you've become someone else. Why did you do that?"

She was able to think about it herself and finally she told him: "I was afraid to face you alone, across the table from you. I think you are very disappointed in my inability to do anything and that you're just waiting for an opportunity to break up with me and abandon me. I was terrified to be alone with you because I think you despise me and are just waiting to leave me."

Steven started to cry and said: "I would never abandon you. I love you and I want to do whatever I can for you. In fact, it felt to me as if you were playing some game with me, just using me, as if it was you who have really been abandoning me the last year or two..."

Now they are both crying and unable to talk...Eventually he repeats: "I love you. I would never abandon you..."

It occurs to her to say: "I was so afraid that you would abandon me like everyone else has, that I just kept trying to abandon you first..."

When she came for her session and related this to me, Susan was in tears. She kept repeating: "He said he would never abandon me...Nobody else ever said that to me before and really meant it..."

Later in the sessions she reported that, after that evening with Steven, she had been able for the first time in her life to concentrate for a sustained period on doing some work; she had stayed up two nights in a row to complete a project she had become impassioned about. I suggested that she could accomplish this because, after the conversa-

tion with Steven, she felt for the first time that she had a safe and secure base to operate from. She agreed and said that she felt changed—
that she was never again going to doubt that he was holding her in his
mind.

I must admit that I felt somewhat skeptical about this—it seemed
too dramatic and there had been other times when I felt Susan to be
somewhat histrionic. But in fact the improvement held up for a long
time, and I began to believe that something had really changed.

While I was surprised at the rapid and dramatic way this occurred, I have, over the years, seen the same effect in a number of
other cases. I recall seeing a blocked writer, a challenging patient but
one who, because of his extraordinary sensitivity and intelligence,
was able to explain the process with great clarity. He said:

"It was about the shock of disconnection—feeling that I mattered
or was an essential part of the world of someone all important, and
then it was clear that I really wasn't at all. At that time I didn't have
these words, just the inchoate, visceral sensation. I understood that it
was about an early experience that I meant almost nothing to my
mother, that she had no true connection to me, and therefore my
connection to her was based on false grounds that easily crumbled
and gave way, and this was replicated with you."

He went on to explain that the replication had occurred when I
became ill and had to stop working for a while. His experience, which
unhappily had more than a grain of truth to it, was that I had badly
neglected to make adequate provisions to see him or help him deal
with the shock of this abrupt and unexpected disconnection, a disconnection that so unfortunately replicated the essential traumatic
situation of his life.

He continued: "Also, there's the problem of words disconnected
from meaning—it's like when Superman swoops down and clasps
you in his arms—something that's physical and absolutely clear, versus words like "I love you" that are disconnected or not reinforced by
anything to make them real. If you couldn't catch me when I fell,
what could your words about connection or attachment really mean?
In that way talking on the telephone was of little use or relief to me,

whereas your physical presence would have made a great difference."

This man was considerably more traumatized than Susan, but eventually an internal presence was established that enabled him to go on and manage his life in a somewhat more connected and integrated way.

But my own difficulties in fully understanding this patient's need for my physical presence when I had disconnected because of illness, even though he repeatedly kept telling me about it, and my equal difficulties in fully believing the extent of Susan's incapacities, or even of her almost miraculous recovery, has led me to some thoughts about counter-transference difficulties with these patients.

We tend to think of psychosomatic issues as those in which the mind somehow influences the body, but I believe that we should equally well include those in which the body somehow influences the mind. Perhaps a better way of saying this is that events are occurring simultaneously in two different registers.

In any case, I believe, because of the development of this and similar cases that we should not just think of someone with an attachment problem who may also have visual and cognitive difficulties, but that it is legitimate and even imperative to think about this holistically as a psychosomatic disorder.

I was not the only one who at first overlooked Susan's visual and cognitive defects, as well as her sense of existential isolation and deadness: the first two had been noticed since she was in kindergarten and there had been sporadic half-hearted attempts at remediation, although her two previous therapists had not taken them really seriously and her last analyst had finally accused her of not trying hard enough.

But I also, as well as the examining neuropsychologist, found it difficult to believe the extent of her visual and learning deficits, and I also found it hard to believe in the quickness of her recovery, although the crucial experience of believing that someone was really there for her came only after a year of doing visual-motor exercises and almost two years of daily analysis.

So, just as at first I found it difficult to really believe that cognitive confusion or feelings of unreality could be caused by visual or processing difficulties, so it seemed equally difficult to really believe that a fantasy of being held in someone's mind could so dramatically affect the ability to read, to reason and to act effectively. But I now think that in this particular case I had to actually *do* something before Susan, who had never been able to believe that she was being held in mind, could believe that I was seeing her accurately and hearing her and holding her in mind in a way that would be mutative for the treatment.

There is a wonderful paper by Pierre Marty (2010), the French psychosomatician, on the narcissistic difficulties aroused in the observer by the patient's psychosomatic problems. He says that psychosomatic processes are difficult to believe because, firstly, one has to believe in the power of the psychic world to make events happen in the real world and, secondly, because one has to believe that a cause can lead to an effect without being able to specify or sometimes even imagine the intervening steps. We depend so much on concrete visual imagery to conceptualize causation that psychosomatic disorders, where this visual imagery may be lacking, can be difficult to imagine. Finally, it is difficult and painful to believe that human beings can harm, mutilate or destroy their own bodies with mere thoughts.

In a word, believing in psychosomatics is a challenge to our narcissism because it threatens and subverts our own world view and makes us anxious about the very stability of our own self. It makes us anxious about our own body, which is vulnerable not only to threats that are seen, but also to threats unseen and even unthought-of. So we may disbelieve or makes jokes about psychosomatic patients because the anxiety they provoke is so mysterious and deeply rooted.

I was reluctant at first to believe in the extent of Susan's disabilities and later even more reluctant to do some of the managing that seemed so necessary, but I realized I must do what seemed so clinically indicated and think about it later. This is part of an ongoing attempt to think about it later.

But to conclude my story: Susan seemed to be making good progress in her analysis until her boyfriend was obliged by circumstances to make a permanent move to another part of the country. After much panic and alarmed discussion, she moved along with him and now lives almost across the continent. We did phone sessions for a while but, just as with the man previously cited, words over the phone were not as useful as being physically present in a live body. Nevertheless, the improvements in her sense of feeling real and alive seemed to be holding up despite the disruption and dislocation. A friend found her an appropriate job in a large audio-video studio, which she was able to accept and has been growing into for some time now. She and Steven finally got married and she tells me that she feels she has re-entered the stream of life.

But as I have thought more about the case over the years, I feel I have come to understand some things that were unclear to me at that time. About two years into the analysis the following incident occurred. Susan was sitting up, which she did from time to time, and we were thus face to face when I reached for my water bottle to take a drink. But I had not replaced the bottle cap tightly and, as I was drinking, water was dribbling onto my pants and shirt and it took me a moment to notice this and correct it.

Meanwhile Susan had turned her head away, and afterwards she said: "I saw what was happening and I could have said something, could have stopped it, but instead I looked away."

I suggested that she didn't want to see me make a fool of myself or be a loser. She said that was exactly right and we talked for a while about how this must have replicated so many events in her childhood, watching her parents screw things up and being unable to stop them and even feeling responsible for it. This led to that iconic moment when she showed her mother the drawing with the dirty word and her mother, as predicted, simply refused to see what was in front of her eyes, just as she had refused or been unable to accurately view her daughter.

The next day Susan went back on the couch, but I didn't say anything about it at the time because I felt she still too desperately needed to keep me in an idealized position. In the end this never got fully analyzed, but thinking about it has led me to wonder if there are at least two needs that have to be fulfilled for the child to grow up with a normal sense of feeling real and alive.

The first is the need for an idealized Other, for which Susan was able to use me when her own denigrated parents proved to be unsuitable for the task.

The second is the need to be accurately viewed by this idealized Other who recognizes and signals just how real and alive you feel to them. I am essentially imagining this as a psychobiological process. In the same way that the sight of another pigeon leads the female pigeon to secrete hormones that begin the process of ovulation, and in the same way that the onset of darkness leads a human being to secrete melatonin that begins the process of falling asleep, so the mirroring and recognition by an idealized Other of a realistically perceived self, through pathways we have not yet understood but that may include the secretion of oxytocin, leads the child to feelings of being recognized, feeling alive and feeling real. But of course I am saying no more than Kohut (1971), Lacan (1949) and Winnicott (1971) have already said about feelings of aliveness.

Another way of talking about this is to say that in the early years of treatment there was a deeply mutual affective interpenetration between Susan and me that enabled her to feel more real and alive and to talk spontaneously with me.

Although Susan dismissed her family, left them far behind and considered them as losers from an early age, she had simply substituted her boyfriend for the bad maternal object from which she had never really separated, and thus she could never feel entitled to a life of her own.

I think that every act of looking accurately is an act of separation, and that Susan was never looked at accurately by her parents and could never accurately look at them, in ways both concrete and symbolic, ways that were intertwined in the psyche-soma.

I have also come to realize that when I listened to her material and thought it sounded "organic" and spontaneously suggested she see a neuropsychologist, I was not only making a concrete practical suggestion but also making a psychological interpretation. I was saying in effect that I was not going to be taken in by her false self but that I understood she had some real problems and that I would try to address them. Thus I was looking at her unflinchingly for the first time, and although it was not good news, it came as a great relief for her to no longer be obliged to continue the masquerade that was fooling even her. Unknown to me at the time, my concrete intervention concerning her neuroanatomy had metamorphosed into a psychological interpretation of some complexity.

So although the analysis helped her to deal with the merging of things in the concrete perceptual realm that had previously been undifferentiated, it never got a chance to thoroughly deal with them in the intrapsychic realm, especially in the transference. In retrospect, I believe that Susan's decision to move was a good one, and that my extra-analytic interventions probably would not have interfered with a completed analysis. But I am discussing it here largely because it provides interesting material about the central role of feelings of realness and aliveness in their relation to the psyche-soma, at a time when so many of our patients seem to present with infinite variations on a false-self paradigm.

REFERENCES

Bach, S. (1977). On the narcissistic state of consciousness. *International Journal of Psycho-Analysis* 58:209-233.

Bach, S. (2006). *Getting from Here to There: Analytic Love, Analytic Process.* Mahwah, NJ: The Analytic Press.

Kohut, H. (1971). *The Analysis of the Self.* New York: International Universities Press.

Lacan, J. (1949). Le stade du miroir comme formateur de la fonction du Je, telle qu'elle nous est révélée dans l'expérience psychanalytique. In *Ecrits.* Paris: Le Seuil, 1966, pp. 93-101.

Marty, P. (2010). The narcissistic difficulties presented to the observer by the psychosomatic problem. *International Journal of Psycho-Analysis* 91:347-360.

Winnicott, D. W. (1971). *Playing and Reality.* New York: Basic Books.

CHAPTER 12

The Disembodied Self:
Dysregulation and Feelings of Unreality[1]

> When I consider others I can easily believe that their bodies express
> their personalities and that the two are inseparable. But it is impossi-
> ble for me not to feel that my body is other than I, that I inhabit it
> like a house, and that my face is a mask which, with or without my
> consent, conceals my real nature from others. - "Hic et Ille"
>
> *W.H. Auden, Encounter, April 1956, p.38*

When I started clinical psychology graduate school in 1955,
I recall asking one of my professors what was the best
way to go about choosing a psychoanalyst. He told me to
take the analyst into a stable and observe how the horses reacted to
him. He meant, of course, to choose emotionally and instinctively,
and not to choose intellectually as, for example, by comparing cre-
dentials. This seemed an excellent piece of advice, but I could never
figure out a way to lure my prospective analysts into a stable. So I decided that, instead, it was I who would have to learn to think
instinctively like a horse, and here are some of the reflections that this
has engendered.

It seems that the body lives in homeostasis, both internally and externally, with the environment. The sign that this is working properly

---

[1] The Norbert Freedman Memorial Lecture at IPTAR, April 2016

is a feeling of well being. They say that on a glorious sunny morning in Paris Samuel Beckett was walking through the park with a friend and the friend remarked: "A day like this makes one feel glad to be alive," to which Beckett responded: "I wouldn't go that far."

And in fact Beckett's letters are filled with multiple complaints about the misery of being alive and the poor state of his body, with many apparently psychosomatic ailments. So when the homeostasis becomes disrupted, then changes in experience occur, ranging from simple bodily unease or psychosomatic complaints to hallucinations at the extreme.

These experiential changes can occur in any modality. Visually, we can experience hallucinations, macropsia and micropsia, diplopia, blurring, etc. Aurally, we can experience loss of hearing, loss of word discrimination, tinnitus, etc. Tactually, we can experience tingling of the fingers, loss of feeling or "things may just not feel the same." Our olfactory system may cease to register smells, or may register pleasant or unpleasant smells that no one else can corroborate. Our food may seem tasteless, burning hot or inedible. Our mind may experience brain fog or acute perceptions of anxiety, depression or mental distress. Our gut can display a variety of symptoms from diarrhea to constipation. Our body may feel painful, shaky, tingling, disoriented, etc. These are only a few of the signs that the body's relationship to its internal or external environment has been disturbed.

Changing our relationship to the external environment or to our perception of the external environment may require direct action. I vividly recall, while interning at Jacobi Hospital, being sent to give psychological tests to a lovely young woman named Carmen who was being confined in the isolation room because she was in a frenzied panic. I abandoned the testing when she told me she was panicked because of dozens of snakes that were wriggling around in the corner of the isolation room. So I picked up a broom and methodically began to kill the snakes. When I finished, she threw her arms around me and said I was the only doctor who had helped her. I was thrilled because she was very attractive and because I wasn't even a doctor yet, not having completed my internship.

But dealing with the internal environment is often far more complicated. Internal homeostasis is largely controlled by the nervous system, primarily the hypothalamic-pituitary-adrenal or HPA axis and the autonomic nervous system, a system that was only discovered in the early 1900s and still remains somewhat mysterious. You will doubtless recall the formulation that the sympathetic system is geared towards action and fight or flight, whereas the parasympathetic system is geared towards relaxation, digestion and sleep. When these two systems are in homeostasis and working harmoniously, it generally feels good to be alive.

Unfortunately, trauma victims and children who have experienced adverse childhood events, people who have been raised in an emotional snake pit amidst poverty, neglect, violence, alcoholism, drugs and child abuse, people like my patient Carmen, see snakes all the time. Their sympathetic nervous system has been conditioned to be in a state of constant overdrive and they are in perpetual autonomic imbalance.

When we see patients with autonomic imbalance, or dysautonomia, one of our first tasks is to help them restore their homeostasis. Of course many psychoanalysts have been doing this all along, without either paying attention to it or perhaps conceptualizing it in some other way, such as calming a very anxious patient by explanation, reassurance or drugs, or prescribing frequent sessions to calm the patient, or by creating some variety of a holding environment. When we help a hyperventilating patient to calm down by taking slow, deep breaths, we are directing her attention away from the snakes in her mind to the imbalance in her body, a very effective way of calming someone down.

Sandor Ferenczi was among the first to observe the apparent splitting of body and mind as a result of an immediate or cumulative trauma. Since then many clinicians have noted patients who report that during physical abuse or a severe illness or a traumatic accident, they have had a typical out-of-the-body experience in which their reporting self flies out of the body or up to the ceiling, leaving their traumatized body to suffer alone while they observe it from outside.

As a result of advances in psychoanalytic thinking and also an immense amount of work done in allied fields on post-traumatic stress disorder and trauma in general, we now have some better ideas about how to help these individuals heal their feeling of living with a Cartesian split between mind and body.

To situate this psychoanalytically, these are usually non-psychotic patients who have been variously described as traumatized, difficult or challenging, a-symbolic, concrete, alexithymic, schizoid, split-off, dissociated, insecurely attached, etc.

These patients may seem strange to the observer because they are often out of touch emotionally, but they are neither delusional nor do they become psychotic if treated. They report feelings of observing their life rather than living it. They may be facile with words but the words have little meaning for them: it seems as if the beta elements are not being metabolized into alpha elements (Bion, 1967). Thus, they often experience existential anxieties about time and space: they may feel they work hard but finish nothing, or find that they have spent their entire day in some altered state. Like Beckett's characters, they are unable to situate their body comfortably or find a place in the world where they feel they belong or that feels safe to them. Above all, life has lost it's meaning: it feels like just words or just events without any real purpose or significance.

We know that to help them heal this Cartesian split, we must provide them not only with an explanation of what happened to them, but more importantly we must provide them with an experience of reality. So we begin with the body because, as Freud noted, the ego is first and foremost a body ego and feelings of reality are always connected to bodily experience. These patients are almost always dysregulated in such basic areas of bodily functioning as eating, sleeping, breathing, hydrating, orienting, exercising, etc. They carry their body along in their mind but as if it were a foreign object that does not really belong to them. Consequently, they also feel as if reality does not belong to them; objects and people do not *feel* real to them and they do not know how to belong or to situate themselves in a world that always seems strange, alien and Other.

Ordinary patients are sufficiently regulated by their regular analytic appointments and their developing connection to the analyst, but these challenging patients who seem to feel either dead or in a perpetual panic state have lost a secure relationship to time, space and the continuity of life: they have lost their trust in the physical world and in people, and these parameters must be specially dealt with. The management of this type of mind-body split has been extensively discussed by analysts such as Ferenczi (1988), Winnicott (1965), Marty (1968), Ogden (1989), Ellman (2007) and many others, as well as by traumatologists such as van der Kolk (2014), Porges (2011), and Putnam (1989).

Because trauma damages the non-verbal bodily substrate, traumatologists who work with holocaust survivors, war veterans and with victims of poverty, violence and childhood abuse often prefer treatment modalities other than psychoanalysis or psychotherapy, and some even disparage any talking cure other than manualized behavior therapies (van der Kolk, 2014). To address this issue would take me far from my subject, but it seems clear to me that many different healing modalities have their proper place and varying effectiveness, depending upon the patient, the therapist, the social situation, the resources available, the goals that both patient and therapist have in mind and many other parameters. Even the best of psychoanalysts such as Freud, Ferenczi and Winnicott have also been healers, whatever their proclaimed intentions, and they have also employed modalities other than the purely verbal when doing psychoanalysis. But I want to return to my main theme, which involves the Cartesian split between body and mind and how this effects embodiment and dysregulation.

In the pre-Renaissance era there was a certain kind of unity between body and mind that may seem naïve to us today, but that preserved a wholeness of experience that we often no longer seem to possess. Barfield (1988) for example, says:

Before the scientific revolution the world was more like a garment men wore about them than a stage on which they moved...It was as if the observers were themselves in the picture.

Compared with us, they felt themselves and the objects around them and the words that expressed those objects, immersed together in something like a clear lake of...'meaning'... (p. 94)

Both Shakespeare and Max Weber (2002) referred to this as a world of physical enchantment, filled with mysterious forces, unknown presences and great meaning.

Compare this pre-Renaissance world-experience with that of the Pulitzer-prize winning poet, Mark Strand (2014), who wrote the following poem[2]:

Keeping Things Whole

In a field
I am the absence
of field.
This is
always the case.
Wherever I am
I am what is missing.

When I walk
I part the air
and always
the air moves in
to fill the spaces
where my body's been.

We all have reasons
for moving.
I move
to keep things whole.

Here the poet has left the holistic world of enchantment where

---

[2] Thanks to Dr. Sujatha Subramanian for bringing this poem to my attention.

things just naturally feel complete, and moved to a divided world whose parts are lost or missing and which he must struggle to control. Rather than feeling connected to the world and immersed in a lake of meaning, he is immersed in confusion and ambiguity and fights to remain connected. His conclusion that he moves to keep things whole reminds me of the many patients I have seen who have been diagnosed with attention disorder, hyperactivity disorder, dissociative disorder and "false self," or others who just lead a frantic life because they feel unable to slow down, as if slowing down puts them in danger of dissolution, disappearance or total annihilation.

Winnicott (1949) has suggested that as a result of trauma the psyche can retreat into the mind, setting up a situation conducive to psychosomatic disorders through the formation of a "head ego" or false self. Then one's feelingful connection to the body and one's meaningful connection to the world is lost, and people become unable to recognize or to name their emotions. Their body, instead of belonging to them, becomes the frightening site of ghosts who return to haunt them with somatic symptoms.

Such was the case with Michael, a young man who came to see me with the chief complaint: "I don't feel alive." And in fact Michael, at the age of 26, seemed to have lost all appetite for life. He did not look or feel depressed; rather, he seemed more schizoid or disconnected, like a walking corpse or a zombie.

He had a recurring dream that he's at a party somewhere. The room is full of people. He is hovering about two feet off the ground and floating around the room, talking to no one, looking at the pictures and inspecting the molding. He is there and not there at the same time. When asked what comes to mind about the dream, he says only that it's a very pleasant feeling.

I have mentioned that levitation dreams and out-of-body experiences are common with abused or traumatized people. I reported one where the patient was very sick as a child and remembers floating up to the ceiling and observing the anxious doctor, his mother crying hysterically and his own feverish body (Bach, 1977). But Michael's dream was unusual because he seemed completely out of touch with the terror and loneliness attached to his experience

Michael was working at a job teaching English to foreigners; a job he had drifted into after graduating from an Ivy League college. After a few months at the job, he was offered a promotion to a higher echelon but he had no real interest in this. He couldn't tell what he wanted to do; it was as if one thing seemed as good as another unless it really hurt.

Since he was good-looking and smart, women often approached him. He had sex with them out of obligation; he functioned well but didn't particularly enjoy it and never grew attached. He often preferred to be by himself, but he wasn't aware of feeling anxious with others and in fact he had friends and had been elected to class positions in both his high school and university. He played with a rock band in school and would sometimes say he was a musician, but he was never really committed to that either.

He had little interest in food and generally ate whatever came to hand. He had an unexplained fear of vomiting, which I later came to understand as a fear of falling apart or annihilation. He was tall and quite thin; well enough coordinated but somehow droopy and seemingly disconnected in his bearing. When he began to use the couch he flopped onto it in an awkward way, arms and legs hanging over, as if he would like to relax into it but didn't quite know how.

He had at times tried drugs and alcohol, but they did not especially turn him on. I began to think that he might be dealing with some profound anxiety about being excited or overstimulated, as if his psychic thermostat were broken or fixed at some low set point that barely kept him warm and alive.

He seemed to want to come and talk because he knew for certain that something was wrong, but he didn't know what it might be. He would speak for a while; recounting events of the day very concretely, and then go silent for a long time. I found that if I asked him what he was thinking about, he would either feel confused or produce a shopping list devoid of all feelings. I learned to hold my peace until finally he spoke about something that felt real. It slowly became clear that he was massively out of touch with his feelings and unable to name them: that he was, in fact, alexithymic. It also became clear that, despite his good reflexes and proficiency in sports, he was also in some way out of touch with his physical body and this, combined with his alexithymia, made him feel that much of what he said and did was suspect or unreal.

He remembered from the age of six or seven having episodes where he became anxious because things felt strange or unreal to him, but he never told anyone about this because he feared they would think him crazy, and he just decided, in his words, "to push through and hope it would go away." I was the first person he had ever spoken to about any of this.

After a few months of analysis he began to report paraesthesias or, as he called them, "dead spots," on his body: places around his mouth or arms or torso where he experienced either a tingling sensation or no feeling at all. He remembered having experienced this before but had not recalled it when he first came. We couldn't seem to connect this with anything specific that he was now feeling or could report.

In the countertransference, the effect on me was also peculiar. I was quite accustomed, in talking with overinflated narcissistic patients, to feel that they were occupying all the space in the office, leaving me with no room or air to breathe. This sometimes resulted in my trying to interpret to them in order to protect myself, or going into hibernation or actually falling asleep. But with Michael, rather than having a counter-reaction, I found myself drifting into an altered state that was neither dead nor alive but hypnotically zombielike. Examining my state afterwards, I could see that I had left my body and feelings behind and that I was floating, like a disembodied observing eye, somewhere up in the void. I took this to be the counterpart or complement of what Michael might be experiencing. I began to wonder what it was that had happened to him or if there might be something bio-chemically or neurologically amiss with him. At his own initiative he went for a complete physical checkup and was pronounced in perfect health.

The narrative that he told of his life seemed to contain no easily discernible traumas. He thought that his relationship with both parents had been good, his childhood happy if somewhat lonely, and his life uneventful. He couldn't really understand his feelings of anxiety, of depersonalization and de-realization, or his overall feeling of not being alive.

As we pieced together the story, it became clear that there were large gaps in his history and a persistent feeling that he had not really been there or lived through even the events that he seemed to remember. There was a continual feeling of boredom as he spoke of these things, a feeling that comes back to me now even as I recount his life. He recalled as a child being entranced with the story of Peter Pan. He felt that he was wandering in the world, lost, without any orientation. I began to feel that we were dealing with some early disorder of attachment.

I thought of Laplanche's (2015) writings about disorders of early libidinization: how normally the mother seduces the child into life with enigmatic signifiers. We know from Spitz's (1945) work the importance of the caretaker's early handling and fondling of the child, and the dramatic pathology of illness and even death that one finds in infants who are medically cared-for but not lovingly touched.

At this same time Michael was talking about not feeling good when girls touched him. Eventually, it developed that his mother had rarely touched him and was not into bodily contact. He remembered that as a young teenager he sometimes fine-cut his wrists in order to feel something. One day his mother had walked in while this was going on and asked if he was OK. When he reassured her that he was fine and had accidentally cut himself, she left without further inquiry.

Michael came from a well-to-do family, had an older brother and was raised by his mother. But his descriptions of both his mother and father continued to remain vague and they did not emerge as real three-dimensional people. Over time it became clear that he didn't really understand them much as people, and we know that if a child doesn't learn to understand his parent's minds, he will have a very difficult time learning to understand his own mind (Bach, 2002). One of Michael's recurring anxiety dreams was that he would not be able to find the right combination to open his locker in the school gymnasium.

After about a year of therapy I went on August vacation. Although

I strongly suggested that we arrange to speak regularly on the phone, Michael did not feel this necessary and never did use the number that I had left him. When I returned, however, he wanted to cut down on the number of sessions. He reported a dream:

> It was like in a science fiction story where I was living in a fake or unreal world. The zombies had come and taken over everything, but I couldn't tell who was a zombie and who was one of the real people left. I made friends with an older man who seemed trustworthy, but then something happens that makes me suspect that the older man is really a zombie in disguise. I wake up terrified that I've been discovered and will die.

Transparent as the dream seemed to me, Michael seemed unable to recognize any transference significance, but he did connect with his fear that he or others could be like zombies and with his anxiety that he might vomit, get sick and ultimately die.

I felt that the dream expressed his basic anxiety about the instability of his objects and of his own self: a concretely expressed fear of dissolution or self-disintegration. But I saw it as considerable progress that he had made some connection to me and that he was reacting to the separation, if at first only unconsciously.

It took years of treatment before Michael could begin to feel, in a reliable way, that he was less like a zombie and more like a human being, and then to be able to go on to make a life for himself in the real world.

I have now followed a considerable number of patients with depersonalization, derealization and bodily detachment symptoms similar to Michael's, and I will try to summarize some of their characteristics. For the moment, they seem to divide into two categories, each dependent on the particular way that the mother-infant dyad had failed as an adequate stimulus provider, stimulus barrier and stimulus regulator.

We believe that children are born with innate predispositions that can vary along one continuum from high endogenous to low endogenous stimulation. Ellman (2009) has graphically described how an infant born with high endogenous stimulation might find a mother's normal reactions overstimulating and aversive, and how the mother might feel so narcissistically injured by this rejection that the system continues in permanent dysregulation. This is equally true for infants born with low endogenous stimulation, who might need greater than normal responsiveness. But I do not have reliable data on these early predispositions and therefore will only speak about a system within which the infant experiences over or under stimulation.

The trauma of the first group that Michael belonged to and which I call the understimulated system, was that too little of a positive nature had happened with their primary caretakers. In general these patients came from an understimulated and love-deficient environment, were touched only in mechanical ways that were not sexually libidinized, rarely experienced affective contact with their caretakers nor the kind of affective interpenetration that could be assimilated and enjoyed, and thus they felt uninhabited by their mothers or by anyone else. As an extreme example of this group, one might think of Spitz's infants who were medically cared-for but untouched and often became ill or developed marasmus. While the conditions for my group were not as extreme as in the orphanage, they generally seemed anxiously avoidant or resistant as infants, and as adults they seemed to avoid intense relationships or quickly withdraw from them. If we can imagine, as Sidney Blatt (1990) did, all psychopathologies as tensions between attachment and autonomy, this group showed problems of avoidant attachment and were philobatic (Balint, 1968), that is, they felt more secure in the empty spaces between objects.

The trauma of the second group which I call the overstimulated system, was that too much had happened with their primary caretakers. In general they came from a loud, sexualized, overly stimulating environment, they were overtly intruded upon or even beaten or molested, and they felt emotionally overwhelmed by their caretakers. Contrary to the understimulated group who felt uninhabited by their caretakers, this group felt so overly inhabited by their caretakers that they could never break away. They were constantly in relationships but of a sadomasochistic kind and always in danger of spousal abuse or breakup up of the relationship. In terms of attachment and autonomy, this group had problems with separation and differentiation and was ocnophilic (Balint, 1968), that is, they felt most secure when attached to objects.

As an example of this group I will mention Gloria, a remarkably intelligent, competent and attractive young woman who came to see me in a state of paralysis after graduating from a prominent university. She was gifted not only intellectually but also artistically, and had already won some important competitions. But she had been brought up in a family of high functioning professionals who were closely symbiotic. Her mother had wiped her at the toilet until latency and dictated her choice of clothing, friends and activities until the analysis began. Even away at college she spoke to her mother several times a day, and everything new that she tried was preceded by the thought: Would my mother approve this or permit this?

By contrast with the understimulated patients, Gloria was held, stroked and caressed too much by both mother and father, but her body did not feel as if it belonged to her and she would feel obliged to ask permission from her mother for everything she did to her body. At the same time that the mother was so overpoweringly present, she was also thoroughly inconsistent and would unexpectedly abandon Gloria for other siblings or threaten to leave or to kill herself. So Gloria's body became inhabited by a toxic introject that could never be relied on and her body itself was there but did not belong to Gloria.

To summarize this in an extremely oversimplified way, the understimulated patients can find no living caretaker inside, no reliable internal representation, and so they must keep themselves stimulated in order to ward off anxieties about loss and annihilation of self. The overstimulated group has internalized a toxic caretaker so that they can feel their body, but the body belongs to their caretaker and not to them. So long as they cling to the toxic mother of pain, they can exist with conflict in a body that does not belong to them. But as soon as they experience happiness or meet someone who loves them, they feel panicked, empty and alone, because happiness or a loving object means abandoning the mother of pain with whom they have been living in symbiosis. In this way feeling good makes them feel bad and they feel as equally disembodied as the deprived or understimulated group who have never had an adequate embodied internalization in the first place.

I have been describing two groups of patients, on opposite poles of a continuum from attachment to autonomy, both of whom feel disembodied but in different ways. The first group, those traumatized by deprivation or understimulation, may feel depressed, bored, very lonely, not really alive or even suicidal. Because they have not adequately introjected a reliable caretaking figure and feel disembodied, they may try to re-establish a sense of whole physicality by staying in constant motion and by such methods as head banging, self-pummeling, hair pulling, fine cutting, piercing, skin lesions, loud music, amphetamines or, at a higher dydadic level, sadomasochistic enactments in which they are stimulated and abused by others.

At the other end, those traumatized by excessive stimulation may feel clinging, needy, anxiously paranoid and profoundly conflicted. They do not feel disembodied, but the body they are in belongs not to them but to an ambivalent protective figure that is or can suddenly become toxic. It is only when they attempt to escape from this toxic internalization that they feel in danger of disembodiment, because their body has been owned by someone else, they have never developed a true capacity to be alone, and happiness or a connection to a loving person makes them feel they are losing their mother of pain and are alone, abandoned and falling apart. In treatment, this often leads to the difficult situation in which the patient, who in reality seems to be improving, becomes terrified intra-psychically and feels worse and worse.

Of course, in the clinical situation one often finds combinations of these polarities that present themselves at different psychic levels or in different transference constellations.

I should also make it clear that I am talking not only about genetically determined endogenous stimulation but primarily about what we see clinically, that is, the interaction of the endogenous with the environment. This is most often exemplified by the mother who, through her containing, mirroring and marking actions, elicits and returns those mutual responses that make up the emotional environment in which the growing child is immersed like a fish in water.

Sometimes the child may feel like he is drowning or cannot breathe because his emotional environment has become severely disturbed as the result of sudden or cumulative trauma. Then we may see him as a child or an adult in a highly dysregulated state, and it will usually be clear that restoring the homeostasis is the first order of business. As this proceeds and the patient develops more of an autonomous, structured and reflective self, then a more classical interpretive analysis becomes possible. Occasionally the patient will have experienced so much relief merely from restoring the homeostasis that he may not wish to continue, but this decision is often dependent on the analyst's own convictions about the creative potential of further analysis.

I am going to spend only a few minutes talking about the initial phase of treatment with these patients because I strongly believe that understanding the patient well enough is the key that unlocks all questions of technique. But it seemed à propos that just as I was writing this I came across an article in the N.Y. Times about how athletes who are trained in mindfulness of their bodies subsequently experience fewer injuries and far less pain after extreme exertions.

The article defines mindfulness as the sensing and reception of physiological signals from within the body, for example, breathing rates, balance, hunger, thirst, whether you have an itch or a sensation, an inchoate feeling, etc. This means learning to feel what's going on in the body right now, a general receptivity to the whole field of awareness and full engagement with the present moment, a knowledge that these events are time limited and will pass and, as far as possible, a non-judgmental attitude towards them.

But, if you think about it, this seems to be very similar to what good-enough-mothers actually teach their young children from the earliest times: how to know when they're hot or cold, hungry or thirsty, dreaming or awake, where it hurts, that pain is temporary and will heal or get better over time, how to make their body comfortable, how to feel good about it and, generally, how to regulate their homeo-stasis.

Furthermore, it seems obvious that this is precisely the kind of awareness and regulatory functions that the mothers of both of these groups of patients were unable to provide.

So now how does this translate into clinical work if you are prac-ticing psychoanalysis or psychotherapy? Personally, I prefer, if possible, to remain within classical parameters when doing treatment because for me that usually gives the best results. But for that one must be lucky enough to have a setting in which there is environmen-tal support, both psychological and economic, for frequent sessions and regressive periods.

In other settings and circumstances, the therapist might draw at-tention to bodily awareness, to breathing, to symptoms or constrictions, and perhaps even suggest consultations with body workers such as physical therapists, yoga teachers, trauma specialists, etc. Still, I have learned from supervision that simply getting the pa-tient or the therapist interested in bodily states in childhood or encouraging mindfulness about the body often has remarkable re-sults. Very often, if the treatment is going well, it will be the patient himself who brings his body into the discussion and begins to em-body himself, either by focusing on psychosomatic symptoms and anxieties or by initiating reparative work such as exercise, dance, die-tary changes, attempts to regulate sleep and chronobiology, and so forth.

Finally, I should say that in my opinion the psychoanalytic treat-ment must be flexible and creative, that is to say, the analyst must be responsive and alive. A patient who feels that he and other people are not real or alive and seem disembodied, or who feels that his own life has not been real and authentic, will not be cured through a manualized procedure or a by-the-book analysis. One must love life in order to help such people, which is why I dedicate this paper to the memory of our late colleague Norbert Freedman, a lover of life if ever there was one.

REFERENCES

Bach, S. (1977). On the narcissistic state of consciousness. *International Journal of Psycho-Analysis* 58:209-233.

Bach, S. (2002). A mind of one's own: Some observations on disorders of thinking. In *Symbolization and Desymbolization: Essays in Honor of Norbert Friedman*, ed. R. Lasky. New York: Karnac, pp. 387-406.

Balint, M. (1968). *The Basic Fault: Therapeutic Aspects of Regression.* London: Tavistock.

Barfield, O. (1988). *Saving the Appearances: A Study in Idolatry*, 2nd Edition. Wesleyan: New Hampshire.

Bion, W. R. (1967). *Second Thoughts.* London: William Heinemann; reprinted (1984), London: Karnac Books.

Blatt, S. J. (1990). Interpersonal relatedness and self-definition: Two personality configurations and their implication for psychopathology and psychotherapy. In *Repression and dissociation: Implications for personality theory, psychopathology and health*, ed. J. L. Singer. Chicago: University of Chicago Press, pp. 299-335.

Ellman, S.J. (2007). Analytic trust and transference: Love, healing ruptures and facilitating repair. *Psychoanalytic Inquiry* 27:246-263.

Ellman, S. J. (2009). *When Theories Touch: A Historical and Theoretical Integration of Psychoanalytic Thought.* London, Karnac.

Ferenczi, S. (1932). *The Clinical Diary of Sándor Ferenczi*, ed. J. Dupont (trans. M. Balint & N. Z. Jackson). Cambridge, MA: Harvard University Press, 1988.

Laplanche, J. (2015). *The Temptation of Biology: Freud's Theories of Sexuality*, trans. D. Nicholson-Smith. New York: The Unconscious in Translation.

Marty, P. (1968). A Major Process of Somatization: The Progressive Disorganization. *International Journal of Psycho-Analysis* 49:246-249.

Ogden, T. (1989). *The Primitive Edge of Experience.* Northvale, NJ: Aronson.

Porges, S. W. (2011). *The Polyvagal Theory: Neurophysiological Foundations of Emotions, Attachment, Communication, and Self-regulation.* New York: Norton.

Putnam, F. W. (1989). *Diagnosis and Treatment of Multiple Personality Disorder*. New York: Guilford.

Strand, M. (2014). *Collected Poems*. New York: Knopf.

van der Kolk, B. (2014). *The Body Keeps the Score: Brain, Mind, and Body in the Healing of Trauma*. New York: Viking Press.

Weber, M. (2002). *The Protestant Ethic and the "Spirit" of Capitalism and Other Writings*. New York: Penguin Books.

Winnicott, D. W. (1960). Ego distortion in terms of true and false self. In *The Maturational Process and the Facilitating Environment: Studies in the Theory of Emotional Development*. New York: International University Press, 1965, pp. 140-152.

Winnicott, D.W. (1965). The maturational processes and the facilitating environment: Studies in the theory of emotional development. *The International Psycho-Analytical Library* 64:1-276.

CHAPTER 13

Analytic Technique and Analytic Love

In a famous 1906 letter to Carl Jung, Freud wrote, "The [psycho-analytic] cure is effected by love" (McGuire, 1974, pp. 12–13). A little more than a month later, at a meeting of the Vienna Psychoanalytic Society, he again commented, "Our cures are cures of love" (Nunberg & Federn, 1962, p. 101). Indeed, Freud once told a colleague, Max Eitingon, that "the secret of therapy is to cure through love" (Grotjahn, 1967, p. 445).

And yet, as I glance through the catalogs of our psychoanalytic institutes, out of hundreds of courses I could find not one devoted to love and only one with the word love in the title. I am reminded of the old joke about a young fellow with a broken watch who passed a store from which a large model of a watch was hanging. When he walked in to get his watch repaired, the old man behind the counter explained that he did not repair watches, that he was in fact a mohel, a person who performs ritual circumcisions. When the young fellow angrily asked him why he had a large watch hanging outside, the old man replied, "And what else should I hang outside?"

Analogously, there seems to be reluctance on the part of psycho-analysts to display love as the model for what it is that they repair, which, of course, is perfectly understandable from many points of view. No doubt were I to ask the dean at any of these institutes why there are no courses on the nature of love, he might answer, "How can

we teach a course on love? This is a school for mental health professionals where we teach psychoanalytic technique and how to treat
mental health problems. We expect that issues of loving will be dealt
with in one's training analysis!"

And he would be right. When we teach the usual courses on technique, we are placing the emphasis on the agency of the psychoanalyst;
that would no doubt be the appropriate way to teach a technical procedure in medicine, computer science, or shoe repair. But perhaps we
should be placing the emphasis, not on the doctor and his technique,
but on the patient and the patient's sense of agency and empowerment.
There may be a vital difference in whether we relate to our patients
primarily through psychoanalytic technique or primarily through love.
Perhaps love and psychoanalytic technique do not inhabit the same
realm of discourse. For one may teach and sometimes even learn psychoanalytic technique, but love is an act of grace for which one can
only prepare.

Love is a difficult subject for everyone, and for psychoanalysts it is
fraught with problems of transference and countertransference, the weight
of social attitudes and collegial judgments, special ethical considerations,
and even legal concerns. Perhaps that is why psychoanalysts, following in
Freud's shadow, have so often chosen to deal with love as a technical
issue rather than attempting to face love as the controlling force implied in Freud's statement, "The secret of therapy is to cure by love."
Many of the technical terms and concepts of psychoanalysis can be
seen as part of a programmatic effort to specify the parameters of
love in an experience-distant language. This technical language has
both advantages and disadvantages: while it may give us some perspective on our emotions by allowing us to think about them
symbolically and to discuss them with colleagues and patients, it also
tends to deprive our words of life and leaves us with a hollow discourse about the technicalities of loving without the essence of the
thing itself.

I mention this dilemma to show what a vexing topic love is and how
complicated and perplexing our ideas and attitudes about love have been
and still remain. Freud (1915) did write one paper, "Observations on

Transference Love," as part of a series on the technique of psychoanalysis. But here again his emphasis was on the technical management of the explosive and embarrassing situation in which a woman patient might precipitously declare her love for her male analyst. Freud certainly knew about this situation from personal experience. He was clear that the analyst should not return the patient's love, by which he meant that the analyst cannot have sex with the patient; on the other hand, the analyst must not encourage the patient to repress those feelings because they are central to the patient's erotic life and must be relived. Freud advised us to show the patient that her love is not real love but only a transferred or transference love, because of its function as a resistance and also because it is composed almost entirely of archaic love elements from past relationships. But then, in a moment of inspired doubt, he wondered with us if this transference love is in fact really any different from genuine love, which, in his own words, is also "more similar to abnormal than to normal mental phenomena" (p. 168). It seems that he was never able to resolve this quandary to his own lasting satisfaction. We might note here Freud's occasional view of love as a pathological phenomenon, as well as the difficulties he had discussing the analyst's feelings of love apart from their expression in sexual relations.

And, indeed, particularly in those bygone days when psychoanalysis was experiencing a wave of popularity, one frequently heard people say that they would never go into analysis because they did not want to fall in love with their analyst. Now, of course, we know that not everyone who goes into psychoanalysis falls in love with his analyst, just as not everyone who goes into church falls in love with God. In fact, many people, in one way or another, are unable to love and this may be the very reason that brings them into analysis.

There was a time when we heard a great deal about "women who loved too much," women who repeatedly fell head over heels in love with men who cruelly mistreated them, and the popular opinion was that women loved too much and most men did not love enough. Analysis of these cases revealed that there was more than a quantitative factor involved and that some women who seemed to love too much really could not love enough in the right sort of way. And the same applied to men.

One might think that the psychoanalytic situation would be a perfect setting for helping us deepen our understanding about love: here we have two human beings intimately involved with each other in ways that predispose to love and who have also vowed to be completely honest with each other and not to act out love sexually. The analytic setting does, in fact, constitute an ideal love laboratory, but unfortunately the passions aroused by love have all too often interfered with the objective collection of data. We have seen that even Freud, the very inventor of this love laboratory, was tempted to abandon the entire project when a pretty young patient threw herself into his recently married arms, and even years later how he tries to manage a similar situation by telling his patient that her transference love is not real, all the while wondering, with his characteristic honesty and intellectual rigor, whether or not he is telling her the truth.

Whether we are watching Freud (1915) struggle with his discovery of the erotic transference or follow Ferenczi (1932) as he tries to love his patients better than a good mother would, we are witnessing the analyst wrestling with insults to his narcissism and the disturbance of his narcissistic balance by the tensions provoked in the analytic situation. And these men were, after all, the best love researchers we had! Freud and Ferenczi each had a very different kind of tolerance for disturbances of their narcissistic equilibrium, and this difference was one factor that allowed each of them to make their distinctive discoveries. Others, with fewer scruples, simply abandoned themselves to their passions or used the patients for their own satisfactions in more devious and reprehensible ways. As we think about it, we become aware that the powers of the Goddess of Love reach not only to the most sublime of human experience but also to the most degraded.

This thought brings to mind the multifarious so-called perversions of love that have existed since time immemorial. I still remember my consternation the first time I met a patient who told me with great embarrassment that his love object was a carefully preserved rubber raincoat. I recall, too, the mixture of emotions that engulfed me as I first heard the intimate, detailed descriptions of tortures, beatings, mutilations, and other S&M practices that people inflict on each other by mutual consent. It took a great deal of time and self-reflection to work through my initial reactions of fear, horror, loathing, fascination, and shifting identifications before I was able to arrive at a place where I could actually listen to what was being told me and try to understand what it meant. The people who engaged in these practices were sometimes people you might not want to have as friends, but often enough they were people of the highest moral and cultural standards, people you might want to have as friends, people who were tortured by their secret obsessions and their self-loathing. It was only slowly that I began to understand that all of us are really looking for the same thing and that, for reasons that could be uncovered by psychoanalysis, people with perversions have simply strayed onto a false path or taken a wrong turn in their search for the road leading to love. It proved to be a not impossible task to retrace these steps and help many of these people find the path that was right for them, and this success was very gratifying indeed.

But it also taught me that a key issue in doing successful psychoanalysis is how to enter into the experiential world of the patient, the world in which the patient is living—that is, to enter into the patient's psychic reality, which requires leaving behind, as far as possible, one's own fears, memories, values, and desires. Now, that is a tall order under any circumstances, and it seemed particularly difficult to abandon my own desires and values to empathize with someone for whom loving meant pouring hot wax on someone's genitals till they screamed in pain, or for whom being loved meant being fist-fucked or screaming in pain. Sometimes I would find myself knowing how I was supposed to be listening but not really being able to listen, or sometimes I would feel that I was the one being psychically tortured by the patient and was unable to put away my natural reactions and recover my narcissistic equilibrium. But I learned that the important thing was to keep trying, even if I could not always succeed.

My friend Irving Steingart (1995) has written some moving words about how an analyst must learn to love the patient's psychic reality, and I agree with him that in a good analysis the analyst is constantly working toward understanding, and indeed toward loving, his patient's psychic reality.

I would add that in my own experience the patient also comes to understand and love the analyst's psychic reality and that this is part of my definition of what true love is all about. In a good analysis the analyst comes to love the patient's psychic reality including her whole embodied reality. Love in the sense of knowing, appreciating, and admiring without carnal knowledge or seductive feelings but in essentially the same way one appreciates the body and flesh of one's closest friends or one's own children in their entirety.

This reminds me of one of the first patients I ever treated, more than 60 years ago, whom I will call Mrs. Brown. I was a young student when, as my first case at a large clinic, Mrs. Brown was referred to me with the diagnosis of paranoid schizophrenia. When I met her, I found a chronically depressed young woman who weighed close to 300 pounds. She had dropped out of high school, was the mother of two children, and was married to a man who also sounded schizophrenic. I was young and foolish and began the treatment with high hopes—despite the cynicism and cautions of my supervisor. I soon noticed that Mrs. Brown was very intelligent and, perhaps because of this, her attitude toward the treatment seemed as cynical and cautious as my supervisor's. Not much seemed to happen as we slowly got to know each other, and after almost a year had gone by I was still very much engaged but becoming less hopeful. Then one day as I walked into the office with Mrs. Brown and watched her settle in, I did not even notice her weight and I found myself thinking how beautiful she was, as if I were seeing her for the first time. As I now understand in retrospect, from that moment on things began to take off in a most unusual way. Mrs. Brown decided to go back to school. She finished her equivalency, went on to college and then later to graduate school. Along the way she shed her excess weight and divorced her husband. When I last heard, she had moved, remarried, and was teaching at a university out West.

Now of course the original diagnosis may have been incorrect. And, since I was a beginning therapist, I had made many interpretations but even then I had not felt them to be the mutative factor. So for many years I understood this as "merely" a "transference cure," even though it seems to have lasted and was a most surprising outcome to both me and to my supervisor. It is only recently that I think I begin to better understand what happened.

Mrs. Brown was a victim of severe early childhood abuse—physical, sexual and emotional. This had caused her to flee her body and to live emotionally outside it as a prematurely developed paranoid spectator of herself and of events. One might say that she no longer lived in her obese body or owned the feelings attached to it. And it was only when I began in my naiveté to befriend her body or even to love it that she could begin to re-appropriate her body and her feelings and move on in her life. At that time, sixty years ago, none of my supervisors could have explained this to me, and it has taken me a long enough time to understand it myself.

I did do one or two other things that might have been useful to Mrs. Brown. For one thing, I never completely gave up hope that things might change for her and that something good might come from our meetings. And also, whatever else I thought I was doing—and at that point my head was stuffed full of theories about psychoanalytic technique—I was somehow able to allow the hate and love that naturally emerges in the psychoanalytic situation to surface in me without too much denial or repression and just allow them to do their own work.

What do I mean by hate and love that naturally emerge in the psychoanalytic situation? Let me focus on love, since that is what I am discussing, although I do believe that love and hate have an intimate and codependent relationship and that most human beings need easy access to both their love and their hate in order to maintain their narcissistic balance and mental health. For, even if the analyst cannot learn to understand and love the patient's hate for him, he must at least learn to respect it. And I think we must assume that, even during periods of the most intense rage and destructiveness, the patient might usually prefer to love us and be loved by us if only he knew how to manage it.

But picture to yourself two people—who know nothing about each other and have never met before—being brought into a room and asked to look into each other's eyes for as long as possible. Many years ago I tried this at the first meeting of a psychology seminar, and it aroused such powerful emotions in some students that I have never tried it again. One student seemed convinced that, as if by voodoo magic, she would have to fall in love with whomever she was gazing at, a thought akin to the fear of some that going into analysis means falling in love with their analyst.

And yet that is not so strange a fantasy after all. Over the last few decades an immense amount of research has been done on the mutual gazing activities of mother and infant, research that involves filming both mother and child and frame-by-frame analysis of the exquisitely delicate interactions that constitute this apparently simple activity. We have learned that the normal infant is eager to gaze, and that there is something very wrong if a child refuses to look. Yet as avid as the child is to gaze, there is a natural rhythm to this activity and at some point the child becomes overly excited and tries to avert his gaze in order to calm himself down. Those mothers who do not permit their child to look away and so regulate their own excitement may become involved in an interaction that Beebe and Stern (1977) have called "chase and dodge," in which the mother pursues the child with her gaze while he tries to avoid looking at her and ends up frustrated or crying. Consequently, an originally loving interaction may over time become converted into a perverse activity that ends in pain and anger rather than pleasure and love.

But if the mother is sensitive to the baby's internal rhythms and if many other things go well enough, then the baby normally falls in love with his mother just as the mother will normally fall in love with her baby. Since this mutual love occurs in the natural order of things, it may not, after all, be so surprising that some people are still afraid that if they gaze long enough at a stranger who enthusiastically returns their gaze they might become overwhelmed and unable to extricate themselves from an attachment they might otherwise not desire.

In fact, paying very close attention in a particular kind of way has at many times and in many cultures been considered a method of aspiring to a special relationship with oneself, with one's neighbors, or with God. Eastern meditation practice and yoga teach us to pay close attention to our breathing or to the utterance of a single syllable or mantra, while mystics and academics alike may devote their entire lives to the close study of a single text or even a single poem. Such close attention, unswervingly maintained over a long period of time, may come to resemble what we know as prayer, and, if I recall correctly, the French mystic Simone Weil (1950) once maintained that any activity a person may choose, shoe repair, for example, if carried out with a certain quality of attention and sufficient devotion, does indeed become the moral equivalent of prayer.

Psychoanalysts are not engaged in anything so practical as shoe repair. But what might it be like if a psychoanalyst were to try to pay the same kind of close attention to a patient, the kind of attention that might indeed be the moral equivalent of prayer? As I try to imagine this situation, it seems that, first of all, you would have to be thinking about the patient quite a lot, not only during his sessions but also at other times throughout the day so that, in an ongoing way, he would become a constantly living presence in your memory and in your life. Let's call this "living presence." Second, if you were voluntarily going to be living with the patient in your mind so much of the time, it seems to me that you would have to trust that he was basically a good person. Let's call this "basic trust." Third, no matter what his problems or how upset, angry, or unpleasant he might be at any particular moment, you would have to feel that underneath it all the patient is a person for whom you have some real sympathy and with whom you might be able to do some useful work. Let's call this "sympathetic resonance."

If you can find this basic trust in the patient, feel sympathetic resonance with him, and hold him in your mind so that he becomes a living presence, then you have become connected to him in a very special way. In my experience, the effects of this kind of attention and connection maintained over a long period of time can be very profound indeed, for the person with whom you are thus connected, whether patient or friend or lover, begins to feel held together by your attention and to feel that more and more parts of himself are becoming meaningfully interconnected.

People who know us only in passing know only a small portion of us, some particular aspect, perhaps only that part we wish to show to them or to the world. The better people get to know us, the more and more parts of us they get to know. And, if someone can accept and embrace parts of us that may be disconnected and that even we do not want to know about, then that attention can heal us and help us feel more whole.

You may have noticed that I have just given you my personal prescription for love but, unlike a prescription for Prozac or Paxil, it unfortunately cannot be filled at the nearest drugstore. The advantage it has, though, is that you do not need a diploma, a state license, or even a couch to prescribe it. It can be used by anyone, anywhere, at any time—without any ritual or hocus-pocus. But it is definitely not an easy task. Shamans, mystics, saints and other very special people know how to do this, and some have attained this ability only after years of seeking and struggle while others seem just naturally gifted.

For those patients for whom I am able to provide something even vaguely approaching this kind of attention while still maintaining my own narcissistic balance—and I do not always try to do this, and even when I try I am often not successful—the most curious things begin to happen. After a while you find yourself totally emotionally involved in the process and you are no longer doing it because you are a doctor or a paid professional but, rather, because you are caught up in a process that is larger than yourself. A part of you is still able to observe professionally, to reflect and exercise control, but another part is hopelessly entangled, and you simply cannot help it. You have, to speak quite frankly, fallen in love with your patient.

If I had an attorney, he would at this point caution me to strike the last sentence. He would point out that it will not only lose me referrals but that it may very likely invalidate my malpractice insurance. I can well understand why Freud spoke only in private, to his most trusted colleagues, about the role of love in the therapeutic process.

One hundred years later, very little has really changed. Any HMO will still pay thousands of dollars for elaborate magnetic resonance imaging of chronic back pain but not a penny for therapeutic touch. Both the American Psychiatric and the American Psychological Associations have drawn up elaborate protocols for the best evidence-based treatments for specific mental disorders, including cognitive therapy for depression and powerful psychoactive drugs for this and other conditions. No one mentions love, although there is probably as large a body of research on the positive effects of care, attention, and love on the body and mind as there is on the effects of most of these other reimbursable therapeutic modalities.

For example, research in cognitive neurobiology (Schore, 1994; Hofer, 2003) has made it abundantly clear that the mother's language and emotional reactions psychobiologically influence the production of hormones and neurotransmitters in the child's brain, so that the emotional interactions between mother and infant are configured into the developing nervous system. In this way, the mother's mind directly alters the child's body and nervous system. It would seem that a sane society should honor and support its mothers as well as its psychopharmacologists and brain surgeons, for the good-enough mother is subtly creating what the brain specialist can only grossly attempt to repair. Furthermore, I believe that psychoanalysts and therapists need to be constantly aware that their own words and actions also influence the production of hormones and neurotransmitters in the patient's brain in ways similar to the psychoactive drugs, but sometimes with greater precision and fewer side effects. So the power of paying a certain kind of attention or of loving another human being can be very great indeed.

I mentioned earlier some people's concerns that, if they went into analysis, they would inevitably fall in love with their analyst, and I also maintained that not everyone who goes into psychoanalysis falls in love with their analyst. But, in my view, if, after some long period of particularly close attention, patients do in fact fall in love with their psychoanalyst, then they are very lucky indeed. For if they have truly fallen in love with their analyst, then their analyst is very likely to have fallen in love with them, and when this happens, then the world becomes enchanted again, just as it was in days of happy childhood or as we sometimes find it in fairy tales.

Some of you may remember that wonderful scene in Tolstoy's (1877) Anna Karenina when Levin first discovers that Kitty, who previously rejected him, now loves him. Levin writes down only the first letter of each word of a long, complicated sentence, but Kitty immediately deciphers his meaning and responds with an initialed sentence of her own, whose meaning, in turn, he immediately comprehends. Their minds are in that state of perfect sympathetic resonance so characteristic of love, and Levin, neither eating nor sleeping, spends all that night and the next morning in a trance. When he walks through the streets to her house to speak with her parents, the world seems magically enchanted. He watches the children going to school, the pigeons on the street, the rolls in a bakery window covered with flour, and everything he sees takes on a significance of unearthly beings which makes him laugh and cry for joy (pp. 397, 403).

Anyone who is lucky enough to have known the magic of love will recognize this enchantment of the world and understand why people will risk their lives to attain it. It is also understandable why less fortunate people will spend their days in altered states of consciousness—like being high on drugs—to mimic or parody this state. Of course, unlike fairy tales, this re-enchantment of the world may not last forever, but as long as it does last it is marvelous and astonishing, and it revitalizes the world in a way that amplifies its meaning and makes it seem wonderfully worthwhile to be alive. And even when disenchantment takes place, if it occurs relatively slowly and painlessly, as it sometimes does in real life when the bloom of love becomes tarnished by the corrosive action of reality and only the memory of love remains, then people may still feel that something wonderful once happened to them.

Freud maintained that the finding of a beloved person is always a refinding, that we are always seeking to find once again the people we loved in our earliest life. Homer also knew that recognition is the pathway to love, and one of the most touching scenes in all literature takes place when Penelope hesitates to recognize Odysseus, who has come back to her as an unknown stranger after 20 years of wandering.

For seeing comes before words, and perhaps the immediate power of recognition comes from the primordial reciprocity found in mother–infant gazing. But there is another kind of recognition that is also important. I will illustrate with a story I have always enjoyed. There used to be a popular cocktail called a Grasshopper. Well, one day an actual grasshopper walked into the bar at the Ritz and sat down, waiting to be served. The bartender approached him with a smile and said, "We're very pleased to have you here! You know, we have a cocktail named after you." And the grasshopper, equally pleased, replied, "Really, you do? You have a cocktail named Irving?"

From this story we learn that the most important thing to Irving, as well as to the rest of us, is not to be recognized generically as a grasshopper, but to be known in our absolute individual uniqueness as Irving. When we are not recognized or when we are misrecognized, we experience shame and humiliation, but when we are fully recognized in our uniqueness, we experience gratitude and love. This recognition that we seek is complex, for it includes both the feeling that we belong to a category larger than ourselves such as grasshoppers or human beings, as well as the sense that within that belonging we are absolutely special, as we know ourselves to be.

In the early months mother and baby feel at one with each other, for they are in love. We think that it takes a baby about a year and a half to recognize fully its physical separateness from its mother, and perhaps another three or four years to recognize fully its psychic separateness. In those few years the baby has made an extraordinary voyage, from merger and absolute dependence to separateness and interdependence, but it would be a voyage that might end in isolation were it not for our need to refind love.

I believe that when we look for love we search for recognition, for a sign that some person whose uniqueness of body and mind we have glimpsed has also caught sight of our own uniqueness of body and mind and delights in it. When this mutual recognition clicks in, we experience the exhilaration and sense of fulfillment of feeling, even for a moment, that someone truly knows us and that we truly know him. When we have loving sex we feel physically known in that way, and when we have moments of intimacy we feel spiritually known in that way. It is the cumulation of such moments of mutual recognition that makes for good parenting, good friendships, good marriages and even, in my opinion, good psychoanalysis.

REFERENCES

Beebe, B., & Stern, D. (1977), *Engagement–disengagement and early object experiences.* In Communicative Structures and Psychic Structures, eds. N. Freedman & S. Grand. New York: Plenum Press, pp. 35–55.

Ferenczi, S. (1932). *The Clinical Diary of Sándor Ferenczi,* ed. J. Dupont (trans. M. Balint & N. Z. Jackson). Cambridge, MA: Harvard University Press, 1988.

Freud, S. (1915). Observations on transference love. *Standard Edition* 12:159–171.

Grotjahn, M. (1967). Sigmund Freud and the art of letter writing. In *Freud as We Knew Him*, ed. H. M. Ruitenbeek. Detroit, MI: Wayne State University Press, 1973, pp. 433–447.

Hofer, M. A. (2003). The emerging neurobiology of attachment and separation: How parents shape their infant's brain and behavior. In *September 11: Trauma and Human Bonds*, eds. S. W. Coates, J. L. Rosenthal & D. S. Schechter. Hillsdale, NJ: The Analytic Press, pp. 191–209.

McGuire, W. (1974). *The Freud/Jung Letters: The Correspondence between Sigmund Freud and C. G. Jung*, ed. W. McGuire (trans. R. Mannheim & R. F. C. Hull). Princeton, NJ: Princeton University Press.

Nunberg, H., & Federn, E., eds. (1962). *Minutes of the Vienna Psychoanalytic Society, Vol. 1:1906–1908.* New York: International Universities Press.

Schore, A. N. (1994). *Affect Regulation and the Origin of the Self: The Neurobiology of Emotional Development.* Hillsdale, NJ: Lawrence Erlbaum Associates.

Steingart, I. (1995). *A Thing Apart: Love and Reality in the Therapeutic Relationship*. Northvale, NJ: Aronson.

Tolstoy, L. (1887), *Anna Karenina*, trans. R. Pevear & L. Volokhonsky. New York: Penguin Books, 2004.

Weil, S. (1950), *Attente de Dieu*. Paris: Fayard, 1985.

Index

www.ingramcontent.com/pod-product-compliance
Lightning Source LLC
Chambersburg PA
CBHW072052020426
42334CB00017B/1484